*Global Culture and Sport Series*

Series Editors: **Stephen Wagg**, Professor, Leeds Beckett University, UK, and **David Andrews,** Professor and Director of Graduate Studies, University of Maryland School of Public Health, USA

*Titles include*:

Holly Thorpe
SNOWBOARDING BODIES IN THEORY AND PRACTICE

Jonathan Long and Karl Spracklen (*editors*)
SPORT AND CHALLENGES TO RACISM

John Harris
RUGBY UNION AND GLOBALIZATION
An Odd-Shaped World

Pirkko Markula (*editor*)
OLYMPIC WOMEN AND THE MEDIA
International Perspectives

Roger Levermore and Aaron Beacom (*editors*)
SPORT AND INTERNATIONAL DEVELOPMENT

**Global Culture and Sport Series**
**Series Standing Order ISBN 978–0–230–57818–0 (Hardback)**
(*outside North America only*)

You can receive future titles in this series as they are published by placing a standing order. Please contact your bookseller or, in case of difficulty, write to us at the address below with your name and address, the title of the series and the ISBNs quoted above.

Customer Services Department, Macmillan Distribution Ltd, Houndmills, Basingstoke, Hampshire RG21 6XS, England

# The London Olympics of 2012

## Politics, Promises and Legacy

Stephen Wagg
*Leeds Beckett University, UK*

First published 2015 by
PALGRAVE MACMILLAN

Palgrave Macmillan in the UK is an imprint of Macmillan Publishers Limited, registered in England, company number 785998, of Houndmills, Basingstoke, Hampshire RG21 6XS.

Palgrave Macmillan in the US is a division of St Martin's Press LLC, 175 Fifth Avenue, New York, NY 10010.

Palgrave Macmillan is the global academic imprint of the above companies and has companies and representatives throughout the world.

Palgrave® and Macmillan® are registered trademarks in the United States, the United Kingdom, Europe and other countries.

ISBN 978–1–137–32633–1

This book is printed on paper suitable for recycling and made from fully managed and sustained forest sources. Logging, pulping and manufacturing processes are expected to conform to the environmental regulations of the country of origin.

A catalogue record for this book is available from the British Library.

A catalog record for this book is available from the Library of Congress.

*For 'Logsplitter', with love*

# Contents

# Acknowledgements

Thanks, for various help, advice and expressions of interest, to: my daughter Cassie, Helen Lenskyj, Peter Bramham, Gavin Poynter, Andrew James, Jon Dart, Brett Lashua, Dave Edwards, Ron Greenall, Catherine Baker, Jackie Hogan, Annika Oettler, Mark James, Steve Greenfield, Guy Osborn and Anna McMullen at *Labour Behind the Label*; and, for all those things, along with love and companionship, to my partner Saronne Rubyan.

# 1

# The Contemporary Olympic Games – Commercial Juggernaut or the Price of Progress?

When I mentioned to her, in the summer of 2014, that I was planning to write a book about the politics of the London Olympics of 2012, my daughter, worldly-wise and in her later 30s, told me to be careful: these Games were, after all, very popular – no sense, therefore, in my making myself some kind of pariah by criticising them in print. This (perfectly sound) piece of advice prompts a number of important prefatory comments.

First, popularity should never be a bar to critical analysis. The apparently near-universal acclaim for a particular view or event itself raises questions: as a character in James Lee Burke's excellent novel *In the Moon of Red Ponies* remarks, 'My dad had a great expression. He'd say "Son, if everybody agrees on it, it's wrong"'.[1] Second, it's fair to say that public appreciation of this event – as with most such events – cannot be read necessarily as an endorsement of its political circumstances; these circumstances, in the case of London 2012, were seldom subject to sustained public scrutiny. (A substantial minority objected to the Games, in any case.) Third, and related to this, a critical sociology of sport has been well established in international scholarship since the 1980s and the people who practise it are rarely opposed to sports or sports events themselves – merely to their political context. Sociologists have, for example, produced strong and well-grounded critiques of FIFA, the governing body of world football[2]; this, of course, has not precluded their enjoyment of football itself. Nor, indeed, has it prevented them from watching international matches.

---

[1] James Lee Burke, *In the Moon of Red Ponies* (London: Phoenix, 2005), p. 172.
[2] I have principally in mind here the widely admired work of Professors John Sugden and Alan Tomlinson. See, for instance, their *FIFA and the Contest for World Football* (Cambridge: Polity Press, 1998) and subsequent *Great Balls of Fire* (Edinburgh: Mainstream, 1999).

The fourth and final point here is that this critical scholarship long ago embraced the Olympics. An important milestone here was Alan Tomlinson and Garry Whannel's *Five Ring Circus: Money, Power and Politics at the Olympic Games*.[3] The publication of this book in 1984 also marked a watershed in Olympic politics, the Los Angeles Games of that year being the first explicitly for-profit Olympics. Since the McDonalds fast food chain were among the sponsors, some less than sympathetic commentators characterised these Games as 'the Hamburger Olympics',[4] and they have more recently been described as the first neoliberal Olympics.[5]

The last 30 years have seen a growth of critical academic writing on the Olympics and this has gone hand in hand with a burgeoning of anti-Olympic activism in countries where a bid to stage the Olympics has been made or a Games is scheduled to take place. Often these parallel developments have featured the same people and the most prominent and influential of these scholar-activists has been Canadian sociology professor Helen Jefferson Lenskyj.[6] Much of the work of Lenskyj, and of scholars like her, has charted the growth and political implications of a new corporate model for the Olympics – often now described as 'the Olympic industry'. This has resulted in an identifiably new paradigm for studying the Olympic movement in which two simple questions are addressed: who gains from the Olympics, and who loses?[7]

This paradigm seems to have been established around the turn of the twenty-first century. The principal political analysis of an individual Olympics in the late twentieth century was John Hargreaves' *Freedom for Catalonia?*,[8] a study of the Barcelona Games of 1992. This

---

[3] London: Pluto Press, 1984.
[4] See Rick Gruneau, 'Commercialism and the modern Olympics', in Alan Tomlinson and Garry Whannel (eds.), *Five Ring Circus: Money, Power and Politics at the Olympic Games* (London: Pluto Press, 1984), pp. 1–15, p. 2.
[5] Rick Gruneau and Robert Neubauer, 'A gold medal for the market: the 1984 Los Angeles Olympics, the Reagan era and the politics of neoliberalism', in Helen Jefferson Lenskyj and Stephen Wagg (eds.), *The Palgrave Handbook of Olympic Studies* (Basingstoke: Palgrave Macmillan, 2012), pp. 134–162.
[6] Prof. Lenskyj's developing interest in the impact of the contemporary Olympics on comparatively powerless social groups is described in her recent book *Gender Politics and the Olympic Industry* (Basingstoke: Palgrave Macmillan, 2013), pp. 2–4.
[7] See Helen Jefferson Lenskyj, *Inside the Olympic Industry: Power, Politics and Activism* (Albany: State University of New York Press, 2000).
[8] John Hargreaves, *Freedom for Catalonia? Catalan Nationalism, Spanish Identity and the Barcelona Olympic Games* (Cambridge: Cambridge University Press, 2000).

book concerned itself largely with the interplay between the Olympics, Catalan separatism and broader Spanish identity. The Games were seen as a success, not least for Catalan nationalism; as a mega-event they were not seen as problematic. Indeed, Hargreaves' reflections were made broadly from the perspective of the Games' organisers:

> There was almost universal agreement that these Games were successful, if not the most successful games ever held. None of the fears held before the Games – about whether the organisation would be up to standard, the threat of terrorism, and disruption by Catalan nationalists materialised. Neither were there any boycotts or international incidents or major drug scandals. The whole operation was excellently organised, COOB [the Barcelona Olympic Games Organising Committee] made a profit, even the weather improved in time, and Spain won an unprecedented number of medals.[9]

It wasn't until the following Games, in Atlanta, that a fully critical lens was trained upon the Olympics, their local organisers and the likely impact of the Games upon the host city and its inhabitants. Charles Rutheiser's book *Imagineering Atlanta*, published to coincide with the Olympics of 1996, is an important landmark in this respect. Rutheiser, an anthropologist at Georgia State University, wrote about the urban politics of the city of Atlanta and what he saw as the hucksterism that characterised preparation for the 1996 Olympics there. Crucially, Rutheiser raised the matter – hitherto overlooked – of the consequences for local people of the Olympic project. He referred, for example, to the 'massive displacements' that had accompanied the Olympics in Barcelona and, four years earlier, in Seoul. Several hundred thousand people, he noted, had been moved on by the South Korean government in their attempts to make the nation's capital an international showcase in 1988 and large numbers of the poor of Barcelona had been relocated to make way for the Games of 1992. In Atlanta, he suggested, similar 'damage' was being inflicted in the name of 'renewal, redevelopment and revitalization' – damage obscured by 'the manifold labors of myriad imagineers'.[10]

This growing attention to the human costs – the loss of homes, businesses and/or civil liberties – of running the Olympic Games bulwarked

---

[9] Ibid., p. 130.
[10] Charles Rutheiser, *Imagineering Atlanta: The Politics of Places in the City of Dreams* (London: Verso, 1996), p. 282.

the burgeoning political concern with financial costs of staging the Games. This concern was at its strongest in Canada, where the Montreal Games of 1976 were known to have been financially punitive for the city. Montreal's mayor, Jean Drapeau, had famously stated that 'The Montreal Olympics can no more have a deficit than a man can have a baby'.[11] But, in the event, the huge costs of staging the Games had had to be met by the Quebec government and the debts incurred by Olympic preparations (estimated at around 1.5 billion Canadian dollars) were not paid off until late in 2006; meanwhile Montreal's Olympic Stadium, because of its shape known originally as 'The Big O', had long since been renamed 'The Big Owe' by local people.[12] By the end of the twentieth century pressure groups opposing the Olympics had begun to proliferate. Thus, from the conjoining of radical urban anthropology and political activism emerged a new critical paradigm for Olympic Studies; the Sydney Games of 2000 were the first Olympics to be subjected to detailed political scrutiny from this emergent perspective.

As noted, the chief writer here was Helen Lenskyj, a professor of sociology and member of Bread Not Circuses, a coalition of groups formed to oppose Toronto's bid to stage the Summer Olympics of 1996 (and subsequent attempt to bring the 2008 Games to the city). Lenskyj's first substantial Olympic critique appeared in 2000 and effectively sets out the new paradigm. Its title – *Inside the Olympic Industry: Power, Politics and Activism* – is instructive in itself. Few people had hitherto characterised the Olympic movement as an 'industry'; now, in Lenskyj's (increasingly widely shared) perception, it was a commercial juggernaut which, with its collaborators in various host cities, generated corruption, urban landgrabs, environmental destruction and the curtailment of civil liberties. While local media were routinely acquiescent in the IOC's preferred definition of events, opposition to the Olympics was growing worldwide.[13] Two years later Lenskyj brought her wide-ranging critique to bear on the first Games of the new millennium, the Olympics staged in

---

[11] http://www.cbc.ca/news/canada/montreal/quebec-s-big-owe-stadium-debt-is-over-1.602530, posted 19 December 2006; accessed 12 September 2014. For a full account of the political controversy surrounding these Olympics, see Terrence Teixeira, 'The XXI Olympiad: Canada's claim of Montreal's gain? Political and social tensions surrounding the 1976 Montreal Olympics', in Lenskyj and Wagg (eds.), *The Palgrave Handbook of Olympic Studies*, pp. 120–133.

[12] http://www.cbc.ca/news/canada/montreal/quebec-s-big-owe-stadium-debt-is-over-1.602530, posted 19 December 2006; accessed 12 December 2014.

[13] Helen Jefferson Lenskyj, *Inside the Olympic Industry: Power, Politics and Activism* (Albany: State University of New York Press, 2000).

Sydney, Australia's largest and wealthiest city, in 2000.[14] Needless to say, Lenskyj's mode of analysis did not meet with universal approval among scholars. One reviewer, himself a sociologist of sport, pronounced it an 'interesting' if 'sometimes tedious examination of the political forces at work during the preparation and immediate lead up' to the Sydney Games. The tone of the book, he noted,

> is critical of the Olympic movement, and the content has little which will be of interest to the reader who is an avid follower of the games themselves. Nor does it touch on any of the issues which plague the Olympic movement. For those who find themselves in an extremely critical position of modern capitalist society, this will be an important read as it adds to the rant.[15]

Nevertheless, as the reviewer acknowledges,

> the true nature of this book is quite apart from anything Olympic. As large cities in any part of the world embark on mega-projects, be they part of a sport celebration or urban re-development, there will be those whose interests are not well served by the project. These tend to be the powerless in a capitalist system where the holders of power are able to influence the important decisions on which the projects depend.

Some people, he reflects, might see this simply as 'the price of progress'.[16]

As Lenskyj had shown, the price of this 'progress' was rising steeply and it was important to make clear who was paying it. The Sydney Games had been described as the 'best ever'. For instance, the travel writer Bill Bryson wrote of Sydney in *The Times*: 'These Games will go down as being one of the most successful events on the world stage...Congratulations, Australia. You did it. From start to finish, it's been wonderful...The Games would never be – simply couldn't be – as good again...'[17] (Indeed, it is now virtually routine for the latest

---

[14] Helen Jefferson Lenskyj, *The Best Olympics Ever? Social Impacts of Sydney 2000* (Albany: State University of New York Press, 2002).
[15] William McTeer, 'Review of Lenskyj (2002)', *Olympika: The International Journal of Olympic Studies*, Vol. 12 (2003), pp. 63–64, p. 63.
[16] Ibid., p. 64.
[17] Quoted on the 'Cool running' website, http://www.coolrunning.com.au/general/2000e020.shtml; accessed 30 January 2015.

Olympic Games to be declared the best ever, or given some such appellation, and this was certainly true of London 2012: the *Telegraph*, for example, took this view, offering a sample of international press comment as evidence.[18] The same week IOC President Jacques Rogge was no less effusive in pronouncing London now to be 'the beating heart of the world'.[19]) Lenskyj's title – *The Best Olympics Ever? Social Impacts of Sydney 2000* – explicitly questioned this judgement by once again taking the argument beyond the spectacle of the Olympics and raising the matter of who had gained (politically, materially...) from the Games, and who had lost. All of Lenskyj's major findings in this regard were, as this book will show, replicated at London 2012. The Sydney Games, like London, were characterised by biased media coverage, with some of the main media actually co-opted into the Olympics themselves: two media companies, for instance, – Fairfax Media Ltd and Rupert Murdoch's News Limited – were made Olympic sponsors.[20] As Lenskyj argues, most Sydney media acted as pro-corporate voices and boosters for the Games, coverage being dominated by the journalist Glenda Korporaal, who wrote for the *Sydney Morning Herald* and then for the *Daily Telegraph*, part of News Limited. Ms Korporaal had collaborated on book projects with both Rod McGeoch (who had managed the Sydney bid) and Kevan Gosper, Australian Vice President of the International Committee.[21] Moreover, concerted attempts were made to marginalise non-accredited media personnel and those thought likely to be seeking 'controversial background stories': these journalists were given premises away from the Olympic Park and extensively courted by representatives of the Australian Tourist Commission, soliciting promotional 'Visit Australia' stories.[22] Another key feature of Sydney 2000, described in some detail by Lenskyj, was the flurry of legislation during the late 1990s, at both state and federal level, which greatly enhanced police

---

[18] Telegraph Sport, 'London 2012 wins gold medal for best Olympics ever', http://www.telegraph.co.uk/sport/olympics/news/9471860/London-2012-wins-gold-medal-for-best-Olympics-ever.html, posted 13 August 2012; accessed 30 January 2015.

[19] Jacquelin Magnay, 'London 2012 Olympics: IOC President Jacques Rogge praises Games as "beating heart of the world"', http://www.telegraph.co.uk/sport/olympics/9468301/London-2012-Olympics-IOC-president-Jacques-Rogge-praises-Games-as-beating-heart-of-the-world.html, posted 11 August 2012; accessed 30 January 2015.

[20] Jefferson Lenskyj, *The Best Olympics Ever?*, p. 16.

[21] Ibid., pp. 15–16.

[22] Ibid., pp. 31–32.

powers to stop people, search them and move them on, strongly under-mining freedom of assembly and, in particular, provoking the harass-ment of young aboriginals and vagrants.[23] Furthermore, the *Olympic Arrangements Act* of 1995 gave legal protection to the image rights of Olympic 'partner' brands – a now-standard safeguard against 'ambush marketing'.[24]

Amid the apparent criminalisation of poverty, the Sydney organising committee purported to be bringing social benefits such as new housing to the city's socially disadvantaged but, as Lenskyj showed, the main beneficiaries here were developers and the wealthy. The main Olympic Park was sited at Homebush Bay on the banks of the Parramatta River, in inner west Sydney. The nearby Redfern district (known locally as 'The Block') was inhabited mainly by poor aborigine families suffer-ing multiple social problems. Any thought that the Games might bring them material benefits were quickly dispelled: as the Olympics drew near, police drug raids in the area increased markedly[25] and 'contrary to prevailing Olympic myths about housing legacies, all new permanent housing at Homebush Bay was to be sold or rented at market value'.[26] The area became an affluent residential and business district and subse-quently changed its name to 'Olympic Park'. Redfern continued to be a deprived area characterised by strained relations with the police – a riot (seen by some as the worst race riot in Australian history) took place there in 2004.[27]

It's fair to say that much of the pattern identified by Lenskyj at Sydney has become an established part of the Olympic project ever since. The Winter Olympic Games in Salt Lake City in 2002, for instance, have become known principally for two things: accusations of large-scale bribery on the part of the organisers (of which more later); and the supposed role of the businessman and Republican politician Mitt Romney in salvaging the Games from financial disaster – proclaimed in *Turnaround*, his book of 2004.[28] These Games, like subsequent Olympics,

---

[23] Ibid., pp. 50–64.

[24] Ibid., pp. 58–59.

[25] Ibid., p. 92.

[26] Ibid., p. 100.

[27] Aden Ridgeway, 'The underlying causes of the Redfern riots run through-out Australia', http://www.onlineopinion.com.au/view.asp?article=1989, posted 23 February 2004; accessed 30 January 2015.

[28] Mitt Romney and Timothy Robinson, *Turnaround: Crisis, Leadership, and the Olympic Games* (Washington, DC: Regnery Publishing, 2004).

including London, were notable for the arbitrary transfer of public funds to private companies and individuals and the consequent privatisation of public space. Romney negotiated $1.5 billion of federal funds to finance the Salt Lake Games and a good deal of this went, in questionable circumstances, to private contractors. For instance, as Tim Murphy showed in 2012:

> Snowbasin, the site of the downhill skiing championships in 2002, was one of the more notorious examples of a well-connected Utahn getting a sweetheart deal in the name of the Olympics. Earl Holding, a billionaire oil baron, pressured the Forest Service into giving him title to valuable land in Park Valley in exchange for land of 'approximate equal value' elsewhere in the state. But Holding drove a hard bargain; he got Congress to foot the bill for a new—and arguably unnecessary—access road (cost: $15 million), and received more than 10 times the 100 acres that were necessary for the Games. That would allow him to turn what was once protected federal land into a massive, and lucrative, mountain resort.[29]

The Winter Games returned to North America in 2010, when they were hosted by Vancouver. Rob Van Wynsberghe, an education professor at the University of British Columbia, conducted an audit of the event. Once again the main beneficiaries seemed to have been developers and construction companies contracted to build new transport links. Since most of the costs (an estimated $7 billion) had been met by provincial and national governments Van Wynsberghe's overall verdict was 'Residents paid little in direct taxes to get great infrastructure ... it is a good deal'.[30] The principal infrastructural developments had been in the cities of Vancouver and Whistler and had consisted of 'the Sea-to-Sky Highway upgrade, which changed a dangerous, winding mountain road into a safer, faster highway; the construction of the Canada Line, which provided rapid transit to Vancouver International Airport and several communities on the route; and the Vancouver Convention Centre, which gave the city a large, modern conference venue overlooking the

---

[29] Tim Murphy, 'Mitt Romney's Pork Barrel Olympics', http://www.motherjones.com/politics/2012/07/mitt-romney-expensive-olympics-federal-funding, posted 26 July 2012; accessed 30 January 2015.

[30] Mark Hume, 'Vancouver Olympics worth the $7-billion price tag, study says', http://www.theglobeandmail.com/news/british-columbia/vancouver-olympics-worth-the-7-billion-price-tag-study-says/article15036916/, posted 24 October 2013; accessed 30 January 2015.

harbour'.[31] There had been little perceptible effect on tourism, although, in the calculations of the bid team, the tourism industry had been expected to be a major beneficiary – another 'given' in contemporary Olympic politicking. And, aside from some community centres, nor had there been any clear benefits for the socially beyond (referring to the Paralympic Winter Games) 'People are more willing to consider hiring people with disabilities, people are more willing to consider athletes with disabilities true athletes . . . so that is a positive legacy'.[32] There had, however, been social costs – similar to those incurred in Sydney (and later in London) – not considered in this account.

The Sea-to-Sky Highway was taken through Eagleridge Bluffs, a wetland ecosystem and land held to have been stolen from Native Americans. Protesters had moved into the area in April 2006 and First Nations elder Harriet Nahanee, seeking to assert her indigenous rights as an Indian under the Canadian Constitution, had been arrested the following month and in January 2007 sentenced to two weeks in jail; already suffering from cancer, she died a few days after of pneumonia.[33] Indeed, 'No Olympics on stolen Native land' had been the primary slogan in a formidable campaign mounted in Vancouver against the Winter Games.[34] There was also a legal challenge to a by-law (the Vancouver 2010 Olympic and Paralympic Winter Games by-law – the equivalent of the Australian Olympic Arrangements Act of 1995, an act of this nature now being an IOC requirement) passed by Vancouver City Council to coincide with the Olympics, clause 4B of which made it illegal during the Winter Games without authorization to:

bring onto city land any

(i) weapon,
(ii) object, including any rock, stick, or glass or metal bottle useable as a weapon, except for crutches or a cane that a person who is elderly or disabled uses as a mobility aid,

---

[31] Ibid.

[32] Ibid.

[33] 'Eagleridge Bluffs protester dies at 71', http://www.cbc.ca/news/canada/british-columbia/eagleridge-bluffs-protester-dies-at-71-1.687057, posted 26 February 2007; accessed 31 January 2015. See also http://www.firstnations.de/development/eagleridge_bluffs.htm; accessed 31 January 2015.

[34] 'Olympic resistance: indigenous groups, anti-poverty activists, and civil liberties advocates protest 2010 Winter Games in Vancouver', http://www.democracynow.org/2010/2/15/olympic_resistance_indigenous_groups_anti_poverty, posted 15 February 2010; accessed 31 January 2015.

(iii) large object, including any bag, or luggage that exceeds 23 × 40 × 55 centimetres;

(iv) voice amplification equipment including any megaphone,

(v) motorized vehicle, except for a motorized wheel chair or scooter that a person who is elderly or disabled uses as a mobility aid,

(vi) anything that makes noise that interferes with the enjoyment of entertainment on city land by other persons,

(vii) ...any advertising material or install or carry any sign unless licensed to do so by the city.[35]

Conviction under this by-law might carry a fine of up to $10,000 or six months' imprisonment and police were said to have been empowered to enter people's homes and seize protest material.[36] These restrictions were, understandably, seen as a denial of free speech and a breach of civil liberties. They also raised the same serious doubts about the Games' security budget as Lenskyj had raised in relation to Sydney. Both budgets were big – Vancouver's was estimated at a billion dollars – and, like most Olympic security budgets since the murder of Israeli athletes at the Munich Olympics in 1972, had been rationalised as a defence against possible terrorist attack. But, as the by-law made clear, much of the policing at the Vancouver Olympics (as with Sydney and as it would be in London) was concerned with clearing the vicinity of the Olympics of unwanted persons, and with suppressing internal dissent and the advertising material of the sponsors' commercial rivals. Indeed, opponents of the Olympics in Vancouver and Toronto had been visited by plainclothes officers from the Integrated Security Unit, an Olympic operation led by the Royal Canadian Mounted Police in the months prior to the Games.[37] Moreover, as Sophy Chan made clear, in the period before the Games homeless people in Vancouver's Downtown Eastside experienced increased police harassment and many were forcibly removed under the

---

[35] Megan Stewart, with Linda Solomon 'BC Civil Liberties Association files suit against City of Vancouver for Olympics speech restriction bylaw', http://www.vancouverobserver.com/politics/news/2009/10/07/bc-civil-liberties-association-files-suit-against-city-vancouver-olympics, posted 7 October 2009; accessed 31 January 2015.

[36] 'Anti-Olympic signs could mean jail: rights group', http://www.cbc.ca/news/canada/british-columbia/anti-olympic-signs-could-mean-jail-rights-group-1.786577, posted 11 October 2009; accessed 31 January 2015.

[37] Ian Austen, 'Concerns as Canada balances protests and civil liberties', http://www.nytimes.com/2010/02/11/sports/olympics/11protests.html?_r=1&, posted 10 February 2010; accessed 31 January 2015.

'health and safety' terms of Canada's *Assistance to Shelter Act*.[38] (Some version of this police action had been a feature of Olympic Games for over twenty years and would be witnessed once again at London 2012.)

The London *Daily Mail* reported that the Vancouver Games had gone over budget (another regular feature of contemporary Olympic Games) by £2.9 billion.[39] In 2012 Christopher Shaw, a leading critic both of the contemporary Olympic movement and of the Vancouver Winter Games project, confirmed this, pointing out that the sale of lots in the two Olympic villages – a key part of the Games' business plan – had not gone well.[40]

As noted earlier, scholarship critical of the Olympics has grown steadily in tandem with these developments and writing in this vein is now reasonably commonplace across a range of academic disciplines.[41] Indeed, critical scholarly appraisals of successive sport mega-events have recently proliferated.[42] Moreover, these developments in the academic world have been paralleled by a growth in investigative reporting of the possibilities of corruption in global sports governance, best exemplified

---

[38] Sophy Chan, 'Unveiling the "Olympic Kidnapping Act" homelessness and public policy in the 2010 Vancouver Olympic Games', in Janice Forsyth, Christine O'Bonsawin and Michael Heine (eds.), *Intersections and Intersectionalities in Olympic and Paralympic Studies*, Twelfth International Symposium for Olympic Research (30–31 October 2014) International Centre for Olympic Studies, Western University Canada, London, Ontario (2014), pp. 43–47.

[39] Neil Wilson and Tom Kelly, 'The Olympics omen: riots, traffic chaos and £2.4bn overspend … are the Vancouver Winter Games a portent for London 2012?', *Mail Online*, *Daily Mail*, http://www.dailymail.co.uk/news/article-1251291/Fears-London-2012-Olympics-Vancouvers-winter-games-blighted-problems.html, posted 16 February 2010; accessed 31 January 2015.

[40] See Christopher A. Shaw, 'The economics and marketing of the Olympic games from bid phase to aftermath', in Lenskyj and Wagg (eds.), *The Palgrave Handbook of Olympic Studies*, pp. 248–260. For a full account of the Eagleridge Bluffs affair see David Whitson, 'Vancouver 2012: The Saga of Eagleridge Bluffs', in Graeme Hayes and John Karamichas (eds.), *Olympic Games, Mega-Events and Civil Societies: Globalization, Environment, Resistance* (Basingstoke: Palgrave Macmillan, 2012), pp. 219–235.

[41] The fullest representation of this writing between two covers is probably Lenskyj and Wagg (eds.), *The Palgrave Handbook of Olympic Studies*.

[42] For a useful list of these see Richard Giulianotti, Gary Armstrong, Gavin Hales and Dick Hobbs, 'Sport mega-events and public opposition: a sociological study of the London 2012 Olympics', *Journal of Sport and Social Issues*, p. 3, http://jss.sagepub.com/content/early/2014/04/14/0193723514530565, published online 14 April 2014; accessed 16 September 2014.

in the case of the Olympics by the work of the Scottish journalist Andrew Jennings[43] and American writer Dave Zirin.[44]

Thus, at the dawn of the twenty-first century, an (albeit asymmetrical) battle was joined, with the IOC, urban developers, boosters, PR professionals and Olympic 'partners' (i.e. sponsors) on the one side and anti-Olympic activists, supported by sympathetic scholars and writers, on the other. A good example of this could be found in Florida, where a campaign was launched, late in 2000, to bring the Summer Olympics of 2012 to the Tampa-Orlando corridor. Florida 2012 CEO Ed Turanchik claimed that the Olympics 'would be of unprecedented value to the communities in Florida in terms of repositioning the state in the global economy'.[45] Neil Demause of the *Orlando Weekly* was sceptical. Drawing on the writings of Lenskyj, Jennings and Rutheiser and the campaigns of activist groups, he suggested:

> Olympic-caliber athletes, economic windfalls and, best of all, no lingering debts of the sort that have accompanied St. Petersburg's Tropicana Field and Tampa's Raymond James Stadium. It sounds too good to be true. And, according to a growing legion of Olympics critics, it is. In books like Helen Jefferson Lenskyj's *Inside the Olympic Industry* and Andrew Jennings' *The Great Olympic Swindle*, and via such organizations as the Sydney Anti-Olympic Alliance and Toronto's Bread Not Circuses, economists and community activists are raising warning flags that the Games can bring with them an Olympic-sized headache [...] Charles Rutheiser, a John Hopkins anthropology professor and author of the book *Imagineering Atlanta*, notes that while the 1996 Olympics allowed the downtown

---

[43] See Vyv Simson and Andrew Jennings, *The Lords of the Rings: Power, Money & Drugs in the Modern Olympics* (London: Simon and Schuster, 1992); Andrew Jennings, *The New Lords of the Rings: Olympic Corruption and How to Buy Gold Medals* (London: Pocket Books, 1996); and Andrew Jennings and Clare Sambrook, *The Great Olympic Swindle: When the World Wanted Its Games Back* (London: Simon and Schuster, 2000).

[44] See, for example, Zirin's 'The ring and the rings: Vladimir Putin's Mafia Olympics', http://www.theguardian.com/sport/2013/jun/18/putin-kraft-superbowl-ring-sochi-winter-olympics; accessed 16 September 2014. See also Dave Zirin, *Brazil's Dance with the Devil: The World Cup, the Olympics, and the Fight for Democracy* (Chicago: Haymarket Books, 2014).

[45] Neil Demause, 'Gold medal ring toss', *Orlando Weekly* (14 December 2000), http://www2.orlandoweekly.com/news/story.asp?id=2012; accessed 17 September 2014.

gentrification Atlanta business leaders had long sought, the inner-ring residential neighborhoods did not benefit as much as had been hoped from the redevelopment.[46]

Valuable literature reflecting on the London Olympics of 2012 which shares or engages constructively with this perspective has already begun to appear.[47] Indeed, one paper by leading sociologists closes by suggesting how anti-Olympic protests might more effectively be carried out in the future.[48] It goes, perhaps, without saying that this book is also written from this growing perspective of critical Olympic studies and it asks to what extent – and, if so, in what ways – London 2012 corresponded to the pattern increasingly evident in post-1984 Games. (It concerns itself largely exclusively with Summer Olympics, my intention being to write more fully about issues raised by the Paralympics of 2012 elsewhere.) In doing so, it draws quite heavily on coverage of the London 2012 Olympic project by British newspapers, notably *The Independent*. This paper, along with the (similarly liberal) *The Guardian* and others, while enthusing about the Olympic events and competitors, was assiduous in reporting on the politically contentious and/or non-sporting aspects of the Games.

[46] Ibid.
[47] Richard Giulianotti, Gary Armstrong, Gavin Hales and Dick Hobbs, 'Sport mega-events and public opposition: a sociological study of the London 2012 Olympics', *Journal of Sport and Social Issues* (2014) and Phil Cohen, *On the Wrong Side of the Track? East London and the Post Olympics* (London: Lawrence and Wishart, 2013) are good examples. See also Jules Boykoff, *Celebration Capitalism and the Olympic Games* (Abingdon: Routledge, 2014).
[48] Giulianotti et al., 'Sports mega-events and public opposition'.

# 2
# The Games Come to London

This chapter will give a brief account of how the Games came to be awarded to London. The decision to bid for the Olympics of 2012 was taken by a few people at the commanding heights of the governing British Labour Party: Prime Minister Tony Blair and the Secretary of State for Culture, Media and Sport Tessa Jowell, in consultation with a small number of senior staff and confidants. This reflected an established pattern of decision-making in the government of the time, described as 'sofa government' in the media and criticised in the Butler Report of 2007.[1] The chapter will also discuss the implications, real and purported, for the East End of London, where the Games were staged. And it will comment, given the controversies generated in the last three decades by Olympic bids, on how little visible political opposition there appeared to be to the staging of London 2012.

## 'We will help you get more out of life'

It's an axiom now that the Labour Party which took office in the United Kingdom in 1997 had abandoned many of even its most vestigial commitments to combating material inequalities in British society; the party had been 're-branded' as 'New Labour' and the pamphlet *New Labour, New Life for Britain*, published the previous year, is generally seen as an embrace of market economics – 'Thatcherism' in the British political lexicon. In their manifesto for the General Election of 1997, Labour

---

[1] Press Association, 'Blair cabinet "took one decision in eight months"', *The Guardian*, 29 May 2007, http://www.guardian.co.uk/politics/2007/may/29/ tonyblair.labour1; accessed 30 September 2012.

had eschewed their traditional undertakings in the realm of sport and leisure. While in the 1950s and 60s the party had promised plentiful public provision – playing fields, swimming pools and grants for youth centres[2] – now the pledges were more modest and ephemeral: in the broad field of sport and leisure, Labour now said that: 'We will help you get more out of life', an example of which was that the party, if elected, would 'Back [a] World Cup bid'. This acknowledged a trend in the British government's address of sport and leisure which was already well under way: 'sport for all' – the promotion of sports participation for its intrinsic benefits (a policy adopted by governments of all political stripes across the 'developed' world) – was being phased out in favour of an emphasis on elite sport. In 1995 John Major's Conservative administration had issued the policy document *Sport: Raising the Game*, calling for competitive sport to be placed at the heart of the state school curriculum.[3] This policy was reaffirmed in *Game Plan*, a further policy document issued in 2002. This document had been concocted by the government's Department for Culture, Media and Sport in conjunction with its Social Exclusion Unit (established in 1997, on the accession of the first 'New' Labour government). The thrust of *Game Plan* was that competitive sport should bring sport itself closer to the centre of national life and, as such, become a means to 'social inclusion'.[4] The term 'social inclusion', as I have argued elsewhere, was (and remains) ill defined[5] – perhaps intentionally so. In the case of *Game Plan*, it was possible to infer that 'social inclusion' meant (a) that the success of sportspeople, who were often from working and lower middle class families, would, via (invariably televised) international competition, be a highly visible token of an open, 'inclusive' society and (b) that the great mass of the general public would share in this inclusiveness via the 'feelgood factor' promoted

---

[2] See, for example, Labour Party manifesto, General Election of 1964, http://www.labour-party.org.uk/manifestos/1964/1964-labour-manifesto.shtml; accessed 26 September 2014.

[3] http://www.sportdevelopment.info/index.php/subjects/48-policy/844-sport-raising-the-game; accessed 28 September 2014.

[4] http://www.sportdevelopment.info/index.php/subjects/48-policy/61-game-plan-a-strategy-for-delivering-governments-sport-and-physical-activity-objectives; accessed 28 September 2014.

[5] See Stephen Wagg, 'Fat city? British football and the politics of social exclusion at the turn of the twenty-first century', in Stephen Wagg (ed.), *British Football and Social Exclusion* (Abingdon: Routledge, 2004), pp. 14–17.

by British sporting achievements. Crucially, along with, and as part of, 'social inclusion', *Game Plan* promised 'neighbourhood renewal'.[6]

Another important development in British government policy, dating from the Major administration of 1990–97 and bearing directly on the Olympic bid, was the Private Finance Initiative (PFI). Under PFI, promoted by the Treasury but embraced by all the major political parties, private capital was sought for public infrastructural projects, on terms widely criticised as ultimately draining on the public purse.[7] PFI was wholly compatible with the political tendencies and expressed philosophies of the 'New' Labour Party leadership which took office in 1997. How this administration would relate to heavily capitalised international sports events was demonstrated within a few months of the General Election.

Labour came to office with a proclaimed commitment to public 'wellbeing', an analogously vague companion term to 'social inclusion'. As part of this commitment it had undertaken, if elected, to ban tobacco advertising. A few weeks into his premiership, however, Blair had met with Bernie Ecclestone, chief executive of Formula One (F1) motor racing and Max Mosley, president of the Fédération Internationale de l'Automobile (FIA) and agreed that F1 should be exempt from the ban. He had then asked Tessa Jowell, at the time the minister for public health, to sort out the details.[8] Ecclestone had previously donated £1 million to the Labour Party (and a reputedly similar amount to the Conservatives). If nothing else, this was a clear and early indication of Labour's – and, specifically, Blair's – openness to the requirements of what sociologists now routinely refer to as the sport-media-corporate nexus. Jowell, the Labour minister most closely

---

[6] http://www.sportdevelopment.info/index.php/subjects/48-policy/61-game-plan-a-strategy-for-delivering-governments-sport-and-physical-activity-objectives; accessed 29 September 2014. For a full discussion of the trend toward a greater emphasis on elite sport in British government policy, see Mick Green, 'Changing policy priorities for sport in England: the emergence of elite sport as a key policy concern', *Leisure Studies*, Vol. 23, No. 4 (October 2004), pp. 365–385.

[7] See, for example, Andrew Petrie, 'PFIs: the good and the bad – but still on the table', *The Guardian*, 19 May 2010, http://www.guardianpublic.co.uk/pfis-future-new-government-investment; accessed 29 September 2014. See also Allyson Pollock, *NHS plc: The Privatisation of Our Health Care* (London: Verso, 2005).

[8] See, for example, Nicholas Watt, 'Blair under fire as row over F1 and party donation resurfaces', *The Guardian*, 13 October 2008, http://www.theguardian.com/politics/2008/oct/13/partyfunding-tonyblair; accessed 29 September 2014.

associated with procurement of the London Olympics of 2012, has been widely described as a 'loyalist', both to 'New' Labour and to Blair personally, and has thus endorsed the same political priorities. She said in 2006: 'Just as we should be proud of our relationship with the trade unions, so, too, we should be proud that, after years of ideological opposition to the means of wealth creation in this country, New Labour has a relationship with business'.[9]

## Why not London?

Both Blair and Jowell have since described their role in the procurement of the Games in breathless, Dare-To-Dream rhetoric: 'it all began with Tessa Jowell',[10] wrote Blair in his autobiography, for example. The writer Michael Joseph Gross noted that Blair had been concerned both about the likely cost of the Olympics and about the unfortunate conjunction of an Olympic bid with the involvement of British troops in an (internationally decried) invasion of Iraq. Gross recorded this exchange between the Prime Minister and his Secretary of State for Culture, Media and Sport in 2002:

> 'In his memoir, Blair recalls that Jowell lectured him to man up:
>
> "I really didn't think that was your attitude to leadership. I thought you were prepared to take a risk. And it is a big risk. Of course we may not win but at least we will have had the courage to try." When Tessa says this, you feel a complete wimp and rather ashamed. You know she is manipulating you, but you also know it's a successful manipulation.'

As Jowell recalled the exchange, 'He looked at me with his lilac eyes and he said—it was an absolute turning point—he said, "I see what you mean. O.K., darling, I'll think about it and I'll let you know." And the next day he said, "We'll go for it".'[11] Blair went on to assert that the

---

[9] Quoted in Martin Bright, 'A loyalist to the bitter end', *The Observer*, 22 February 2009, http://web.archive.org/web/20090301190650/http://www.guardian.co.uk/politics/2009/feb/22/profile-tessa-jowell-david-mills; accessed 29 September 2014.

[10] Tony Blair, *A Journey* (London: Hutchinson, 2010), p. 545.

[11] Michael Joseph Gross, 'Jumping through hoops', *Vanity Fair*, June 2012, http://www.vanityfair.com/culture/2012/06/international-olympic-committee-london-summer-olympics; accessed 2 October 2014.

award of the Olympics to London had much to do with his personal access to the international corridors of power. In prose reminiscent of mafia pulp fiction, he recalls this meeting with Italian prime minister and media tycoon Silvio Berlusconi:

> The previous August I had gone to visit him at his home in Sardinia to seek his help with the bid. Italy was a key player. He asked me how much it mattered to get the Olympics. 'It matters', I said. 'Greatly?' he asked. 'Greatly', I said. He said, 'You are my friend. I promise nothing but I see if I can help'. Typical Silvio, which is why I like him. Most politicians say 'I promise' but then do nothing. He said 'I promise nothing' but then delivered.[12]

(Blair does not say how Berlusconi delivered.)

In any case, Olympic history, like any other history, is not made simply by prominent individuals trading on each other's friendships or re-enacting scenes from *The Godfather*. As Gavin Poynter, Professor of Social Sciences at the University of East London and a close observer of the London 2012 saga, has argued, the bid for London to host the Olympic Games of 2012 had originated considerably earlier, in British Olympic politics of the 1990s. Birmingham, England's second city, had bid for the Olympics of 1992; Manchester had tried for the 1996 and 2000 Games. Neither bid had achieved the necessary backing, whereupon a number of commentators had asked 'Why not London?'[13] The British Olympic Association had therefore commissioned a feasibility study on a bid for London and this had recommended a site in either the west or the east of the city. In 2001, this suggestion was shown to Ken Livingstone, mayor of London since the previous year. Livingstone had a long history on the left of the Labour Party; as leader of the Greater London Council (GLC) between 1981 and 1986, he had carried out a popular programme of municipal socialism, bringing him personal vilification in the British popular press and the abolition of the GLC by the second Thatcher administration. Between 1987 and 2001 Livingstone had been a Labour MP for Brent in North West London. The 'New' Labour leadership had blocked his attempt to stand for the party in the

---

[12] Tony Blair, *A Journey*, p. 552.

[13] See Gavin Poynter, 'London: preparing for 2012', in Gavin Poynter and Iain MacRury (eds.), *Olympic Cities: 2012 and the Remaking of London* (Farnham: Ashgate, 2009), pp. 183–200, p. 184. See also Mike Lee, with Adrian Warner and David Bond, *The Race for the 2012 Olympics* (London: Virgin Books, 2006), p. 5.

first mayoral election of 2000; his decision to stand as an independent (against the official Labour candidate) had made his expulsion from the party inevitable. With the first Blair administration openly committed to neoliberalism, Livingstone, retaining something of his socialist philosophy, chose East London as the site for any bid, calculating that the Olympics presented the best chance of a material enhancement of the lives of East Enders through any kind of civic intervention. He said later: 'I didn't bid for the Olympics because I wanted three weeks of sport. I bid for the Olympics because it's the only way to get the billions of pounds out of the government to develop the East End'.[14] Livingstone, like many contemporary politicians, clearly subscribed to the notion that 'good' Olympic experience could be 'catalytic' for its host city – a conviction now widely promoted in the more celebratory commentaries on the recent Games in Athens, Sydney and, most especially, Barcelona.[15] His support, albeit that, as a politician who refused to recant his socialist past, he was anathema to the 'New' Labour leadership, seems to have turned the political tide in favour of a London bid.

Opposition to the idea of London staging the 2012 Olympics was strongest in the Treasury and in the Labour cabinet, largely on grounds of cost: in particular, there had been much disputation over the respective financial estimates of the consultancy firm ARUP and senior civil servant Robert Raine.[16] In December 2002 *Observer* journalist Denis Campbell reported that the Blair government would scrap the bid, fearful that it 'would cost too much and lead to endless negative headlines'.[17]

However, in January 2003, Livingstone met Jowell and agreed to raise the council tax on Londoners by £20 for up to ten years in order to part-fund the Games.[18] Understandably, this eased government concerns and, with the financial difficulty apparently disposed of, a number

[14] Chris Mason, 'Who's who: political credit from London Olympics', http://www.bbc.co.uk/news/uk-politics-19179711, posted 9 August 2012; accessed 14 October 2014.

[15] Noted by Gavin Poynter, 'The evolution of the Olympic and Paralympic Games 1948–2012', in Poynter and MacRury (eds.), *Olympic Cities: 2012 and the Remaking of London*, pp. 23–41. See, in particular, pp. 31–36.

[16] Gavin Poynter, 'London: preparing for 2012', pp. 184–185. See also Lee et al., *The Race for the 2012 Olympics*, pp. 10–12.

[17] Denis Campbell, 'Britain's Olympic bid to be scrapped', *The Observer*, 22 December 2002, http://www.theguardian.com/politics/2002/dec/22/london.sportfeatures; accessed 14 October 2014.

[18] Lee et al., *The Race for the 2012 Olympics*, pp. 13–14.

of intertwining arguments in favour of a London bid came into play. First, *Game Plan*, the government's own policy document for sport, had been published only the previous year; it had prioritised elite sport and the importance of staging mega-events, such as the Olympics. Second, a number of sport- or entertainment-related public projects had recently foundered. These included the redevelopment of Wembley Stadium in North London (begun in 2000 and due for completion in 2003, but well behind schedule); the Millennium Dome in Greenwich, conceived by the government of John Major (1990–97) and endorsed by the incoming 'New' Labour administration in 1997, but widely canvassed as an eyesore and a white elephant; the failure in 2000 to procure the football World Cup Finals of 2006; and, most importantly, the plan to build a National Athletics Stadium at Picketts Lock in North London to stage the World Athletics Championships of 2005 – building work had begun in 2000 and the project abandoned the following year. Comparable difficulties in the hosting of the Commonwealth Games in Manchester in 2002 had, according to some, only been averted by a government envoy pressing Manchester City Council into covering the escalating costs of putting on the event.[19] The Games themselves, however, had been widely regarded as a success and 2012, it was now thought, presented a chance for the UK to establish a reputation for the hosting of such mega-events. Third, in 2001 the Summer Olympics of 2008 had been awarded to a city in Asia – Beijing; this raised the possibility at least that the IOC would favour a European city for the following Games. Fourth, by this time the key term in the lexicon of Olympic bids had come to be 'legacy'[20] – the Games should 'put something back' into the host city, once the athletes and television crews had moved on. This notion had become more pressing, partly through the persistent allegations of urban land-grab in relation to the Atlanta Games, but chiefly because of the charges of bribery levelled by the United States Justice Department in 1998 against many of those who had campaigned to bring the Winter Olympics of 2002 to Salt Lake City.[21] The IOC was naturally anxious to dispel the idea that its officials were touting for gifts and to promote a more socially constructive corporate image. Although

---

[19] Ibid., p. 8.

[20] For a full discussion, see Alan Tomlinson, 'Olympic legacies: recurrent rhetoric and harsh realities', *Contemporary Social Science: Journal of the Academy of Social Sciences*, Vol. 9, No. 2 (2014), pp. 137–158.

[21] For a lengthy discussion, see Lenskyj, *Inside the Olympic Industry*, chapters 1 and 2.

much smart money was on Paris to host the Games of 2012, the working class districts of London's fabled East End, popularised in the works of Charles Dickens and others and now suffering the effects of deindustrialisation, could be the basis of a powerful argument when consideration turned to 'regeneration' and 'legacy'. Fifth, in 2003 Prime Minister Blair had committed British troops to join US forces in an invasion of Iraq, which had drawn mammoth protests in 600 cities around the world.[22] This had included a demonstration in London in February 2003 that was widely accepted to be the biggest political protest in British history. US President George W. Bush's (premature) declaration, in early May 2003, that the war in Iraq was over allowed the publicity-conscious Blair – described by one commentator as 'Britain's first postmodern party leader'[23] – to reconsider a bid for the Olympics, perhaps thinking that a resulting national feelgood factor might expunge public anger over the assault on Iraq. As Mike Lee, subsequently 'Director of Communications' for the British bid and a Blair confidant/'New' Labour insider, remarked later, while the war was on 'Blair decided he could not be seen to be considering throwing a sports party'.[24] Following Bush's 'Mission Accomplished' speech, though, the priority might well become an Olympic bid and, if it were successful, the advantageous presentation of self on the part of the main political actors. This, in the main, meant marginalising scorned leftist Ken Livingstone: 'Jowell knew', recalls Lee, 'that she couldn't allow him [Livingstone] to steal the glory from the government should the Olympics get the green light'.[25] Moreover, there was clear evidence that substantial swathes of both the British polity and the British public were supportive, in principle, of the project. Iain Duncan Smith, the leader of the Conservative opposition in the House of Commons, had urged the government to go ahead[26] and a recent opinion poll conducted by ICM in December 2002 had suggested that over 80% of British people were of like mind.[27]

---

[22] See Joris Verhulst, 'February 15, 2003: the world says no to war', in Stefaan Walgrave and Dieter Rucht (eds.), *The World Says No to War: Demonstrations against the War on Iraq* (Minneapolis: University of Minnesota Press, 2010), pp. 1–19.
[23] Andrew Rawnsley, *Servants of the People: The Inside Story of New Labour* (London: Penguin, 2001), p. 6.
[24] Lee et al., *The Race for the 2012 Olympics*, p. 15.
[25] Ibid., p. 13.
[26] See, for example, Campbell, 'Britain's Olympic bid to be scrapped'.
[27] See Chetan Dave, *The 2012 Bid: Five Cities Chasing the Summer Games* (Bloomington, IN: Author House, 2005), pp. 34–35.

Finally, Blair needed to know that London had a realistic chance of a successful bid. By the spring of 2003, private confirmation had been given that this was the case. IOC President Jacques Rogge had given Jowell such an assurance at a meeting in Lausanne in January and Mike Lee, then considering leaving his post at UEFA to join the London bid, received a similar undertaking from Rogge's advisor Christophe de Kepper.[28] (While one imagines that such assurances are commonplace in IOC dealings, it's unlikely that either Jowell or Lee, as seasoned political networkers, would have proceeded – or that Lee would have resigned his current post – without some strong indication that London was actually in the running.)

As suggested earlier, 'New' Labour administrations were characterised by (highly undemocratic) 'sofa' government. In keeping with this political *modus operandi*, and as intimated earlier, the decision to bid to bring the Olympic Games to London in 2012 appears to have been taken by Blair, Jowell and their close advisors. The latter category routinely included 'a number of leading entrepreneurs'.[29]

## Insider dealing: the London bid and the politics of legacy

Herbert Marcuse, the German Marxist philosopher of the Frankfurt School, said in the early 1960s that 'the language of politics tends to become that of advertising'.[30] This is now the common-sense of political discourse, with considerable power, influence and credit being accorded to 'political strategists', 'directors of communication' and 'spin doctors', all of whom are essentially advisors on presentation. The contest to procure the Olympic Games is a large scale political campaign, much like any other, being, in effect, a competition between several highly resourced and well connected publicity machines. Britain's campaign for 2012 bears this out.

Britain's bid was initially led by the American businesswoman Barbara Cassani, best known in the commercial world as founder and chief executive of British Airways' low budget airline *Go*. Cassani had been appointed apparently for her 'start-up' skills and, under her stewardship, the first phase of the bid – dealing with the location of events, establishing relationships with corporate 'partners' and other 'stakeholders', the proposed building of infrastructure and overall budget projection for

[28] See Lee et al., *The Race for the 2012 Olympics*, p. 14, pp. 23–24.

[29] Ibid., p. 7.

[30] Herbert Marcuse, *One Dimensional Man* (London: Abacus, 1972), p. 92.

the Games – was accomplished, leading to London's selection as one of the five candidate cities in the spring of 2004. Cassani then resigned and subsequent commentary strongly suggested that she lacked the presentation techniques and 'networking' capacity necessary for the next phase of the bidding process. At Cassani's departure, *The Guardian* journalist Paul Kelso wrote of her rumoured distaste for the masculine IOC culture and for the 'schmoozing' that the job would now require:

> It is the second phase of the bid, selling London's virtues and persuading the 126 members of the IOC that the city will stage a successful games, where she and others felt she would be found wanting.
>
> The process of persuasion required to win a games is hard work but no hardship, taking place as it does largely in the bars of five-star hotels in some of the world's most scenic locations, but it does require a natural lobbyist, something Cassani plainly is not. She loathed the IOC's bar culture, one member of the bid team indicated, and lacked the bonhomie required to charm the curious mixture of politicians, businessmen, minor royalty and potentates that make up the IOC membership.
>
> According to Rod McGeoch, the Australian credited with winning the 2000 games for Sydney, one of the first rules of Olympic lobbying is never to leave the bar while there is a single IOC member still present.[31]

Mike Lee, the bid's principal media strategist, later confirmed that the preferred candidate for Cassani's role had been Sir Christopher Meyer, former British ambassador to the United States: Meyer and his wife were 'archetypal networkers, ideal for the round of Olympic meetings and sports events where they would be called upon to meet and greet important people and push London's case'.[32] At any rate Cassani's eventual replacement, her deputy Lord Coe, was seen as far more suited to this task and to the environment in which it would have to be carried out. Sebastian Coe was an Olympic gold medallist, former Conservative MP (and advisor to the party leader William Hague) and a wealthy businessman, owning a string of health clubs and earning big money from personal appearances, speeches and 'image rights'. As an ambassador for

---

[31] Paul Kelso, 'Why Cassani had to call time, gentlemen, please', *The Guardian*, 20 May 2004, http://www.theguardian.com/sport/2004/may/20/Olympics2012. politics; accessed 15 October 2014.
[32] Lee et al., *The Race for the 2012 Olympics*, pp. 25–26.

the sportswear brand Nike, which had sponsored him as an athlete, he was wholly at home in the sport-media-corporate nexus. (In 2012 Complete Leisure Group, the company Coe owned and used as a vehicle for his public appearances, was sold to the global marketing company Chime Communications, Coe becoming chairman of its sports marketing subsidiary, CSM Sport and Entertainment at a salary of £350,000 per year.)[33] Most importantly, Coe's stock was high at the IOC, his having swallowed his own right-wing sympathies to defy the call of the Carter and Thatcher administrations for a boycott of the Moscow Olympics of 1980; he'd won gold in the 1500 metres there. Lee knew of the high regard in which Coe was held by recently retired IOC President Juan Antonio Samaranch and thought that Coe might even be groomed as a future President of the IOC itself.[34] Key observers have suggested that Coe's 'insider' status and 'schmoozing' capacities were crucial in appeasing the IOC hierarchy when, in November 2004, a BBC *Panorama* documentary claimed that, far from banishing the suspicions of corruption raised by Salt Lake, bribery had been, and remained, *de rigueur* in the Olympic bidding process; Salt Lake boosters appeared in the programme, arguing that they had only done what had been required of them.[35] The possible (or continuing) betrayal by the IOC of its own charter and stated ideals might have been thought to be an important matter for public scrutiny, but Olympic bid culture, oblivious to the truth or otherwise of the allegations, defined it as only an issue of publicity. Veteran Olympic marketing strategist Michael Payne said later:

> *Panorama* came out with a sting about how London could buy votes. It was all anybody was talking about. London was radioactive – you wouldn't have even been seen sitting next to someone from the bid. You would have got the most outrageous odds on London winning. Nobody in their right mind gave them a chance.[36]

[33] Roger Blitz, 'Coe on marks for £12m image rights deal', http://www.ft.com/cms/s/0/0cb1b4bc-1ec9-11e2-be82-00144feabdc0.html; accessed 15 October 2014.
[34] Lee et al., *The Race for the 2012 Olympics*, pp. 30, 61.
[35] Transcript of the programme available at http://news.bbc.co.uk/nol/shared/spl/hi/programmes/panorama/transcripts/buyingthegames.txtranscript; accessed 17 October 2014.
[36] Alex Kay, 'London had blown it! Coe saved Olympic bid from disappearing without a trace', *Daily Mail*, 27 July 2012, http://www.dailymail.co.uk/sport/olympics/article-2179761/London-2012-Olympics-Sebastian-Coe-saved-bid–Michael-Payne.html; accessed 17 October 2014.

Coe's concern had been simply to 'gauge the scale of the reaction and to reassure them [IOC Members] that the London bid was not involved in the making of the programme in any way'.[37]

For Lee, the *Panorama* furore simply added weight to his argument that, with the scandal of Salt Lake still preoccupying the IOC, impression management would be more important than ever, traditional gift-giving now being out of the question.[38] The resulting impression management strategy would be determined by professional boosters, such as Lee himself, often in dialogue with specialist Olympic 'consultants' who used their contacts with IOC personnel to write reports and furnish advice based on the current thinking of Olympic officialdom.[39] (Lee himself worked subsequently as strategist on the successful bids of Rio de Janeiro for the Olympics of 2016 and Qatar for the football World Cup Finals of 2022.)[40]

Lee and his team set about fashioning a 'narrative' about London and the Olympics:

> We needed to break new ground in terms of developing a modern campaign, which needed to have communications and marketing at its heart because there was a real possibility that direct contact with the [IOC] members would be very limited. [...] It was essentially like an international political campaign. We needed to understand our audiences and develop a global election manifesto. [....] We also set about developing key themes that we could reinforce through presentations and communications events. The core elements were regeneration of the East End of London, the diversity of London, the legacy of the Games, use of London landmark iconic sites and what the Olympics could offer British and world sport. Early on we also began to develop an idea of Games for the next generation.[41]

The intense reiteration of this 'narrative' culminated in a team presentation to the IOC in Singapore in July 2005 by the British Princess Royal, Coe, Craig Reedie (Chair of the British Olympic Association), former British Olympic athlete Denise Lewis, Blair, Livingstone and Jowell.

---

[37] Lee et al., *The Race for the 2012 Olympics*, p. 79.
[38] Ibid., p. 33.
[39] Ibid., pp. 81–82.
[40] Mike Scott, 'Mike Lee, the Englishman behind Qatar's World Cup success', *The Guardian*, 2 December 2010, http://www.theguardian.com/football/2010/dec/02/mike-lee-qatar-world-cup-bid; accessed 15 October 2014.
[41] Lee et al., *The Race for the 2012 Olympics*, pp. 33–34.

In the team presentation, Coe's speech, the result of months of marketing strategy discussions, is likely to have been the most significant. It offered the IOC, given its current commitments and political anxieties, everything that it wanted to hear. He promised a 'magical atmosphere', which he immediately translated into a guarantee of a new Olympic Park, containing nine state-of-the-art venues and an athletes' village where competitors would 'live within sight of the Olympic Flame'. He also openly recognised the 'needs of all those upon whom the athletes depend', assuring IOC members, sponsors, media personnel and others that 'we already have legally-binding agreements which guarantee low, fixed prices for all Olympic Family [hotel] rooms. With no minimum stay'. But the bulk of Coe's remarks drew on the chosen and by-now well honed 'narrative' of 'the next generation' – here invoked as a self-evident legacy for the Games.

Coe introduced a number of young British sportspeople to the audience. These included Amber Charles, a 14-year-old Afro-Caribbean schoolgirl basketball player from East Ham who been chosen to deliver the London bid to IOC headquarters in Lausanne in 2004. Why these children, instead of 'businessmen and politicians', Coe asked the gathering, rhetorically.

> It's because we're serious about inspiring young people. Each of them comes from East London, from the communities which will be touched most directly by our Games. And thanks to London's multi-cultural mix of 200 nations,[42] they also represent the youth of the world. Their families have come from every continent. They practise every religion and every faith. What unites them is London. Their love of sport. And their heartfelt dream of bringing the Olympic Games to our city.[43]

These carefully chosen remarks involved the suspension of contemporary politics, in both  the British Parliament (wherein doubts about

---

[42] Back in January 2004 Livingstone had stated that London was the premier 'world city', since over 300 languages were spoken there: 'No other city in the world has the scale of diversity we have here. In a sense, therefore, London represents the Olympic ideal of destroying the barriers that divide us and bringing people together'. See http://news.bbc.co.uk/sport1/hi/olympics_2004/olympics_2012/3393681.stm; accessed 19 October 2014.

[43] All quotations from Lord Coe's speech are taken from a transcript of the address given to the 117th International Olympic Committee Session, Singapore, 6 July 2005. This transcript is held in the British Olympic Association archive collection (Bid by the city of London, 2004–2005), held by the University of East London.

'immigration' and 'multiculturalism' were frequently raised by nearly all parties) and the IOC (who were gifted the symbolic removal of the 'businessmen and politicians' with whom they now routinely dealt). In their place was positioned a platoon of sport-loving ethnic minority children from East London, styled here as a cultural melting pot. These children thus became a symbol of globalism and universality, representing the people of tomorrow, transcendent of nationality, religion, politics or business and bonding the world through sport. In this rendering London embodied the contemporary, media-oriented version of the Olympic ideal of nations communing in athletic competition, Amber Charles and her young 'next generation' colleagues its unimpeachable legacy.

To hammer the point home, the British team then cued a five-minute film, showing young African urchins watching a purported London 2012 Olympics on an open-air TV and seeing a Nigerian (i.e. the adult that they might become) win a gold medal. Further footage shows a series of child-sportspeople (a swimmer, a cyclist, a runner) in various, apparently deprived locales around the world morphing into Olympic winners. The film closes with the promise 'LONDON WILL INSPIRE THE CHAMPIONS OF TOMORROW'.[44]

In sum, the British bid uses children and images of childhood to define London, sport and the Olympics on terms now favoured by governments and by the global sport marketing elite. London's East End is presented as a microcosm of the world's hungry and diverse masses. Here, sport is equated with elite sport and, thus, as a possible way out of poverty. Children such as the ones we are shown may one day win a gold medal at the Olympics, witnessed by a global television audience. If so, they will have access to the social world already inhabited by Lord Coe and the IOC – the world of corporate sponsorship, sports marketing and image rights. All they need for this is, not material help, but to be 'inspired'. Young Amber was photographed with each member of the London delegation – Jowell, Coe, Livingstone..., but, most notably, David Beckham, the living apogee of sports marketing.

It's worth bearing in mind here that this campaign was supported by politicians and public figures who in other contexts would have been quick to condemn the exploitation of children. In Britain in the early twenty-first century, leading spokespeople promoted and/or participated

---

[44] 'Inspiration': Production Company: New Moon Television; Executive Creative Producer: Caroline Rowland; Director: Daryl Goodrich. The film can be viewed at http://vimeo.com/28366735; accessed 17 October 2014.

in a succession of moral panics about the purported vulnerability of children to, among other menaces, child traffickers and pornographers; sex
abusers; the marketers of inappropriately sexualised clothing; and the
publishers of equally inappropriately 'adult' fiction.[45] However, there
was little compunction about the exploitation of children as promotional adornments by the British Olympic bid team in Singapore; once
again, in this respect, as in a number of others discussed later in the
book, London 2012 represented the (unacknowledged and somewhat
hypocritical) suspension of 'politics as usual'. In any event, some of the
multi-ethnic party of young East Enders would, as this book will later
make clear, have strong grounds for feeling that they'd been used.

---

[45] All issues explored in Stephen Wagg and Jane Pilcher (eds.), *Thatcher's Grandchildren? Politics and Childhood in the Twenty-First Century* (London: Palgrave
Macmillan, 2014).

# 3
# 'It Remains Unclear How Local People Will Benefit...': Post-Bid, Pre-Games – Prognostication and Protest

## Sport for all? A new East End? The debate over likely 'trickle down'

Understandably, the award of a third Summer Olympics to London attracted a good deal of comment in the seven years between the IOC's decision and the Games themselves. Commentary centred largely on the purported legacy of the Games, in two principal areas: the nature of the promised 'regeneration' of the East End of London (and any accruing benefits to East Enders) and the (by now, much trumpeted) predicted surge in the number of young people/would-be Olympians inspired by the Games to take up sport.

As we have seen, by the time cities came to contend for the Olympics of 2012, the notions of 'regeneration' and 'legacy' had become the IOC's main imperative; they sat alongside more established considerations, such as modern amenities (a priority since the Berlin Games of 1936, suspended only in the case of the 1948 'Austerity Games') and factors likely to enhance the Olympics as a television event. In 2004 the Cassani team found itself able to offer all of these. London proposed a brand new, state-of-the-art Olympic Park, incorporating the competitors' village. Specific events would be staged at several of the city's world-famous landmarks: Wembley stadium, Lords' cricket ground, Wimbledon's All England Tennis Club, Hyde Park, Regent's Park and Horse Guards Parade. The Olympic Park would be a showpiece of regeneration, since it was to be conjured seemingly out of an apparently neglected area of the East End; Paris' bid, by contrast, was organised around the already-existing Stade de France, which had staged the football World Cup Final of 1998.[1] Moreover, an 'ethical pledge' signed in November 2004 by Coe and Livingstone, following a campaign by the East End pressure group London Citizens, had appeared to guarantee a range of benefits to local people from the Games. The *London Evening Standard* reported that, among other things,

> [u]p to 11,000 jobs would be created by hosting the Olympics, and the deal involves ensuring contractors draw as much of their work-force as possible from the local community. They would be paid a 'living wage' – likely to be around £6.60 an hour. Half of the 9,000 homes to be built in the Olympic Park would be designated for low-paid workers, such as teachers and NHS staff.

Significantly, Coe had stated, following the pledge, that the Olympic bid was now 'eminently more winnable'.[2] Equally significantly, how-ever, as the writer Anna Minton has pointed out, the Olympic Delivery Authority, set up to manage preparations for London 2012 under the London Olympic Games and Paralympic Games Act of 2006, subse-quently refused to honour the pledge, claiming that it was 'illegal to dictate the terms of contracts struck under open tender'.[3] The abandon-ment of this pledge was also noted by the New Economics Foundation, which in 2008 published a detailed and doubtful assessment of probable benefits to the East End:

> It remains unclear how local people will benefit from the assets that are left behind after the Games. The enormous debts built up by Olympic delivery will have to be repaid, and the easiest way to do this will be to sell off Olympic assets to the highest bidder. Serious doubt has already been cast on the projections used by the Govern-ment to calculate the £1.8 billion which could be raised by land sales after the Games to repay public and National Lottery money used to buy land for the Olympic site. Given the current slowdown in the housing market, there will be even more pressure on the London

---

[1] http://news.bbc.co.uk/sport1/hi/olympics_2004/olympics_2012/3402847.stm; accessed 19 October 2014.

[2] Ross Lydall, 'East End to strike gold', *London Evening Standard*, 10 November 2004. See http://www.standard.co.uk/news/east-end-to-strike-gold-7224974.html; accessed 19 October 2014.

[3] See Anna Minton, 'The London Olympics: a festival of private Britain', *The Guardian*, 24 January 2012, http://www.theguardian.com/commentisfree/2012/jan/24/london-olympics-festival-private-legacy; accessed 19 October 2014.

Development Agency (LDA) to maximise revenues. In January 2008, the office of the London Mayor revealed that it had already reneged on its promise that 50 per cent of homes on the Olympic Park would be affordable.[4]

Not wholly discouraged either by the outcry among the IOC-impression-management nexus that had greeted their *Panorama* programme or by the nationalistic media euphoria that had followed the award of the Games to London, in 2007 the BBC permitted investigative journalist David Conn to examine the key claims on which the London bid had been based. Conn tackled the twin issues of legacy – urban renewal and increased sports participation. Using the recent 2002 Commonwealth Games in Manchester as a blueprint for the kind of regeneration that might now await the East End of London, Conn pointed out that £341 million had been expended on a stadium for the Games, now occupied by elite football club Manchester City. There was some limited community access to the stadium, but local researcher Adam Brown told Conn 'I don't get a sense that people feel a great sense of ownership...'; at the same time, sports participation in the area had gone down. Conn found East Enders who anticipated similar outcomes from the London Games: for example, Johnny Walker, Chairman of the Hackney and Leyton [football] League, lamented that the football pitches on Hackney Marshes would be concreted over by 2011 and replaced by a coach park. Amateur footballers would be making way for what was, effectively, professional sport – an 'act of criminality'.

On the matter of accommodation, there was new private housing in East Manchester, but a corresponding decline in social housing and a lengthening of waiting lists. Local people had formed a committee to fight compulsory purchase orders; they felt they were being 'squeezed out' – one spoke of 'the ethnic cleansing of the working class'.

Conn also challenged Coe on the pivotal question of increased sports participation, Coe simply insisting that it would come and that young people principally took to sport because they were inspired by champions. London 2012, said Coe, would bring 'what I've always, always wanted – more young people into sport'. But no evidence existed,

---

[4] Josh Ryan-Collins and Paul Sander-Jackson, 'Fools gold: how the 2012 Olympics is selling East London short, and a 10 point plan for a more positive local legacy', New Economics Foundation, London, 2008, pp. 4–5, http://www.bl.uk/sportandsociety/exploresocsci/businesseconomics/economics/articles/fools_gold08.pdf; accessed 20 October 2014.

replied Conn, that an Olympics had brought a sustained increase in sport or physical activity.

> Conn: 'Does that not worry you – that the research doesn't bear out the theory?'
>
> Coe: 'Well, first of all, I think it's not quite as clear-cut as you make it. But, even if I accept broadly the premise, why I think it can be different [is] I'm not sure that, in any previous Games, there was as much thought given to legacy across all its manifestations as we are giving it here now. I will go to my grave instinctively knowing that the best driver of participation is a well-stocked shop window, ideally full of medallists, world champions. They do more to drive participation than almost anything else. That's not to say you don't fund participation, but all participation funding in the world, on its own, will not produce more people in sport.'
>
> Conn: 'Is that based on evidence or is that based on your own instinct?'
>
> Coe: 'It's based on evidence and my own instinct. I know that the greatest driver for sports participation is because there is a role model.'

Matt Jackson, a researcher at the Institute of Public Policy Research, cast further doubt on this argument. His finding had been that, generally speaking, inspiration to take up sport did not 'trickle down' to people from champion performers. On the contrary, they were put off by spectacles of elite athletic performance and made to feel inadequate; they settled instead for becoming 'couch potatoes'. Indeed, as Jackson pointed out, in 2002 the government's own *Game Plan* had acknowledged that sport mega-events brought little in the way of increased participation.[5]

In the British parliament, the all-party House of Commons Committee of Public Accounts reflected this confusion. In a report of 2006 they had argued that the UK medal tally in the Athens Olympics of 2004 had not met expectation and that future funding should be linked more closely to results.[6] Two years later the same committee stated that

---

[5] All remarks quoted here were transcribed from a tape of the programme 'A sporting chance', BBC Radio Four, 17 April 2007. I'm grateful to the BBC and the help of Adrian Goldberg for the opportunity to listen to it seven years after its original broadcast.

[6] House of Commons Committee of Public Accounts, 54th Report of Session 2005–06, *UK Sport: supporting elite athletes*, HC 898.

'the focus on winning medals could distract the Department [of Culture, Media and Sport]'s attention from encouraging ordinary people to participate. There is no clear evidence that elite sporting achievement influences people to take up sport in the long term....'[7]

Two years later, in Beijing to acknowledge the 'handover' of the Olympic Games to London, Labour Prime Minister Gordon Brown compounded this confusion. Apparently anxious to dispel any suspicion of lingering socialist sensibility within the 'New' Labour project, Brown followed Coe in adopting the language of champions:

> We want to encourage competitive sports in schools, not the 'medals for all' culture we have seen in previous years, [...] In sport you get better by challenging yourself against other people. A lot of sports are team games where people have to work together but they play against other teams.

There would, he claimed, be public health benefits from London 2102, but these could only come via the now widely invoked formula of Olympic inspiration: the Games, Brown stated, 'will inspire fitness and help tackle obesity. The Olympics can inspire people. More people will give up smoking, less people will become obese'.[8] Brown, like most parties to the promotion of London 2012, was trying to square the circle, communing in the now-dominant Olympic rhetoric of 'inspiration' and grafting on to it a highly improbable social benefit. Commenting on Brown's forecast of a decline in obesity and smoking, socialist commentator Yuri Prasad responded that

> there is plenty of evidence to suggest that the opposite will be the case. As the cost of the London Olympics has spiralled to £9.3 billion, funds are being diverted from local sports projects that involve many thousands of people – few of whom engage with sport in order to win a medal. The big money is now being directed towards creating 'centres of excellence' in selected sports where a few hundred potential success stories will be groomed in the hope of Team GB winning a few more medals.

---

[7] House of Commons Committee of Public Accounts, 42nd Report of Session 2007–08, *Preparing for sporting success at the London 2012 Olympic and Paralympic Games and beyond*, HC477, p. 2.
[8] Deborah Summers, 'Bring back competitive school sports: Brown', *The Guardian*, 25 August 2008, http://www.theguardian.com/education/2008/aug/25/school sports.olympics2012; accessed 24 October 2014.

As an example, he judged that the building of the 2,500-seat Olympic
Aquatics Centre in Stratford 'will speed the demise of nine local swimming pools in London – including the best pool in the host borough of
Waltham Forest, which is short of the £75 million it needs each year to
remain open'.[9]

It's fair to say that, as preparation for the Games progressed, the official language of Olympic legacy generally remained as unspecific as the
vocabulary employed by Coe in the above exchanges. Ex-Prime Minister Blair, for instance, was similarly vague in 2010: 'People talked about
the Games needing a legacy, which normally meant facilities that didn't
close as soon as the Games were over. I took it to mean something that
would make a positive difference to the world'.[10] The bulk of criticism
of the Olympic project meanwhile concentrated – as is routinely the
case with Games in the postmodern era – on the escalating costs of
it. In 2008, for example, journalist Ed Howker published an apparently
well-sourced article telling of serious concern in the British corridors of
power at the rising costs of the Games (already, at £9.3 billion, triple the
original estimate) and the salaries being paid to officials – £557,440, for
example, to Paul Deighton, a multimillionaire ex-banker with Goldman
Sachs and now chair of the Olympic Organising Committee.[11] Indeed, a
poll taken only six months before London 2012 found that under half
of respondents felt the Games would be worth the cost to the public
purse.[12]

A number of close scrutineers, however, were prepared to postpone
judgement on the Games and, in particular, on the crucial question of
legacy.

Chief among these latter was a team of researchers at the London
East Research Institute (LERI). This institute was housed in the University of East London, which was based in Newham, the same borough
as the Olympic Park. *Olympic Cities: 2012 and the Remaking of London,*[13]
edited by Gavin Poynter and Iain MacRury of the LERI, was published in
2009 and could be seen as the most cogent and thoroughgoing academic
appraisal of the approaching Games and their likely impact.

[9] Yuri Prasad, 'Bluster aside, these games won't deliver', *Socialist Worker*, 30 August
2008, p. 4.
[10] Tony Blair, *A Journey* (London: Hutchinson, 2010), p. 551.
[11] Ed Howker, 'A gold medal muddle', *Independent*, 22 October 2008, pp. 12–13.
[12] Andrew Grice, 'Public still slow to warm to this summer's Olympics', *Independent*, 29 March 2012, p. 4.
[13] Gavin Poynter and Iain MacRury (eds.), *Olympic Cities: 2012 and the Remaking
of London* (Farnham: Ashgate, 2009).

While it acknowledges some of the arguments of critical Olympic scholarship, the tone of the book is broadly optimistic and/or properly agnostic about the benefits that London 2012 might bring. While some essays note the onset of commercialism and the growing contradiction between Olympism and branding,[14] Poynter argues that 'Commercial Games' constitute only one possible outcome (as against 'Catalytic Games', which bring better infrastructure and national self-promotion, and 'Dynamic Games', which signal the hosts as major economic powers)[15] and various contributors (like a large number of academic writers on the Olympics) accept individual Summer Olympics – Seoul (1988),[16] Barcelona (1992)[17] and Athens (2004)[18] – broadly on the IOC's own terms, judging them to have been successes. The only serious reservation is over Atlanta (1996), where the Games were held to have been utilised to 'commence a process of urban renewal that marginalised community groups and local forms of political accountability while "privileging investors' interests"…'[19] With regard to London 2012, the book expresses a guarded confidence. Gavin Poynter, for example, approved the partnership between public bodies (central government, the Lord Mayor of London's office, the British Olympic Association – all represented by the London Organising Committee for the Olympic Games; Transport for London; the Olympic Delivery Authority; the local authorities of Greenwich, Hackney, Newham, Waltham Forest and Tower Hamlets…) and private ones (the Olympic Development Authority, responsible for building the Olympic facilities, was a private consortium). He suggested that, unlike for Atlanta, 'the agencies engaged with London 2012 are not dominated by a coalition of primarily commercial interests'[20] and that there had been an over-emphasis

---

[14] See, for instance, Iain MacRury, 'Branding the Games: commercialism and the Olympic City', in Poynter and MacRury (eds.), *Olympic Cities*, pp. 43–71.

[15] Gavin Poynter, 'The evolution of the Olympic and Paralympic Games 1948–2012', in Poynter and MacRury (eds.), *Olympic Cities*, pp. 23–41.

[16] Hyunsun Yoon, 'The legacy of the 1988 Seoul Olympic Games', in Poynter and MacRury (eds.), *Olympic Cities*, pp. 87–95.

[17] Ferran Brunet, 'The economy of the Barcelona Olympic Games', in Poynter and MacRury (eds.), *Olympic Cities*, pp. 97–119.

[18] Roy Panagiotopoulou, 'The 28th Olympic Games in Athens 2004', in Poynter and MacRury (eds.), *Olympic Cities*, pp. 145–162.

[19] Gavin Poynter and Emma Roberts, 'Atlanta (1996): the Centennial Games', in Poynter and MacRury (eds.), *Olympic Cities*, pp. 121–131, p. 130.

[20] Gavin Poynter, 'London: preparing for 2012', in Poynter and MacRury (eds.), *Olympic Cities*, pp. 183–199. See pp. 187–189.

in the media on the financing of the Games. In effect, endorsing Ken Livingstone's position, he concluded:

> The hosting of the 2012 Games lends legitimation to a programme of state-led urban renewal on a significant scale and in a time-frame that is more rapid than the normal 'organic' process of urban regeneration [...] Set in this context, the costs associated with the Games are less 'madness' or 'scandal' and more a public investment in a process of social re-engineering of London's east end.[21]

## The bailiffs and the blue fence: the East End responds

In the East End itself, meanwhile, there was much disquiet and considerable protest following the approval of London's bid in 2006, most of it unrecorded in the mainstream national media. Much of it concerned the expropriation of East Enders, many of whom lost their homes and/or their livelihoods and sources of pleasure. While it was quite widely made known that 1.5 million people had been displaced to make way for the Beijing Olympics of 2008,[22] this may have been because China was a command economy, run by the Communist Party and therefore, in mainstream media assumption, the claimed antithesis of Western freedoms. East End displacements, however, and protests against them – mounted as they were by people (council tenants, small businesses, travellers...) conspicuously lacking in political power – might rate only a small paragraph in a British broadsheet or an item on local television news. Nevertheless, in 2005 the Geneva-based Centre on Housing, Rights and Evictions (which had earlier recorded the Beijing displacements) found itself monitoring the largest compulsory purchase order (CPO) in British history, issued by the London Development Agency (LDA) on land in the East End of London.[23]

CPOs have become a routine feature of Olympic preparation and among the people most vulnerable to them are tenants in the designated areas, who are not entitled to compensation.[24] In November 2005

---

[21] Ibid., pp. 196–197.

[22] See, for example, Lindsay Beck, 'Beijing to evict 1.5 million for Olympics: group', *Reuters*, 5 June 2007, http://www.reuters.com/article/2007/06/05/us-olympics-beijing-housing-idUSPEK12263220070605; accessed 20 October 2014.

[23] See Craig Hatcher, 'Legacies of dislocation on the Clays Lane Estate', in Hilary Powell and Isaac Marrero-Guillamon (eds.), *The Art of Dissent: Adventures in London's Olympic State* (London: Marshgate Press, 2012), pp. 197–206.

[24] Ibid., pp. 199–200.

the tenants of the Clays Lane estate in Stratford, East London, were served with CPOs, the site having been earmarked for the Olympic Village. Over 1,000 people were forcibly evicted from homes or businesses in the Stratford area[25] in the early summer of 2007 and the LDA was claiming to have met little resistance. The British *The Guardian* reported:

> The London Development Agency (LDA), which had a £1.4bn budget for land assembly, had expected fierce protests and resistance to one of Britain's biggest compulsory purchase orders. But it is now confident that the whole site will be under its control by July 2 – with 93% secured through agreement, rather than legal enforcement. Gareth Blacker, the LDA's director of development for the Olympics, said yesterday: 'We are not envisaging a huge number of evictions, but there might be one or two as a sign of protest'.[26]

Protests, 'fierce' or otherwise, had, however, been numerous, taking the form of demonstrations, the formation of action groups, the inauguration of websites – some critical of the Olympics in general[27] and some covering specific East End struggles, such as the campaign to save the Carpenters estate in Stratford[28] – and representations to government.

These various efforts were, on the whole, unsuccessful, but instructive. Several important themes emerged.

First, local authorities in the East End seemed to have had 'regeneration' plans for the area that pre-dated the award of the Olympics and, thus, to have availed themselves of the coming Games as a pretext. Residents of the Clays Lane estate had been told by the LDA back in 2003: 'We've got plans for this area, and we're going to demolish this estate whatever happens'[29]; after the Olympics, Newham Council attempted

---

[25] Ibid., p. 197.

[26] Andrew Culf, 'Olympic evictees go without a struggle', *The Guardian*, 21 June 2007, http://www.theguardian.com/society/2007/jun/21/communities. olympics2012; accessed 21 October 2014.

[27] See, for example, the Counter Olympics Network, http://counterolympics network.wordpress.com/; accessed 21 October 2014. The more generic Games Monitor, http://www.gamesmonitor.org.uk/about; accessed 21 October 2014 had been founded in 2006.

[28] See http://savecarpenters.wordpress.com/about/; accessed 21 October 2014.

[29] Julian Cheyne, resident of the estate 1991–2007, in conversation with Charlotte Baxter, *The Guardian*, 2 June 2008. See 'Displaced by the Olympics', http://www.theguardian.com/uk/2008/jun/02/olympics2012; accessed 21 October 2014.

to sell the Carpenters estate to University College London for a new campus.[30]

Second, the pervasive reaction of local residents faced with eviction was that they were losing their sense of community – the thing they valued most and which could not be compensated for: at one demonstration a protester held a placard reading 'CLAYS LANE: THE REAL OLYMPIC VILLAGE'.[31]

Third, many of the expropriated residents of this part of London's East End did not anticipate that the Games' material legacy would benefit people like themselves. Seventy-five-year-old Ron Rowen, ex-Royal Navy and the Fire Service, was expecting in 2007 to be led out of his home by bailiffs. He told Rachel Williams of *The Guardian*: 'After the Olympics the property mob will move in. You'll get a lot of people with money here and it will never be the same again. I want to keep it like this'.[32] The following year, Julian Cheyne, obliged the year before to leave his home on the Clays Lane estate, said:

This is about regenerating east London, but not for the people who live there now. It's being done for a completely new population, a much richer population who will enjoy the canals that were once used for industrial purposes but are now available for them to live next door to and enjoy the river views and so on. Our community was shattered. It fell apart very rapidly once this started, as people were concerned about finding a place to go.[33]

Fourth, a section of the Olympic zone – specifically the Lower Lea Valley – was apparently, in effect, nobody's in particular, much of it

---

[30] Negotiations with UCL collapsed in 2013, by which time planning powers for the area had transferred to the Mayor and the London Legacy Development Corporation. At the time of writing, the group Carpenters Against Regeneration Plans (CARP) is still active, albeit in abeyance, awaiting the planners' next move, according to Joe, CARP spokesman, telephone interview, 21 October 2014.
[31] Powell and Marrero-Guillamon (eds.), *The Art of Dissent*, p. 213. See also Cheyne and Baxter, 'Displaced by the Olympics'.
[32] 21 June 2007, http://www.theguardian.com/society/2007/jun/21/communities. olympics2012; accessed 21 October 2014.
[33] Cheyne and Baxter, 'Displaced by the Olympics'. See also Richard Giulianotti, Gary Armstrong, Gavin Hales and Dick Hobbs, 'Sport mega-events and public opposition: a sociological study of the London 2012 Olympics', *Journal of Sport and Social Issues*, p. 3, http://jss.sagepub.com/content/early/2014/04/14/0193723514530565, published online 14 April 2014; accessed 16 September 2014.

wild and untended. As space, this made it attractive to many local people but, politically, less easy to defend. This terrain, according to the writer Anthony Iles, was 'formed by strips of common land, canals and marshes separating the Metropolitan Borough of Hackney from the Victorian suburbs of Newham, Walthamstow and Leyton [and] was an agricultural, then industrial area characterised by railways, greenhouses, warehouses and light manufacturing until the end of the Second World War'.[34] Thereafter it became 'a place where people make their own entertainment, from allotment holders, footballers, anglers, kite flyers, ramblers, cyclists and nature lovers to ravers and free party-makers, under-age drinkers, graffiti artists and scooter thieves' – marginal groups, engaged in activities that took place 'without planning or costly amenity'.[35] Such an aggregation – a world away from Lord Coe and his legion of inspiring elite athletes – was clearly not going to detain the Olympic project. They did not go down without a fight, however, nor, in some cases, a dignified lament, but they could too easily be made to seem like quaint romantics, affordable casualties in the cause of economic progress and national celebration.

In the late summer of 2007 an 11 mile, blue-painted fence went up around this site. The Olympic Delivery Authority said it had been erected for 'health and safety reasons, primarily…' but *The Guardian* reporter Andy Beckett found it to be policed with some severity – a local sculptor called Silke Dettmers told him she had been arrested for taking photographs of it.[36] His *The Guardian* readership would very likely have sided largely with the sculptor, harassed for her artistic curiosity, but Beckett made it clear that local opinion wasn't wholly behind lovers of the Lea Valley landscape. A Lithuanian carpenter, working on the site, was impatient with such sensitivities and told Beckett: 'I don't know when they're going to start the action. The environmental people mess everything up. They find some pigeon nest, and all work stops'.[37] A community of travellers – the social grouping with the least political influence in the whole of Europe – was moving, reluctantly, to another site.

The plot-holders of the Manor Gardens Allotment Society appeared to fare better. Perhaps benefiting from the bedrock public sympathy

---

[34] Anthony Iles, 'The Lower Lea Valley: from fun palace to creative prison', in Powell and Marrero-Guillamon (eds.), *The Art of Dissent*, pp. 150–159, p. 150.
[35] Ibid.
[36] Andy Beckett, 'Cordon blue', *The Guardian*, 21 September 2007, http://www.theguardian.com/society/2007/sep/21/communities; accessed 21 October 2014.
[37] Ibid.

for private cultivators and the consequent popularity of television gardening programmes, those tilling the Manor Gardens Allotments at Hackney Wick (now within the designated Olympic Park) attracted considerable local media attention.[38] They were allowed to tend their allotments for a time, even after the blue fence had gone up, given alternative land and promised that they would be restored to their original plots after the Games. (Tessa Jowell, perhaps sensing strong public support for allotment holders, in London and elsewhere, protested the reneging on this specific promise in 2014.[39] She doesn't appear to have condemned the breaking of any other promises made ahead of London 2012.) The greatest media coverage, though, was accorded to Iain Sinclair, a novelist, filmmaker and poetic chronicler of London life, who wrote in coruscating (if sometimes elusive) prose about the militaristic intrusions upon his East End. His media access was used for commentary, rather than activism, and this commentary evoked principally despair. He wrote a long essay for *London Review of Books* in which he observed: 'The opponents of the Grand Project, this unoccupied City of Illusions with its vivid blue frontier, its plywood scarf, are a community bonded in loss'.[40]

Fifth, the vigorous representations of local people were swallowed up in consultations and purported official enquiries, the outcome of which it was not difficult to predict. Thus, the political pattern of expropriation identified by various writers in relation to preceding Olympics was repeated to various tribunals and then ruled to be of no relevance. David Rose, the inspector chairing the inquiry into the consequences for private tenants of compulsory purchase orders in the East End, ruled: 'I am not convinced that the experiences of former Olympic cities around the world, with different social contexts, administrative and regulatory mechanisms and specific characteristics, has any material bearing in

---

[38] For example, BBC1 television's *Inside Out* programme provided a sympathetic report on the campaign to save the allotments: 30 October 2006. This can be seen on YouTube, https://www.youtube.com/watch?v=Q-aNwauzO3Y; accessed 21 October 2014.

[39] 'Tessa Jowell – Joan of arc of the allotments?', http://www.gamesmonitor.org.uk/node/2178; accessed 21 October 2014.

[40] Iain Sinclair, 'The Olympics scam', *London Review of Books*, Vol. 30, No. 12 (19 June 2008), pp. 17–23, http://www.lrb.co.uk/v30/n12/iain-sinclair/the-olympics-scam; accessed 21 October 2014. See also Iain Sinclair, *Ghost Milk: Calling Time on the Grand Project* (London: Penguin, 2012) and 'A Pox on the Games' (Iain Sinclair interviewed by John Walsh), *Independent Magazine*, 2 July 2011, pp. 24–27.

anticipating social outcomes in the Lower Lea Valley'. He cited 'the pro-vision of a significant number of affordable housing units' and insisted that, besides, '[a]ny pressures on land values and accommodation arising from the Games' would have to be weighed against 'the very substantial benefits that the project will bring...'.[41]

The mainstream media, meanwhile, attended mainly to the sorts of argument, identified by Lenskyj, which now routinely characterised the narrating of Olympic preparation. These included the vocabulary of the 'ticking clock',[42] via which audiences are reminded that the Games' infrastructure must be ready on time. For example, in the sum-mer of 2009 an article in the *Independent on Sunday* by blogger and Olympic supporter Alan Hubbard assured readers: 'The clock is ticking but we're setting a good pace'.[43] A year later Hubbard followed up with the even more heartening 'Two years to go and London is so ahead of the Games'.[44] Beyond this, while ostensibly prepared at least to give the Olympic critique a hearing, the columnists of the liberal broad-sheet press had a counter-argument up their sleeve: opponents of the Olympics could readily be branded as cultural snobs (leading spokespeo-ple had, for instance, accused the government of diverting money from the arts to pay for the Olympics[45]) and no fun. This depiction was given a greater airing as the Games drew closer. *The Independent* was typical. 'Don't believe the killjoys of London 2012' was the headline of an article by columnist Mary Dejevsky in the spring of 2010. 'Let the privilegentsia huff and puff with more or less gentility', wrote Dejevsky. 'They can move out for the summer if they feel that strongly and leave the rest of us to enjoy the global party'.[46] Two years on, and with the Games a fortnight away, fellow columnist John Walsh could be found styling the

---

[41] Martin Slavin, 'Scenes from public consultations', in Powell and Marrero-Guillamon (eds.), *The Art of Dissent*, pp. 214–219, p. 216.

[42] Helen Jefferson Lenskyj, *Olympic Industry Resistance: Challenging Olympic Power and Propaganda* (Albany: State University of New York Press), p. 18.

[43] Alan Hubbard speaks to Sebastian Coe, 'The clock is ticking but we're setting a good pace', *Independent on Sunday*, 26 July 2009, pp. 12–13.

[44] Alan Hubbard, 'Two years to go and London is so ahead of the Games', *Independent on Sunday*, 25 July 2010, pp. 18–19.

[45] See, for example, Andrew Culf and Charlotte Higgins, 'Arts leaders turn on Jowell over Olympics', *The Guardian*, 23 April 2007, p. 1.

[46] Mary Dejevsky, 'Don't believe the killjoys of 2012', *Independent*, 2 April 2010, http://www.independent.co.uk/voices/commentators/mary-dejevsky/mary-dejevsky-dont-believe-the-killjoys-of-london-2012-1933797.html; accessed 11 February 2015.

various anti-Olympic arguments as events-in-themselves ('Synchronised Grumbling', 'Throwing the Hammer of Sarcasm' . . . ) and calling for an end to the 'moaning':

> When it comes to the Olympics 2012, we're all paid up members of the Grouch club. There isn't a single area of this massive project that we haven't thoroughly dissed and agreed to disparage. And now that it's here at last, coming over the cloudy horizon in a flood of striving humanity – athletes, boxers, horsemen, cyclists, gymnasts, hoop-shooters, javelin launchers, shot-putters, jumpers, vaulters, sprinters – we have to face an awkward truth: we're probably going to love it.[47]

Finally, a day or two before London 2012, in an article that also appeared on the *World Post* website, a third *Independent* columnist, Christina Patterson, applied a hefty (if somewhat tortuous) tug to her readership's heartstrings. Stating that Olympic athletes were 'from all around the world, and sometimes from poor families, and sometimes from poor families in some of the poorest countries in the world, and you think about where they started, and where they are now, what you think is that all is not lost'. Patterson continued:

> You think that some people in the world can carry on thinking that it's good to be famous just for being famous, but many, many other people can carry on thinking that what matters isn't who you are, or if you're famous, but what you do with what you've got. What we'll see, for the next three weeks, will remind us that the most spectacular feats in the world don't cost money. And that, for all the worry and embarrassment, will be £9 billion well spent.[48]

In this remarkable formulation, Olympic protesters were therefore, in effect, despising the world's poor and its athletic strivers. These (highly trained and variously funded) strivers will have been as surprised as

[47] John Walsh, 'Let the moaning end and the Games begin', *Independent*, 13 July 2012, pp. 8–9, p. 8.
[48] Christina Patterson, 'This party in the park could prove to be £9bn well spent', *Independent*, 25 July 2012. See also Christina Patterson, 'Why the Olympics could be £9 billion well spent', *World Post*, 25 July 2012, http://www.huffingtonpost.com/christina-patterson/why-the-olympics-could-be_b_1702144.html; accessed 22 October 2014.

anyone to learn that their feats, spectacular and otherwise, did not 'cost money'. There are perceptible signs of strain and (in the case of Patterson) emotional blackmail in these arguments – a tacit acknowledgement, perhaps, that important criticisms of the Olympics were still in play and needed, for the time being at least, to be dismissed in what was now assumed to be 'the national interest'. This, needless to say, was not a strand of argument new to contemporary Olympic debate – indeed, it seems to have been introduced in relation to London 2012 comparatively late. Critics of Sydney 2000 were branded 'unpatriotic' or 'Un-Australian'[49] and support for the Beijing Games in 2008 was deemed by the Chinese government to be a patriotic duty.[50]

---

[49] Helen Jefferson Lenskyj, *The Best Olympics Ever? Social Impacts of Sydney 2000* (Albany: State University of New York Press, 2002), p. 24.

[50] Anne-Marie Broudehoux, 'The social and spatial impacts of Olympic image construction', in Helen Jefferson Lenskyj and Stephen Wagg (eds.), *The Palgrave Handbook of Olympic Studies* (Basingstoke: Palgrave Macmillan, 2012), pp. 195–209, p. 202.

# 4
# Looking for Inspiration: The Politics of the Olympic Flame at London 2012

The rituals of the Olympic Games are a case study in the invention of tradition. In particular, from the time of the founding of the modern Olympics in the late nineteenth century to the contemporary deliberations of IOC marketing strategists, some kinship to the rites of the original festival in ancient Greece has been either claimed or implied. At the centre of this mythologising has stood the Olympic flame, which was never more prominently displayed than at London 2012.

## The Olympic flame: origins and destinations

Academics – particularly historians of the ancient world – have queued up to refute a range of suggestions that the modern Olympics have accurately borrowed from the original events staged on Mount Olympus.[1] While the IOC continues to insist that the Olympic torch relay was one of these original events,[2] the evidence is to the contrary. Classics professor Mark Golden recently wrote: 'the torch relay, moving and effective as it is, had no purpose in an ancient festival rooted at one site, and even the lighting of the Olympic flame is modern...'.[3] Indeed, the

---

[1] A prominent commentator here has been Paul Cartledge, Professor of Greek Culture at Cambridge University. See his 'Olympic self sacrifice', *History Today*, Vol. 50, No. 10 (2000), http://www.historytoday.com/paul-cartledge/olympic-self-sacrifice; accessed 31 October 2014.

[2] See the IOC website, http://www.olympic.org/olympic-torch-relay-origin-values-ceremony; accessed 5 November 2014.

[3] Mark Golden, 'The ancient Olympics and the modern: mirror and mirage', in Helen Jefferson Lenskyj and Stephen Wagg (eds.), *The Palgrave Handbook of Olympic Studies* (Basingstoke: Palgrave Macmillan 2012), pp. 15–25, p. 17.

inauthentic nature of the Olympic torch ritual is quite widely acknowledged. In early April 2008, for example, with the torch on its way to
Beijing, British political journalist Andy McSmith reasserted the (equally
quite widely held) view that the Olympic torch ritual had been devised
for the so-called 'Nazi Olympics' of 1936 in Berlin: 'There is a two-word
answer to those who think the Olympic torch is a symbol of harmony
between nations that should be kept apart from politics – Adolf Hitler.'[4]
McSmith credited Carl Diem, the Berlin Games' chief organiser, with
developing the idea from pagan mythology, which 'could hardly fail to
appeal to the Nazis'.[5] The apparently Nazi origins of the relay were aired
once again at London 2012 but this time, perhaps predictably given
the virtually monolithic support by the British media for the Games
themselves, observations of this kind seem to have surfaced only in the
socialist press:

> The Olympic torch 70-day relay across Britain is being heralded as a
> moment of celebration. The International Olympic Committee pres-
> ident Jacques Rogge said the relay will 'promote peace and make our
> world a better place'. There's just one problem with that – the modern
> torch relay was invented as a Nazi propaganda tool. [...] The torch
> made its way [...] through Bulgaria, Yugoslavia, Hungary, Austria and
> Czechoslovakia to Berlin. Before long Hitler's troops made the same
> journey in reverse.[6]

Several years earlier, two Olympic historians strongly supportive of the
Games had sought to adjust the widespread attribution of the Olympic
torch idea to Diem and the Nazi propagandists. Their purpose was simply to place alongside Diem, as contributors to the fashioning of the
'most elaborate and glorious sport spectacle known to us in modern
times' the names of two Dutchmen, Jan Wils and Johan Wienecke, who
were involved in the preparation of the Amsterdam Games in 1928, and
the Greek archaeologist Alexander Philadelpheus, who had raised the
possibility of lighting the torch using the sun's rays.[7]

---

[4] Andy McSmith, 'Aryan ideals, not ancient Greece, were the inspiration behind
flame tradition', *The Independent*, 8 April 2008, p. 3.
[5] Ibid.
[6] 'The troublemaker' column, *Socialist Worker*, 19 May 2012, p. 2.
[7] Robert K. Barney and Anthony Th. Bijkerk, 'The genesis of sacred fire in Olympic
ceremony: a new interpretation', *Journal of Olympic History*, Vol. 12, No. 2,
pp. 6–27, pp. 6 and 8, http://library.la84.org/SportsLibrary/JOH/JOHv13n2/
JOHv13n2f.pdf; accessed 31 October 2014.

In 1998 Janet Cahill noted:

> In the past two decades, the official Olympic Games Organising Committee reports have increasingly depicted the flame ceremony and torch relay as being central elements of the Olympic Games. The first in-depth description of the Olympic flame and torch relay was found in the official report of the 1984 Games in Los Angeles.[8]

Cahill, who acted as consultant to the Olympic Games Business Unit at the Australian Tourist Commission during the Sydney Olympics of 2000, also observed that there had been a considerable lengthening of the time devoted to the Olympic relay between the financially ill-fated Olympics in Montreal in 1976, when only a few days were set aside for the torch to make its progress, and subsequent Games such as those staged in Los Angeles in 1984 and in Atlanta in 1996, for which the time allotted had risen to 'a few months' – a period which facilitated 'a build-up to the Opening Ceremony, as well as extra mileage for sponsors of the Olympic Games to advertise the forth-coming event'.[9] However, as with so many arranged marriages between sport and marketing, the commercialising of this variously confected Olympic ritual had often failed to gain full acceptance and had had to be tempered. Reflecting on the Atlanta Games and looking toward the next Olympics in Sydney, Cahill wrote:

> it may be debated that the essence of what the sponsor is 'buying' in its sponsorship is being eroded by misuse. The culmination of this is the 1996 Olympic torch relay to Atlanta which became nicknamed in the press as the 'Coca Cola torch relay'. Sydney Organisers have recognised that the dilution of the flame and torch symbols and their direct association with the Olympic Games affects more than the sponsors. Games organisers rely on the torch relay to build good community feeling for the Games and draw the community as a whole into the Olympic Games experience. Therefore in 2000, the torch relay will not be associated with one major sponsor thereby limiting the name-association with the event.[10]

---

[8] Janet Cahill, 'The Olympic flame and torch: running towards Sydney 2000', in R. Barney, K. Wamsley, S. Martyn and G. MacDonald (eds.), *Global and Cultural Critique: Problematizing the Olympic Games Proceedings of Fourth International Symposium for Olympic Research* (London and Ontario: International Centre for Olympic Studies, 1998), pp. 181–190, p. 183, http://library.la84.org/Sports Library/ISOR/ISOR1998u.pdf; accessed 2 November 2014.

[9] Ibid.

[10] Cahill, 'The Olympic flame and torch', p. 185.

In the event, the torch relay for the Sydney Games was sponsored by AMP, an Australian financial services company – a company which, by its very nature and unlike, say, Coca-Cola, would be more interested in gaining kudos within the business world than in maintaining a profile in a mass consumer market.

Beside this, the Beijing Olympics of 2008 had demonstrated how, for its sponsors, the torch relay could be a double-edged sword. These Games had promised to be a honeypot for Olympic partners with the expectation, most importantly, of access to an emergent market of 400 million urban consumers in China. The torch relay for Beijing was sponsored by Coca Cola, the South Korean home electronics conglomerate Samsung, and Lenovo, a Chinese multinational computer technology company with headquarters in China and the United States. It was scheduled for a long haul, beginning on 24 March, culminating on 8 August and traversing twenty countries on the way. On its arrival in London, however, in early April the torch was met by angry demonstrators protesting the Chinese government's abuse of human rights, particularly its repression in Tibet, annexed by China in 1951. In a series of tussles a number of attempts were made to grab the torch or extinguish it – attempts repelled with some force by Chinese security guards and the Metropolitan Police.[11] (Chinese security guards, of course, should ordinarily have no authority to act in this way in the United Kingdom. Intentionally or otherwise, this seems to have been still another example of the now-familiar granting of Olympic immunity.) The following day, despite the presence of 3,000 police, there was similar mayhem in Paris, where the mayor had to cancel a scheduled reception ceremony for the torch, which was taken onto a bus for safe-keeping.[12]

The Ethical Corporation, a company providing advice to 'businesses around the globe to do the right thing by their customers and the world',[13] had seen this coming:

> Corporate sponsors of the 2008 Beijing Olympics are facing a tough challenge to protect their own reputations as a worldwide campaign breaks out against the host country. An intensifying campaign against China's crackdown on ethnic protests in Tibet, the jailing of activists, suppression of human rights and its role in Darfur is calling

---

[11] Jerome Taylor, '35 protesters arrested as Olympic torch is paraded through London', *The Independent*, 7 April 2008, p. 2.

[12] 'Protests cut short Olympic relay', *BBC News*, 7 April 2008, http://news.bbc.co.uk/1/hi/world/europe/7334545.stm; accessed 3 November 2014.

[13] http://www.ethicalcorp.com/about-us; accessed 2 November 2014.

on sponsors to act. [...] The most immediate threat for brands is
expected from the activists trying to use the Olympic torch relay to
make their point, as witnessed at its launch in Greece and during legs
in Istanbul, London, Paris and San Francisco. Tensions have been
expected to peak when the torch is taken to Mount Everest, passing through Tibet, a gesture that pro-Tibet groups call provocative.
Boycotts of ceremonies, heavy security arrangements and images of
activists scuffling with police, violence and arrests have resulted in
regular negative publicity for China, and the sponsors. This is all bad
news for Coca-Cola, Samsung and Lenovo – the three sponsors of
the torch relay. A group of 153 pro-Tibet organisations has written to
Coca-Cola chief executive Neville Isdell asking him to withdraw from
sponsorship and to request the organisers to drop Tibet region from
the relay route.[14]

Coca-Cola could not, of course, have been expected to renounce their
sponsorship of this purported symbol of international peace and had
responded in the only way that, in the circumstances, they could
have been expected to respond. Spokeswoman Kelly Brooks had stated:
'We remain committed to supporting the torch relay, which provides
a unique opportunity to share the Olympic values of unity, pride and
inspiration with people all over the world'[15] – but the buffeting of the
torch in 2008, coupled with the dangers of too-brash commercialism
evidenced at Atlanta in 1996, will very likely have given the Olympic
torch strategists of London 2012 pause for thought. After all, the British
government's human rights record was scarcely blameless, following its
occupation (along with the United States) of Afghanistan (since 2001)
and Iraq (since 2003), its military support for the armed overthrow of
the Libyan government in 2011 and the heavy policing of urban riots in
London the same year.[16] Moreover, in the wake of the banking crisis of
2008 and drastic 'austerity' measures taken in Britain by the newly established Conservative-Liberal Democrat Coalition, two groups of political
activists had begun to take direct action – UK Uncut (founded 2010) had

[14] Rajesh Chhabara, 'Olympics 2008: Beijing games – sponsors enter rings of fire',
*Ethical Corporation*, 8 May 2008, http://www.ethicalcorp.com/communications-
reporting/olympics-2008-beijing-games-%E2%80%93-sponsors-enter-rings-fire;
accessed 3 November 2014.
[15] Ibid.
[16] See http://www.theguardian.com/uk/series/reading-the-riots; accessed 3 November 2014.

demonstrated at the premises of businesses engaged in 'corporate tax avoidance'[17] and the following year Occupy London (formed in sympathy with the Occupy Wall Street movement in New York) had tried to camp outside the London Stock Exchange. This might cause individual Olympic partners to be concerned, but as the UK Uncut website pointed out, the whole Olympic project carried tax exemptions for its corporate supporters:

> The Olympic site has become the world's newest temporary tax haven. Instead of funding our vital public services, or refunding the British public for paying for the Olympics, billions of pounds of profits made by multinational companies with monopoly rights to exploit the Games will flow directly into the pockets of shareholders and CEOs. The Games' 'partner organisations' including the likes of McDonald's and Visa have a temporary exemption from both UK Corporation Tax and UK Income Tax. According to a report published by Ethical Consumer, Olympics-related corporate partners and service providers are due to make £2.7bn in revenues this summer. They will be avoiding over £600m in tax.[18]

UK Uncut had announced a series of street parties across the country to precede the Olympics and to 'resist the cuts and celebrate a future that is decided by us, not a handful of billionaires'.[19] This specific announcement will have come too late to influence the planning of the torch relay, but public disquiet at the reductions in public spending (defined as 'savings' by the government) and the minimal tax paid by huge companies were established items for public conversation after 2008.

With all this in mind, the imperatives seem to have been to protect the sponsors from the scourge of any unseemly publicity and at the same time to attract as much approbation as possible to the torch itself by judicious selection of its bearers.

---

[17] Mark Townsend, 'High street stores hit in day of action over corporate tax avoidance', *The Observer*, 19 December 2010, http://www.theguardian.com/uk/2010/dec/19/uk-uncut-tax-avoidance-protests; accessed 4 November 2014.
[18] UK Uncut, 'An Olympic tax dodge', 14 July 2012, http://www.ukuncut.org.uk/?s=olympic+; accessed 4 November 2014.
[19] UK Uncut, 'Press release: UK Uncut to hold protest "Great British Street Parties" before the Jubilee and Olympics', 12 April 2012, http://www.ukuncut.org.uk/?s=olympic+; accessed 4 November 2014.

## Dumb generalisations? The Olympic torch at London 2012

On 10 May 2012 the Olympic torch was lit, as is now customary, in a ceremony at the ancient Temple of Hera at Olympia performed by actresses dressed as vestal virgins. Losing no opportunity to underscore the Greek-ness of the ceremony, and its culmination in the UK, organisers had arranged for the torch to be handed over to Greek swimming world champion Spyros Gianniotis, who had been born to a British mother in Liverpool. Gianniotis later passed it to 19 year old boxer Alexander Loukos, who held it together with Spyros Philipas, president and chief executive of Greek car dealers BMW Hellas. Loukos, whose father was Greek, had been another of the East End children brought by the London bid team to Singapore to support their chosen theme of young-people-to-be-inspired. At the ceremony Coe delivered a speech, from which the *Newham Recorder*, local paper in a borough where part of the Olympic Park now stood, selected the following words:

> Sport has enduring and universal appeal, and the timeless Olympic values transcend history and geography; values, which, I believe, in these challenging times are more relevant than at any time before, particularly to young people all over the world. This is the second time representatives of the UK have gathered here to celebrate the lighting of the Olympic Flame. In 1948, shortly after the Second World War, my predecessor stood where I am today and made the first tentative steps in turning the world from war to sport. We find ourselves in challenging times again and turn to sport once more to connect the world in a global celebration of achievement and inspiration.[20]

IOC President Jacques Rogge also contributed a speech:

> The United Nations has unanimously called upon the world's nations to build a vision of peace and prosperity. The torch bearer will carry this flame to London and spread the message of sport's capacity to spread peace and build a better world. This flame will travel from the birthplace of the ancient Olympic Games to the country that gave us the spirit of fair play.[21]

---

[20] http://www.newhamrecorder.co.uk/news/london_2012_we_turn_to_sport_to_connect_the_world_seb_coe_at_olympic_flame_lighting_1_1373791;   accessed 3 November 2014.

[21] Gregg Bakowski, 'London 2012 Olympics: torch lighting ceremony – as it happened', *The Guardian*, 10 May 2012, http://www.theguardian.com/sport/

The influential writer and urban ethnographer Phil Cohen has characterised these remarks (perfectly) as 'dumb generalisations'[22] but they are, of course, purposely and carefully crafted dumb generalisations, containing the appropriate cocktail of Olympic and national myths and warm-sounding invocations. Specifically, sport does not have a universal appeal; Olympic values are not timeless, nor do they (nor can they) transcend history or geography; if 'these times' are 'challenging' because of such factors as poverty, disease, war or famine, then the (notoriously vague and changing) values of Olympism have little perceptible relevance, in this age or any other; sport cannot bring peace; in no sense can the world be said to have turned 'from war to sport' in 1948; nobody could sensibly argue that Britain gave the world 'the spirit of fair play'. But these enunciations conform to the rules, not of rational proposition, but of advertising. Few people in the world were going to object to words and phrases such as 'peace', 'prosperity', 'better world' and 'fair play'; they have what Coe claimed for sport: 'universal appeal'. Similarly, the thought of 'young people' being 'inspired' toward 'achievement' – a reiteration of the Coe team's chosen slogan – could be expected to meet little opposition. These dumb, but warm and inoffensive, generalisations, symbolised by the torch and its relay, were thus a valuable commodity, available to sponsors seeking favour with a global audience. As Olympic Partners endorsing the flame this time around, and thus purchasing the right to be associated with these heartening words, phrases and images, Coca Cola and Samsung were joined by the banking group Lloyds TSB, which, together with HBOS and the Royal Bank of Scotland, had received £37 billion of bail-out money from Gordon Brown's Labour government in 2008.[23]

The relay would last 70 days, during which the torch would be carried by 8,000 people, accompanied by seventy security guards. Once it arrived in the UK it would, according to the proud boast of the organisers, visit 74 locations and 'would come within a one-hour journey of 95% of people in the UK'.[24]

---

blog/2012/may/10/london-2012-olympics-torch-lighting-ceremony;   accessed 3 November 2012.

[22] Phil Cohen, *On the Wrong Side of the Track?: East London and the Post Olympics* (London: Lawrence and Wishart, 2013), pp. 256–257.

[23] Graeme Wearden, 'British government unveils £37bn banking bail-out plan', *The Guardian*, 13 October 2008, http://www.theguardian.com/business/2008/oct/13/marketturmoil-creditcrunch; accessed 3 November 2014.

[24] BBC News, 'London 2012 Olympic torch relay route revealed', 18 May 2014, http://www.bbc.co.uk/news/uk-13426353; accessed 3 November 2014.

Two factors seem to have sealed the apparent success of the relay as an event: the astute selection of torchbearers and the role of the BBC.

The recruitment of torchbearers was organised centrally around the London Organising Committee's stipulated key word – 'inspire'. A large allocation – well over half the total – of torchbearing opportunities were, expectably, allocated to sponsors, who were eager – and instructed in how – to exploit the theme of inspiration. Specifically 1,360 places went to each 'presenting partner' of the relay and a further 913 to other Olympic corporate sponsors.[25] Other allocations were made via the IOC itself, the British Olympic Association and the London Organising Committee (LOCOG), the latter inviting nominations via the slogan 'Moment to Shine', which they had market-tested as a 'strapline' and trademarked in February 2011.[26]

Similarly, Coca Cola (a 'presenting partner' since Barcelona in 1992) chose the strapline 'Future Flames' via which to seek inspirational young torchbearers. Two years ahead of the Games Simon Baldry, Managing Director, Coca-Cola Enterprises Ltd, told the company's website:

> We're focused on building long term category plans with our customers to grow soft drink sales in Great Britain. We know that our sponsorship for London 2012 will energise this work. Adding the London 2012 Olympic Torch Relay will accelerate this, and enable us to connect CCE's trade partners with our worldwide Olympic sponsorship at a local community level in the build up to the 2012 games.[27]

TSB and Samsung, likewise, put out a call for inspirational nominees.

The resulting procession of torch carriers divided broadly into three categories.

First, there were those who were widely acknowledged, at community or national level, to have genuinely heroic or inspirational qualities – they had raised large sums of money for charity perhaps, or coped

---

[25] Paul Bradshaw, 'Olympic torch relay places – how were they allocated? Get the data', http://www.theguardian.com/sport/datablog/2012/jul/26/olympic-torch-relay-places#zoomed-picture; accessed 5 November 2014.

[26] John Reynolds, 'Locog tests "Moment To Shine" strapline', *Marketing*, 15 April 2011, http://www.marketingmagazine.co.uk/article/1065753/locog-tests-moment-shine-strapline; accessed 5 November 2014.

[27] http://www.cokecce.co.uk/news-media/news-releases/2010/coca-cola-to-present-london-2012-olympic-torch-relay-bringing-the-olympic-flame-to-millions-of-people-across-the-uk.aspx; accessed 5 November 2014.

with the effects of a debilitating illness, or otherwise impressed the people of their locality with their determination. When the torch passed through Leicester in the English East Midlands, for example, the local paper featured 20 year old Lucy Davies on its front page; Lucy, from the nearby village of Barwell, had Ehlers-Danlos syndrome, a condition affecting the skin, ligaments, cartilage and blood vessels, and stood up briefly from her wheelchair to receive the torch and pass it on. She said the experience had been 'totally amazing'[28] – an approximation to the expressed sentiments of most of these young nominees.

Second, invitations found their way by various routes to a range of local and national celebrities drawn from a range of fields – principally sport (Gordon Banks, goalkeeper in England's World Cup winning football team in 1966, carried the torch outside Wembley Stadium, tennis players Andy Murray, Tim Henman and Venus Williams held it at the All England Club in Wimbledon...); music (Beverley Knight, John Legend, Will.i.am of the band Black Eyed Peas...); film (Rupert Grint of the *Harry Potter* franchise, Sir Patrick Stewart from the *Star Trek* movies...); television (Matt Smith, then starring in the BBC's longstanding science fiction drama *Dr Who*, carried the torch in Cardiff, Joanna Lumley and Jennifer Saunders, of the situation comedy *Absolutely Fabulous*, took the torch between the London boroughs of Lambeth and Kensington, *Strictly Come Dancing* compere Sir Bruce Forsyth held it outside the BBC in London's White City...) and the arts (the artist Tracey Emin held it in her home town of Margate...). Given the displacements and consequent ill feeling caused by the coming of the Olympics to the East End of London, particular attention seemed to have been accorded to this part of the route. Paloma Faith, a singer with a twenty-something/thirty-something demographic who, though born in Stoke Newington (North London) had made her name on the East End cabaret scene,[29] carried the torch through the borough of Newham; Olympic gold medallist (in 1984) Tessa Sanderson, who ran a sports academy in Newham, also carried it there; hip hop songwriter and record producer Dizzee Rascal carried it through his home district of Tower Hamlets; triple jumper Phillips Idowu, like Dizzee an East Ender ('born, raised and schooled in East London'[30]) of Nigerian parentage, took the torch

---

[28] *Leicester Mercury*, 'OLYMPIC SPIRIT', 3 July 2012, pp. 1–2.
[29] See http://www.outmag.co.uk/site/index.php?option=com_content&view=article&id=347:paloma-faith&catid=19:main-news; accessed 5 November 2014.
[30] Owen Gibson, 'After its journey across Britain, the torch is held aloft in London', *The Observer*, 22 July 2014, p. 2.

into the Westfield shopping centre next to the Olympic Park; and footballer Fabrice Muamba, born in Zaire but schooled in Walthamstow, East London, was given the torch in Waltham Forest, another Olympic borough. (Muamba had attracted huge international sympathy when he suffered a cardiac arrest during a televised football match between Bolton Wanderers and Tottenham Hotspur four months earlier.)

These two groups – the Inspiring and the Celebrities – together helped to deliver the Olympics to the mass media in advance of the Games themselves. A great many – indeed, virtually all – members of each group were independently newsworthy. Moreover, the bravery and altruism represented by the bearers of the first group provided a powerful pretext for abandoning any critique of the relay or the approaching Games. Owen Gibson, one of a number of journalists allocated places in the relay, wrote of his experience:

> To my left on the bus is 81-year-old June O'Regan, nominated by her grandson for arranging charity luncheons near where we both live in Charlton, south-east London. As the convoy carrying our cohort of torchbearers weaves through Eltham's streets, she waves furiously at the never-ending stream of people she knows among those lining the streets. Also on my left, in his matching dazzling white outfit, is Jaco van Gass, a South African who sold everything he owned to travel to the UK and join the Parachute Regiment. In 2009 he lost his left arm and part of his left leg in Helmand on his second tour of Afghanistan. Last year he trekked to the North Pole as part of a Walking for the Wounded expedition and has now set his sights on Everest. [...] It's hard to say without sounding as though you've bought wholesale into the sometimes cloying 'moment to shine' rhetoric of the organisers, but in the company of such individuals any residual cynicism about the relay tends to melt away.[31]

Moreover, among the mass media, the BBC needed no second bidding to embrace the relay. In June 2004, before the award of the 2012 Olympics to London, the BBC had announced that it had been awarded the UK TV, radio and online rights to cover the 2010 Winter Olympics from Vancouver and the 2012 Games. Peter Salmon, BBC Director of Sport,

---

[31] Ibid.; see also Owen Gibson, 'Olympic torch relay gives ordinary people their moment to shine', *Guardian Observer*, 21 July 2012, http://www.theguardian.com/sport/2012/jul/21/olympic-torch-relay-moment-shine; accessed 5 November 2014.

had said: 'We're delighted to continue to bring this most prestigious of sporting events to audiences throughout the UK. [...] And whether it's Paris, New York, Madrid or even London in 2012 the BBC will relish its involvement in the biggest and best sporting competition on earth'.[32] Having found this 'biggest and best sporting competition on earth' on their own doorstep, the corporation was not inclined to leave any aspect of the Games unreported. BBC local radio stations followed the torch's progress every step of the way as it crossed their constituencies. For example, the torch's 100 mile passage from Coventry to Leicester, via Northampton, on 2 July was monitored throughout the day by local radio and internet 'torchcam', beginning at 6.45 in the morning and lasting until 6.54 at night – coverage of over 12 hours. Regular bulletins amplified the message of local good works and links between the local and the global. Here is a sample of the day's coverage:

> Now running through his hometown under some colourful bunting strung across the street is 45-year-old Andy Wightman. Andy is a very highly qualified karate teacher, who trains youngsters at a number of local clubs.
>
> 11.10: With the torch now is Philip Highley, 73. Among Philip's many fundraising activities with the Rotary Club is a 1,200-mile journey criss-crossing Britain with the aid of his bus pass.
>
> 11.12: Our final Northampton torchbearer is Carlo Bini from Rome. Carlo is noted for the day he helped trapped and injured passengers at a train crash in the Apennine Mountains in Italy.
>
> 11.15: Sorry again for the loss of pictures but we are now due to go into convoy mode for the 20-minute drive to Wellingborough.
>
> 11.31: The torch is due into Wellingborough shortly – and then will visit Isham, Kettering, where it stops for lunch, Geddington, Corby, Dingley, Market Harborough, Lubenham, Foxton, Kibworth Harcourt, Oadby and finally Leicester.
>
> 11.33: The relay enters the outskirts of Wellingborough.
>
> This market town was named after the Saxon chieftain Waendel. In the early 80s it achieved fame as the birthplace of the 'goth rock'

---

[32] BBC Press Office, 18 June 2004, http://www.bbc.co.uk/pressoffice/pressreleases/ stories/2004/06_june/18/olympics.shtml; accessed 5 November 2014.

movement and its leading band Bauhaus. The town is also birthplace
of Sir David Frost.

11.34: Wellingborough's first torchbearer is 17-year-old Nicola
Kenton from Rushden. Nicola has a medical condition that causes
her joints to dislocate very easily. Despite this, she is a keen swimmer
at her local club.

11.37: Wellingborough native Kathy Randall is now with the torch.
Kathy, 63, donated a kidney to her brother-in-law recently but hopes
to run in a half-marathon to raise awareness of organ donation.[33]

Needless to add, the relay runners, thus recruited, also delivered a
nationwide roadside audience to the relay's sponsors, costs in each
locale having been met by the local authorities: in the spring of 2013, for
instance, it emerged that over £230,000 of public money had been spent
'paving the way for the Olympic torch relay to pass through Leicester
and Leicestershire'.[34]

The 'presenting partners' of the relay sought to exploit the event
in two ways. First, they approached the roadside spectators with routine commercial blandishment. 'Crowds have lined up six deep on the
sides of dual carriageways, and draped flags over motorway bridges in
scenes of enthusiasm which Lord Coe probably didn't dare hope for',
wrote journalists Tom Peck and Charlie Cooper. 'But it is also a corporate juggernaut. The torch's main sponsors arrive an hour in advance of
the flame, handing out flags, inflatable noise-making devices covered
in branding, and, of course, souvenir bottles of a certain ubiquitous
American soft drink made from vegetable extracts'.[35] The 'presenting
partner' promotion teams were given detailed instructions as to 'activation activities' (TSB favoured 'Recorded music and juggling, stilt-walkers,
acrobatics and audience interaction', Samsung specified 'Main focus on
distributing keepsakes for crowd interaction and Torch arrival notifica-
tion'); location (Coca Cola suggested 'pedestrian environments where

---

[33] http://www.bbc.co.uk/torchrelay/day45; accessed 5 November 2014.

[34] *Leicester Mercury*, 27 March 2013, http://www.leicestermercury.co.uk/Olympic-
torch-relay-cost-Leicester-city-pound-102/story-18532161-detail/story.html;
accessed 5 November 2014.

[35] Tom Peck and Charlie Cooper, 'The torch relay: golden moment or flaming
nuisance?', *The Independent*, 26 May 2012, pp. 18–19. See also http://www.
independent.co.uk/sport/olympics/the-torch-relay-golden-moment-or-flaming-
nuisance-7789295.html; accessed 6 November 2014.

possible. Targeting key spots along route including customer car parks, parks, town squares'); number of operating staff (varying between 2 and 6 persons) 'with teams "leapfrogging" ahead of each other'; and vehicle specification (TSB favoured ice cream vans, Samsung went for quad bikes).[36]

Coca Cola supplemented their Future Flames programme with 'Move to the Beat' (another trademarked strapline), a campaign to engage the youth market by bringing suitably young and London-based musicians together with Olympic sportspeople under the company banner: 'The ambition of Move to the Beat™', said the company's press release, 'is to bring teens closer to the Olympic Games and to sport in general. Harnessing teens' passion for music, and drawing inspiration from London's musical heritage, the campaign fuses London music with Olympic sport to connect young people to London 2012'.[37] The campaign entailed four gigs; an Olympic song (recorded by Peckham-born Katy B and North London DJ and musician Mark Ronson; a documentary about the making of the song, in which Ronson meets five Olympic athletes; a Facebook app; and a pavilion on the Olympic site, named the 'Beat Box'.[38] Availing itself of the Coe team's chosen rhetoric, Coca Cola claimed that this initiative formed part of a 'commitment to sustainability [which] is motivating teens across the country to get excited about sport, and inspiring them to lead active, healthy lifestyles'.[39] (As Lenskyj, Boykoff and others have pointed out, 'sustainability' found its way into the Olympic vocabulary in the early 1990s[40]; it is often, as here, little more than a word that

---

[36] London 2012 Olympic torch relay: presenting partner advance activation – ancillary activities to the Olympic torch relay, http://www.local.gov.uk/c/document_library/get_file?uuid=f03b420d-5287-460c-bb44-919a7f0a4cb7&groupId=10180; accessed 6 November 2014.

[37] Andrew Sung, 'Coca-Cola launches Move to the Beat™London 2012 Olympic games campaign with unveiling of beat wall', 16 February 2012, http://www.coca-colacompany.com/press-center/press-releases/coca-cola-launches-move-to-the-beat-london-2012-olympic-games-campaign-with-unveiling-of-beat-wall; accessed 6 November 2014.

[38] 'Move to the Beat of London 2012', http://www.coca-cola.co.uk/olympic-games/move-to-the-beat-london-2012-mark-ronson.html; accessed 6 November 2014.

[39] Ibid.

[40] Helen Jefferson Lenskyj, *Inside the Olympic Industry: Power, Politics and Activism* (Albany: State University of New York Press, 2000), pp. 155–171; Jules Boykoff, *Celebration Capitalism and the Olympic Games* (Abingdon: Routledge, 2014), pp. 39–42.

Olympic partners know that they must insinuate into their publicity material.)

Second, however, the various partners, with the connivance of the organisers, sought to sprinkle Olympic fairy dust upon themselves and upon the culture of commerce *per se*: when the torch was in certain hands sponsorship, wealth, executive position and the whole lexicon of business was implied to be 'inspirational'. While this may have passed under the radar of the BBC's generally euphoric commentary, it did not escape the attention of the press. Arbitrary as it might seem, given the overall vacuity of official Olympic rhetoric, Tom Peck of *The Independent* decided to tax Coe with his 'dumb generalisation', enunciated at the flame-lighting ceremony: 'He promised', wrote Peck,

> that the torch relay would 'lift the spirits and hopes of people across Britain and across the world'. He continued: 'We promise to protect the flame; to cherish its traditions and to stage an uplifting torch relay of which we can all be proud and which can inspire a generation. We will involve young people from all backgrounds, cultures and faith groups in the torch relay, reflecting London's immense diversity and creativity as a global destination and voice for young people.[41]

Moreover, partners had been instructed that bearers should be 'young people, or have stories inspiring to young people'.[42] This was difficult to square with the selection of a regiment of Chief Executive Officers, PR strategists, marketing managers, IT specialists and salespeople, drawn mainly from the partner companies themselves and their clients, who had been set alongside the Inspiring nominees:

> Coca-Cola has heavily promoted its 'Future Flames' campaign, allocating torch-relay places to the likes of 15-year-old Jordan Clarke, who had a liver transplant at the age of eight and has since raised more than £12,000 for Birmingham Children's Hospital. But among the nominations the company gave to its own staff and partners are Julia Zeen, who designed its Olympic pin badges, and Ben Alun-Jones, who has been 'developing concepts' for the interior of Coca-Cola's Olympic Pavilion.[43]

---

[41] Tom Peck, 'Seb Coe promised an "uplifting torch relay to inspire a generation". So are these really the role models to do it?', *The Independent*, 5 June 2012, pp. 8–9, p. 8.
[42] Ibid.
[43] Ibid., p. 9.

Britain's wealthiest man Lakshmi Mittal, CEO of the multinational steel manufacturer ArcelorMittal, was to carry the torch (through the affluent London boroughs of Kensington and Chelsea on 26 July) and his son was similarly honoured. Mittal had claimed to be taking the torch on behalf of 'the 270,000 people around the world who are part of the ArcelorMittal family'.[44] Adidas, the official supplier of sportswear to the Olympics, had been similarly careless of the selection criteria: one of their nominees had ' "made a fantastic contribution to the Adidas group business". Another "breathes Adidas... Her positive attitude and 'money in [the] till' approach is legendary" and a third mentioned "achieving my sales targets in every market I have worked in" '.[45]

Press condemnation of these nominations went across the political spectrum. *Socialist Worker*, organ of the Trotskyite Socialist Workers' Party, remarked that the Olympic torch had become 'a rich man's plaything'[46] but the right wing *Daily Mail* was equally outraged. *Mail* reporter Harry Mount wrote

The Latin motto of the Olympic Games is 'Citius, altius, fortius' – faster, higher, stronger. Well, you can throw in another adjective: greedier. For as the Olympic torch makes its way around the country, the ideals of amateurism and selfless endeavour are gradually being blotted out by the grotesque demands of the Games' commercial sponsors. [...] Torchbearers were supposed to be local heroes, chosen to represent every corner of the United Kingdom that the torch passes through. Instead, we have the unedifying spectacle of sponsors handing out torch relay slots as corporate goodies. The torchbearers were accompanied by big commercial sponsorship juggernauts: the red Coke open-top bus, followed by the Samsung blue and white one, with the green Lloyds TSB bus bringing up the rear, all with their own music. The spirit of Chariots of Fire, it is not. And the tragedy is that the Olympic torch relay could have been immensely moving, if it hadn't been so crudely hijacked in this way.[47]

---

[44] Ibid., p. 8.

[45] James Ball, 'London 2012: torchbearers picked by sponsors keep flame of commerce alive', *The Guardian*, 6 June 2012, http://www.theguardian.com/sport/2012/jun/06/torchbearers-nominated-olympics-sponsors; accessed 6 November 2014.

[46] 16 June 2012, p. 2.

[47] Harry Mount, 'Flames of greed: how the Olympic spirit has been hijacked by commercialism', *Mail Online*, 6 June 2012, http://www.dailymail.co.uk/debate/

Mount was, of course, invoking a higher Olympism, comparing this spectacle unfavourably with the recent celebration of the British Queen's Diamond Jubilee and condemning the 'vacuous celebrity culture' that had allowed popular cultural figures such as the X Factor winners the Jedward twins into the relay team.[48] This was perfectly in keeping with the profession of the right wing press to uphold apparently exalted, non-material values (monarchy, high culture, community spirit...) against tawdry commercialism. But the broader point, once again, is that the conjoining of sport (here symbolised by the Olympic torch) and marketing has never gained full public acceptance and has had, for the most part, to have been smuggled into the Olympics behind a smokescreen of 'dumb generalisations'. And, as Peck and Cooper observe, 'despite the best attempts of Coca-Cola, Samsung and Lloyds TSB – the torch relay's three sponsors – to commercialise, sanitise and otherwise hijack for their own ends the country's lengthiest street party, each area the relay has passed has been lent its own distinct flavour'.[49]

article-2155590/Flames-Greed-How-Olympic-spirit-hijacked-commercialism. html; accessed 6 November 2014.
[48] Ibid.
[49] Peck and Cooper, 'The torch relay', p. 18.

# 5
# 'Isambard Kingdom Brunel Wasn't a Marxist': The Opening Ceremony of London 2012

In her insightful article of 2003, the sociologist Jackie Hogan noted that, in their post-1984, Hollywood form, Olympic opening ceremonies were 'elaborately staged and commercialized narratives of nation'; these narratives necessarily contained 'ideological tensions'.[1] The commercial value of these ceremonies is not in doubt. *Sky News* reported late in 2011 that: 'The opening and closing ceremonies of the London 2012 Olympics could net broadcasters up to £5bn in advertising, organisers have said'.[2]

This chapter will entail a discussion of 'Isles of Wonder', the spectacle devised by the film director Danny Boyle and a creative team appointed by LOCOG in 2010 to open the Summer Olympics of 2012. 'Isles' took place on 27 July and, according to the California firm FiveCurrents, one of the companies responsible for staging it, had a cast of 18,000;[3] Reuters news agency estimated the global television audience for this event to have been around 900 million viewers.[4] The chapter will assess the ceremony, which was widely praised, in relation to the politics of the time, both British and Olympic. To do so it will review a range of responses to

---

[1] Jackie Hogan, 'Staging the nation: gendered and ethnicized discourses of national identity in Olympic opening ceremonies', *Journal of Sport and Social Issues*, Vol. 27, No. 2 (2003), pp. 100–123, pp. 102–103.
[2] 'Olympic ceremonies "worth up to five billion"', *Sky News*, 5 December 2011, http://news.sky.com/story/906632/olympic-ceremonies-worth-up-to-five-billion; accessed 12 November 2014.
[3] http://fivecurrents.com/projects/ceremonies-celebrations/london-2012-olympic-paralympic-ceremonies/; accessed 9 November 2014.
[4] Avril Ormsby, 'Olympics-London 2012 opening ceremony draws 900 mln viewers', 7 August 2012, http://www.reuters.com/article/2012/08/07/oly-ratings-day-idUSL6E8J78H620120807; accessed 9 November 2014.

the event and, in that regard, pay particular attention to (often interconnected) then-current debates about: the writing and teaching of history; the welfare state; popular culture; 'race' and national identity; and imperialism. The principal argument will be that in order to fulfil its task of engaging a global audience – and, indeed, a national one – a number of key signifiers of Britain and Britishness would have to be omitted and, to reiterate an earlier point, items of the ceremony would fly markedly in the face of much established political orthodoxy in the United Kingdom at the time – something that could, of course, be said equally for other aspects of the 2012 Games.

### The truth but with adrenaline? The opening ceremony – prescription and prospect

The Olympic Charter is brief on the matter of the ceremony to open the Games. It provides a simple sentence to be enunciated by the host country's head of state in declaring the Olympics open and asserts the IOC's customary denial of politics:

> During the entire period of the Olympic Games, including all ceremonies, no speeches of any kind may be held by any representative of any government or other public authority, nor by any other politician, in any venue placed under the responsibility of the OCOG. During the Opening and Closing Ceremonies, only the IOC President and the President of the OCOG are entitled to deliver short addresses.[5]

Beyond this, Olympic planners are referred to the IOC's protocol, which in regard to the opening ceremony, requires organisers, first, to reflect the 'tradition and humanistic principles of Olympism and [...] assure the continuity of the Olympic tradition and ritual from city to city and Games to Games'[6] and, second, to 'capture the flavour and culture of the host nation. The Opening Ceremony is the one true, global beginning of the Games, and a chance to highlight the people and traditions of a

---

[5] Olympic charter (latest version, in force from 9 September 2013), p. 98, http://www.olympic.org/Documents/olympic_charter_en.pdf; accessed 9 November 2014.
[6] International Olympic Committee, *Technical Manual on Ceremonies* (Lausanne: IOC, November 2005), p. 27, http://www.gamesmonitor.org.uk/files/Technical_Manual_on_Ceremonies.pdf; accessed 9 November 2014.

city, region and nation'.[7] And there is a reminder that this is primarily a media spectacle: 'A successful Opening Ceremony often sets the tone of the Games in the media, and shows the world the face of a nation, its people, and its culture, setting the stage for the drama, inspiration and celebration of humanity that is the celebration of the Olympic Games'.[8] The IOC must approve the creative concepts behind the ceremony a year in advance and a full script with three months to go.[9]

Boyle's appointment was announced in June of 2010. Some sensible suggestions can be made as to why he was chosen. From a working class Lancashire-Irish family, Boyle lived in Mile End, not far from the Olympic site. He had, for many, established himself as a film director in 1996 with *Trainspotting*, a comedy-drama about heroin addicts in the urban squalor of an economically depressed Edinburgh in the 1980s; voted the fourth best British picture of all time in 2004,[10] it had brought him a young and/or liberal audience and, unlike Coe, some credibility as a figure outside the British political and cultural Establishment – a vital consideration for an event designed to touch so many hearts and minds. Most importantly, perhaps, in 2009 Boyle had gained huge success with *Slumdog Millionaire*, which had won an Academy Award for Best Picture and been popular in North America, Europe and across the Asia Pacific region.[11] Crucially, *Slumdog* (about a slum boy in Mumbai who wins the Indian version of the TV programme *Who Wants to Be a Millionaire?*) had had precisely the same rags-to-riches, Third-World-to-First narrative as the film presented by the Coe team in Singapore. It had also been criticised for endorsing a Western and imperialistic perspective on shanty town poverty in the 'under-developed world'. Academic and anti-poverty activist Mitu Sengupta had been among those arguing that *Slumdog* ignored the community spirit, entrepreneurial activity and capacity for resistance that characterised life in such slum areas. She wrote of the film:

> Perhaps the crucial ingredient of *Slumdog*'s success among Western audiences and Indian middle classes is not its 'feel good' tenor, but

[7] Ibid., p. 27.
[8] Ibid.
[9] Ibid., pp. 31–32.
[10] See http://news.bbc.co.uk/1/hi/scotland/3518815.stm; accessed 10 November 2014.
[11] See http://en.wikipedia.org/wiki/Slumdog_Millionaire#cite_ref-92; accessed 10 November 2014.

its understanding of poverty as the product of aberrant local cultures that must be shaken off and replaced by liberal modernity. Despite appearances to the contrary, *Slumdog*'s stunning sweep of the box office and awards circuit signals the West's celebration of itself – of its long-standing ideals and cherished myths, along with some newer ideals and myths that reflect the West's neoliberal present. The largely uncritical acceptance of *Slumdog*'s triumphalism in India, on the other hand, indicates the acquiescence to such ideals and myths by the country's upwardly mobile middle classes.[12]

A colleague described Boyle to *Vogue* magazine in precisely the same vocabulary as that being disseminated by the Coe team:

'Danny is a very earnest man in the sense that he cares deeply about social issues, but he is never dour, never pessimistic,' says Tessa Ross, of Film4, the British company that developed *Slumdog Millionaire*. 'What he wants to do is inspire people, and the way he does that is by portraying the truth but with adrenaline – because he himself is optimistic.'[13]

Boyle and his assistants were to act in tandem with American agency FiveCurrents and the British firm Unspun.[14] Both FiveCurrents and Unspun describe themselves as 'creative' agencies, 'creative' being a code word in contemporary commerce for branding, presentation and the gamut of high level impression management. FiveCurrents had worked on previous Games in Beijing, Athens and Atlanta. Unspun, according to their website, are 'a leading strategic change and engagement agency', whose business is 'Defining a compelling narrative, with a strategic idea at its heart'. They were involved in the London bid and, perhaps predictably, the words 'inspire' and 'inspiring' feature prominently on

---

[12] Mitu Sengupta, 'A million dollar exit from the anarchic slum-world: Slumdog Millionaire's hollow idioms of social justice', *Third World Quarterly*, Vol. 31, No. 4 (2010), pp. 599–614, p. 610.

[13] Hadley Freeman, 'Danny Boyle: Olympic opening ceremony artistic director', *Vogue*, 27 July 2012, http://www.vogue.com/865344/danny-boyle-olympic-opening-ceremony/; accessed 12 November 2014.

[14] Chantelle Thorley, 'Locog creates consortium to produce £40m Olympic ceremonies', *Event*, 18 June 2014, http://www.eventmagazine.co.uk/locog-creates-consortium-produce-40m-olympic-ceremonies/article/1010916; accessed 10 November 2014.

their website.[15] They had the strong links to big corporations and to the political British political Establishment that artistic figures such as Boyle appeared to lack. Their corporate clients included several global companies (HSBC, KPMG, Nissan, Vodaphone, EDF…) as well as an Olympic partner (Coca Cola). Sir Michael Lockett of Unspun had worked extensively for the British Conservative Party, organising the staging of a number of party conferences, running Prime Minister John Major's presentation unit during the 1992 General Election and assisting with David Cameron's campaign for the party leadership in 2005, as well as supervising the Party at the Palace concert for the Queen's Golden Jubilee in 2002.[16] Sara Donaldson of Unspun later said of her company's role: 'We worked alongside the LOCOG brand team on the ceremonies to ensure all costumes were on-brand and approved'.[17]

Days before the opening ceremony was to be broadcast press stories appeared telling of friction between Boyle and Olympic Broadcast Services, who were responsible for televising the event. There had, reportedly, been an uneasy compromise:

> A second OBS director will be in control of the protocol parts of the ceremony, including the athletes' parade, in which neutrality is an issue with the International Olympic Committee (IOC) insisting that all 204 countries are given airtime. Tensions over this compromise have flared in recent days, with a debate over who could have control of certain camera positions for the ceremony.[18]

The accuracy of these comments is hard to determine, but it will certainly have done Boyle's – and the event's – credibility no harm for him to have been seen to be defending his 'vision' against interfering

---

[15] See http://unspunlondon.co.uk/home/; accessed 10 November 2014.
[16] Gordon Rayner, 'The Diamond Jubilee pageant, the Shard, the Olympics: no job's too big for Michael Lockett', *The Telegraph*, 5 July 2012, http://www.telegraph.co.uk/culture/art/architecture/9375908/The-Diamond-Jubilee-pageant-the-Shard-the-Olympics-no-jobs-too-big-for-Michael-Lockett.html; accessed 10 November 2014.
[17] See http://www.beyond2012.org.uk/opening-and-closing-ceremonies-costumes/; accessed 10 November 2014.
[18] Paul Kelso, 'London 2012 Olympics: opening ceremony tensions with Danny Boyle will be resolved, says Locog', *The Telegraph*, 19 July 2012, http://www.telegraph.co.uk/sport/olympics/news/9412027/London-2012-Olympics-opening-ceremony-tensions-with-Danny-Boyle-will-be-resolved-says-Locog.html; accessed 11 November 2014.

semi-officialdom. Already an egalitarian aura had begun to settle around Boyle and his project (an aura strengthened by Boyle's refusal of a knighthood the following year – 'It's just not me', he said, stressing that the ceremony had been a collective effort on the part of a 'cast of thousands'[19]). As a perceptive profile of Boyle observed the day before the ceremony, LOCOG might have put the occasion

> into safer, staider hands – a Cameron Mackintosh [producer of successful musicals such as *Les Misérables*, *The Phantom of the Opera*, and *Cats*] or a Richard Curtis [scriptwriter of *Four Weddings and a Funeral*, *Bridget Jones's Diary*, and *Love, Actually* and founder of *Comic Relief*], say, peddling the rose-tinted opposite of Boyle's gritty vision.[20]

Boyle, it went on, was not tied to a genre – 'not a social realist in the [British film directors] Mike Leigh or Ken Loach vein, nor is he a Hollywood-bound commercialist'[21] – and this would make him more likely successfully to bridge demographics. After all, within its prescribed 'No Politics' remit, the ceremony would have to find some accommodation with a huge audience, embracing old and young, male and female, black and white, left and right, gay and straight, Third World and First. Six weeks before the event itself, Boyle told the BBC's Huw Edwards that, while full of praise for the opening ceremony in Beijing in 2008, the ceremony this time would be 'warmer' and more 'inclusive'.[22] In media commentary after the event Boyle was frequently described as 'left leaning' and was said to have been protected from political interference in his work by Lord Coe.[23]

---

[19] Amanda Williams, ' "It's just not me": Danny Boyle explains he turned down knighthood because he wouldn't have felt right accepting individual award for the Olympics opening ceremony', *Mail Online*, 19 March 2013, http://www.dailymail.co.uk/news/article-2295579/Danny-Boyle-explains-turned-knighthood-wouldnt-felt-right-accepting-individual-award-Olympics-opening-ceremony.html; accessed 11 November 2014.

[20] Steve Rose, 'Danny Boyle: artist, entertainer and all-round good bloke', *The Guardian*, 26 July 2012, http://www.theguardian.com/film/2012/jul/26/danny-boyle-olympic-ceremony-director; accessed 13 November 2014.

[21] Ibid.

[22] 'London 2012: Boyle describes opening ceremony "meadow" ', *BBC News*, 12 June 2012, http://www.bbc.co.uk/news/uk-18409682; accessed 13 November 2014.

[23] Owen Gibson, 'Olympics chief Lord Coe rejects return to frontline politics', *The Guardian*, 13 August 2012, http://www.theguardian.com/sport/2012/aug/13/olympics-chief-lord-coe-politics; accessed 19 November 2014.

## 'THIS IS FOR EVERYONE'? The ceremony

Boyle's creative team included another film director – Stephen Daldry, responsible for the popular *Billy Elliott* (about a miner's son who becomes a ballet dancer and comes out as gay); Paulette Randall, a Londoner from a Jamaican family, who had been artistic director of black theatre company Talawa and had worked on TV comedies *Desmond's* and *The Real McCoy* featuring black and/or Asian performers; Hamish Hamilton, a director of concerts for leading bands; and Frank Cottrell Boyce, a children's author. The composition of the team thus predisposed the ceremony toward diversity, inclusivity and popular culture as themes. Conservative London mayor Boris Johnson said of them: 'They exemplify some of the greatest attributes we have – creativity, vision, and intelligence – which will be critical to ensuring shows that are as stunning as they are uniquely British'.[24]

Boyle and his associates decided that the most attractive and least contentious motifs of Britishness would include: a glimpse of rural England; Britain's experience of the Industrial Revolution; the National Health Service; and Britons' contribution to global popular culture – entailing pop songs, TV programmes, films, comedy and the World Wide Web, whose creator (unbeknown to commentators on NBC television in the United States, who said 'If you haven't heard of him, we haven't either'[25]) was English computer scientist Sir Tim Berners Lee.

The ceremony began with a film clip of a helter-skelter journey down the River Thames from its source. The audience heard the Eton Boating Song, the Sex Pistols singing 'God Save the Queen' (now emptied of its original transgressive import and, along with 'London Calling' by The Clash, which featured later on, 'repurposed as generally emblematic of "the UK" '[26]) and the theme from BBC Television's *East Enders*. As the

---

[24] 'London Millionaire! Danny Boyle set to take charge of opening ceremony at 2012 Olympic Games', *Mail Online*, 17 June 2010, http://www.dailymail.co.uk/sport/olympics/article-1287392/London-Millionaire-Danny-Boyle-set-oversee-opening-ceremony-2012-Olympic-Games.html; accessed 13 November 2014.

[25] Emma G. Keller, 'NBC lambasted over banal butchering of opening ceremony – and rightly so', *The Guardian*, 28 July 2012, http://www.theguardian.com/media/us-news-blog/2012/jul/28/nbc-olympics-opening-ceremony; accessed 13 November 2014.

[26] Noel Murray, 'The 2012 Summer Olympics: opening ceremonies', 27 July 2012, http://www.avclub.com/tvclub/the-2012-summer-olympics-opening-ceremonies-82935; accessed 13 November 2012.

ceremony progressed the nation would be defined increasingly by its popular media culture.

The camera alighted on a grass-covered hillock (depicting Glastonbury Tor in Somerset), around which actors dressed as eighteenth century English rustics were playing cricket. This signalled the first major segment of the ceremony entitled 'Green and Pleasant Land'. A children's choir sang William Blake's 'Jerusalem', from which the words 'Green and pleasant land' are taken, and film was shown of similar choirs singing 'Danny Boy' in Northern Ireland, 'Flower of Scotland' in Scotland and 'Bread of Heaven' in Wales. (No doubt taking a cue from LOCOG's chosen 'Inspire a generation' rhetoric, the Boyle team deployed children and young people in considerable numbers.)

Onto the mock-up tor now strode English actor Sir Kenneth Branagh dressed as the famed Victorian engineer Isambard Kingdom Brunel. Branagh-Brunel, accompanied by a platoon of actors playing top-hatted, nineteenth century industrialists, read from Shakespeare's *The Tempest* and moved swiftly to usher in the Industrial Revolution. This second scene, called 'Pandemonium' (the word used by John Milton in *Paradise Lost* for the capital of Hell and used here to convey the horrors of early industrial life), in which Britain was portrayed as the 'workshop of the world', was dramatised by percussionists while men and women, representing the new industrial proletariat, rushed hither and thither, pulling large levers and raising giant, belching chimneys. Branagh strode among them with a swagger and a cigar, the camera finally settling on him in self-satisfied pose, his feet wide apart. Meanwhile the proletariat were working at a mock blast furnace to forge the five Olympic rings and, as they did so, a number of groups from British history – suffragists, the unemployed men who marched from Jarrow to London in 1936, Caribbean immigrants arriving in 1948 on the *Empire Windrush*, Chelsea Pensioners, a colliery band, a 1970s DJ float, a steel band, The Beatles as they'd dressed for the cover of *Sgt. Pepper's Lonely Hearts Club Band* and a group of London's Pearly Kings and Queens – entered the stadium. This sequence plainly acknowledged the working class, feminist, black and migrant popular cultural strands in British history.

The next segment – 'Happy and Glorious' – consisted of a short film in which actor Daniel Craig (as 'James Bond'), watched by a gaggle of schoolchildren and to the strains of the Dam Busters March, escorts the Queen to a helicopter. Stuntmen dressed as 'Bond' and the Queen then descended by parachute into the arena. This was a clever device, downplaying the (objective) social gulf between a vastly wealthy hereditary figure and her subjects now facing significant cuts to public services and presenting her in the subjective – as a 'good sport'. It also show-cased Britain as the home both of the James Bond franchise and of a purportedly irreverent humour.

'Second to the right, and straight on till morning', effectively the fourth instalment, is probably the one that garnered the most public attention and subsequent comment. To the music of Mike Oldfield's *Tubular Bells*, his best-selling album of 1973, nurses (male and female, black and white) danced around hospital beds with their child patients. On BBC television commentator Barry Davies announced gravely that 'no society can legitimately call itself civilised' if it were to deny med-ical aid to anybody 'because of lack of means'.[27] The children were then lain down to sleep, but began to read beneath their bedclothes. The children's author J.K. Rowling now read aloud from J.M. Barrie's *Peter Pan* and a mood of children's fantasy was created, summoning some of the most noted villains of children's literature – the Child Catcher from the adaptation by Roald Dahl of *Chitty Chitty Bang Bang* by Ian Fleming, Cruella de Vil from Dodie Smith's *The Hundred and One Dalmatians*...A number of Mary Poppins figures then descended, banished the monsters and danced with the children (once again male and female, black and white, and thus faithful to the LOCOG styling of the East End as a cultural 'melting pot') to Oldfield's music, before the children retired to bed.

There was then another comic interlude in which the London Sym-phony Orchestra (LSO), playing the theme from *Chariots of Fire*, the British Olympic film drama of 1981, and conducted by Sir Simon Rattle, is found to include the hapless Mr Bean. Mr Bean absent-mindedly plays one note on his keyboard while fantasising about beating the fabled *Chariots* runners in their famous run along the beach by taking a car ride for most of the way and barging the leader over at the finish line. Once again, Britain was posed as the fount of slightly irreverent comedy and its experts as 'game for a laugh'. This comedy trope, in which a star performance is undermined by a clueless but persistent interloper, was popularised by English comedians Morecambe and Wise and recalled in particular their Christmas Show of 1971 during which Morecambe, at the piano, plays a ruinous version of Edvard Grieg's A Minor Piano Concerto with the LSO and then informs conductor Andre

---

[27] Four hours of the BBC broadcast of the ceremony is available to watch on YouTube: http://www.youtube.com/watch?v=4As0e4de-rI; accessed 13 November 2014.

Previn that he's playing 'all the right notes, but not necessarily in the right order'.[28]

The last major stage in the opening pageant, entitled 'Frankie and June say...thanks Tim', celebrated the British-in-their-media. Essentially a hymn to British popular and youth culture, the sequence took the standpoint of the consumers, rather than the producers, of this culture. In the sequence a mother with her young son arrives in a Mini Cooper. They enter a mock-up of a modern British house, the son apparently preoccupied with his I Pad. Clips from a number of British TV programmes, music videos and films are played, beginning with the famously mistaken reassurance to the nation by BBC weatherman Michael Fish in 1987 that a hurricane was not imminent. The house contains a happy, mixed-race family, with children dancing in their bedrooms, gazing into their mobile phones or watching situation comedies on TV. Groups of adolescent men and women appear and, texting each other feverishly, contemplate a night out. A middle-aged voice is heard issuing the peremptory words, heard at one time or another in millions of households: 'You're going nowhere dressed like that, young lady'. The troupe of young people embark on an evening of excitement and young love, while clips of British films (*Gregory's Girl*, *Four Weddings and a Funeral...*) and music from a succession of British bands – The Jam, The Who (singing 'My Generation'), The Kinks, The Beatles, Mud, the Sex Pistols ('Pretty Vacant'), New Order, Frankie Goes to Hollywood, the Eurhythmics, Queen, the Arctic Monkeys – blares out. A young woman in a wheelchair is seen moving her chair to the strains of 'Satisfaction' by the Rolling Stones. A place is found for 'My Boy Lollipop', Jamaica-born black singer Millie Small's hit of 1964. A mass disco, featuring pogoing punks with gigantic Mohican haircuts, culminates in a kiss between the two central black teenagers – Frankie and June. This coincides with a screen sequence of famous film and TV kisses, including one performed by Prince William and Kate Middleton on their wedding day in 2011 and the lesbian kiss of 1994 in the TV soap opera *Brookside*.

In conclusion the party repaired to the 'Green and Pleasant' lot and the house lifted to reveal Sir Tim Berners Lee seated at his computer. Lee then delivered the message 'THIS IS FOR EVERYONE' (implying that he favoured open access to the World Wide Web, his invention) to the LCD

---

[28] The sketch can be seen in full at: http://www.youtube.com/watch?v= R7GeKLE0x3s; accessed 13 November 2014.

(liquid-crystal display) lights attached to the chairs of the audience via Twitter.

Emili Sande (born to an English mother and a Zambian father) now performed 'Abide With Me' (sung at the F.A. Cup Final since 1927 and said to be a favourite of Mahatma Gandhi[29]) while Akram Khan (a Londoner from a Bangladeshi family) led a dance on the theme of mortality.

Despite its largely demotic flavour, the ceremony turned, finally, to the nation's most expectable global stars: David Beckham arrived, James Bond-like, in a speedboat and Paul McCartney sang 'Hey Jude' – a song which, because it was about overcoming fear ('the movement you need is on your shoulder'), was clearly compatible with contemporary 'inspirational' Olympic rhetoric.

## A love letter to Britain or multicultural crap? The opening ceremony – reading and reaction

The Boyle team's rendering of Britain, the British and their culture was widely and understandably welcomed. To portray Britain as the country which pioneered the industrial revolution; which established a welfare state; which benefited from large scale immigration; and which gave the world the works of Shakespeare, the Beatles, the Rolling Stones, punk rock, some feel-good films, Harry Potter and the World Wide Web is a strongly sympathisable perspective. Moreover, the part played in British history by ordinary people had been positioned consistently in the foreground. This placed the display fashioned by the Boyle production team among the less objectionable attempts to portray Britain as – to borrow Benedict Anderson's now widely adopted concept – an 'imagined community'.[30] Much response – of course, transmitted by other media – was very favourable.

'London sets the world alight', said the British *Independent*, 'BOYLE UNVEILS HIS SPELLBINDING VISION'.[31] 'We showed the world we can laugh at ourselves, even to the point of having our most respected national institution parachute into the stadium with a fictional

---

[29] http://www.know-britain.com/hymns/abide_with_me.html; accessed 14 November 2014.

[30] Benedict Anderson, *Imagined Communities: Reflections on the Origin and Spread of Nationalism* (London: Verso, 2006 [originally published in 1983]).

[31] 28 July 2012, p. 1, pp. 4–5.

character', stated an editorial in the *Independent on Sunday*.[32] Simon Barnes of *The Times* agreed:

> London turned down the option to celebrate giants and super-men and power and might and chose instead to celebrate peo-ple... Humour, above all things, humanises and there were elements of self-mockery that suggested that we could make this the humor-ous Games; the Games of humorous humanity in a land in which a joke and a grumble are never far away, and often enough one and the same thing.[33]

Richard Williams in *The Guardian* wrote: 'For four years, following Beijing was thought to be the most thankless task in show business. Danny Boyle made it happen. He made the stadium seem bigger than it is, as big as the world. He gave a party, full of jokes and warmth and noise and drama...'[34]

Ian Garland in the right wing *Daily Mail* judged Beckham's arrival by speedboat as 'the coolest moment of an amazing show and an esti-mated television audience of one billion tuned in worldwide to witness what had been billed as the Greatest Show on Earth'.[35] Andy Dawson in the *Daily Mirror* embraced this broad view: 'Danny Boyle's portion of the ceremony was a jaw-dropping love letter to Britain itself, including the eyes-on-stalks sight of The Queen doing some actual acting, in a brief scene with Daniel Craig's James Bond. [...] Boyle's breath-taking show paid tribute to the things that TRULY make Britain great'.[36] Even *Socialist Worker* was prepared to endorse 'a stunning depiction of the industrial revolution, a view of the Suffragettes and some early trade

---

[32] 29 July 2012, p. 41.

[33] 'Media reaction to London 2012 Olympic opening ceremony', *BBC News*, 28 July 2014, Media reaction to London 2012 Olympic opening ceremony; accessed 14 November 2014.

[34] Richard Williams, 'Boyle's inventive ceremony grabs the licence...and thrills', *The Guardian*, 28 July 2012, http://www.theguardian.com/sport/2012/jul/28/richard-williams-olympic-opening-ceremony; accessed 14 November 2014.

[35] Ian Garland, 'Britain fires up the world: London gets the 2012 Games under way with the Greatest Show On Earth (rounded off by Macca, of course)', *Mail Online*, 28 July 2012, http://www.dailymail.co.uk/news/article-2179920/Olympics-Opening-Ceremony-London-gets-2012-Games-way-Greatest-Show-On-Earth-rounded-Macca-course.html; accessed 14 November 2014.

[36] Andy Dawson, 'Boyle Command Performance is hampered by not-so-clever Trevor', *Mirror*, 28 July 2012, http://www.mirror.co.uk/tv/tv-reviews/bbcs-trevor-nelson-stumbles-but-danny-1177361; accessed 14 November 2014.

unionists, recognition for multicultural Britain and a strong celebration of the NHS'.[37]

British media hurriedly collated supportive media reactions from abroad. 'Across the globe', reported Alexandra Topping in *The Guardian*, 'Danny Boyle's opening ceremony provoked respect, excitement, the occasional whiff of disdain and no little bafflement'.[38] A Chinese journalist, she said, had asked if this was 'the most rock and roll opening ceremony ever'.[39] Moreover,

> [o]n Copacabana beach, nervous Brazilians watched the show they would have to live up to: laughing at Bond, commenting that the Queen looked grumpy, but generally impressed by the spectacle. 'I hope Rio can match this,' said one. 'Perhaps we will be embarrassed after this,' added another [...] Germany's prestigious conservative newspaper the Frankfurter *Allgemeine Zeitung* said that London's hosting of the opening ceremony passed off with 'heart and humour... spectacular, but also thoughtful and touching'. It said: 'Billions worldwide in front of their TV were enchanted by a stylish show that merged the traditional and the modern in colourful images.' Spain's *El Mundo* correspondent John Muller tweeted: 'I think that, despite all their mistakes, it has become clear that without the UK our lives would not be the same'.[40]

The *Times of India* hailed 'a vibrant picture of Great Britain's rich heritage and culture'.[41] And the headline on the BBC's World News website was 'London 2012 opening ceremony wows world media', the text below reporting glowing approval of the event on the part of the Yonhap news agency in South Korea, Singapore's *Straits Times* and *The Australian*. Xinhua, China's state-run news agency, commented: 'With idyllic pastoral scenes, British humour, and fantasy literature, the London Olympics opening ceremony was full of British characteristics.

---

[37] 4 August 2012, p. 5.

[38] Alexandra Topping, 'Olympics opening ceremony: the view from abroad', *The Guardian*, 28 July 2012, http://www.theguardian.com/sport/2012/jul/27/ olympics-opening-ceremony-view-from-abroad; accessed 15 November 2014.

[39] Ibid.

[40] Ibid.

[41] 'Dazzling opening ceremony launches 30th Olympic Games', the *Times of India*, 28 July 2012, http://timesofindia.indiatimes.com/news/dazzling-opening-ceremony-launches-30th-olympic-games/articleshow/15220673.cms;  accessed 14 November 2014.

What lay behind these memorable parts were none other than Britain's well-developed cultural and creative industries'.[42]

Within those self-same cultural industries optimistic noises about the Boyle display as a basis for a fresh, convivial and durable British national identity began to be heard. An impressive debate, for example, was launched on the *Open Democracy* website. Anthony Barnett, founder of *Open Democracy* and a leading contributor to this debate, sought to stress Boyle's own statement in the programme notes to the ceremony:

> We hope ... that through all the noise and excitement you'll glimpse a single golden thread of purpose – the idea of Jerusalem – of the better world, the world of real freedom and true equality, a world that can be built through the prosperity of industry, through the caring nation that built the welfare state, through the joyous energy of popular culture, through the dream of universal communication.[43]

Barnett acknowledged that the whole event was doubtless 'contrived by the public relations industry, about which for once the claim that "Britain leads the world" is all too credible'.[44] But he was convinced, not only that the ceremony had confronted neoliberalism – principally in the form of the Conservative-Liberal Democrat 'Austerity' programme – but that it could be the basis for a political riposte – a 'new Jerusalem': 'What the Olympic opening shows is that a different form of politics from that on offer is possible and would be popular'.[45] Within the same debate Barnett received qualified support from Sunder Katwala, director of British Future, a new think tank dealing with 'issues of identity, immigration and fairness'.[46] Katwala (British born of Indian and Irish heritage) argued from the standpoint of British identity, congratulating

[42] 28 July 2012, http://www.bbc.co.uk/news/world-19026951; accessed 15 November 2014.

[43] Anthony Barnett, 'The fire and the Games: how London's Olympic opening confronted corporate values', *Open Democracy*, 30 July 2012, https://www.opendemocracy.net/ourkingdom/anthony-barnett/fire-and-games-how-london%E2%80%99s-olympic-opening-confronted-corporate-values; accessed 16 November 2014.

[44] Ibid.

[45] Ibid.

[46] Sunder Katwala, 'An island story: Boyle's Olympic opening was irresistibly British', *Open Democracy*, 31 July 2012, https://www.opendemocracy.net/ourkingdom/sunder-katwala/island-story-boyles-olympic-opening-was-irresistibly-british; accessed 16 November 2014.

Boyle for having 'finally exploded the common, but rather thin, objection that there is little to be said about what Britishness is, because it contains nothing that is truly unique' and suggesting 'Shakespeare and the suffragettes, the Beatles and James Bond, Harry Potter and Tim Berners-Lee are our story, our icons, before we share them with the world too. The show also succeeded through a generous pluralism, which refused stale polarisations'.[47] But even Katwala could not avoid tempering his admiration for Boyle's feat by flagging up the matter of crucial *absences* from 'Isles of Wonder'. Some of these absences will now be discussed.

For Katwala, and other writers, the glaring omission was **imperialism**. After all, multicultural Britain, forged in part by the migrants who travelled on the *Empire Windrush* and the Asian and Caribbean families from whom 'Frankie' and 'June' were descended, had not come to the UK by accident; they had travelled (often at the request of the British government) to Britain as the 'Mother Country':

> There are two distinct stories about Britain's place in the world – and this show chose to prioritise one of them, the forge of the industrial revolution, but perhaps to duck the other, the story of a global island's imperial expansion and Commonwealth contraction, and how that was to change Britain irreversibly.[48]

Ranga Mberi, a Zimbabwean journalist, tweeted: '#OpeningCeremony segment supposedly showing the people who built modern Britain. But I don't see many immigrants. OK Britain, we see you flaunting your history. Where's the bit in which you invade, loot, kill and plunder?'[49] But, generally, as the sociologist Annika Oettler noted, media response, across Africa and the 'global north', to the opening ceremony was supportive, with little mention of the colonial past – partly, she suggests, because they reflect the ideological positions of their national political elites, rather than their audiences.[50] Boyle himself had almost certainly wanted to avoid any triumphalist portrayal of the British Empire, but this omission will probably have been made, not because of his left-ish

---

[47] Ibid.
[48] Ibid.
[49] Noted in Topping, 'Olympics opening ceremony'.
[50] Anika Oettler, 'The London 2012 Olympics opening ceremony and its polyphonous aftermath', *Journal of Sport and Social Issues*, published online 1 July 2014, http://jss.sagepub.com/content/early/2014/05/07/0193723514541281; accessed courtesy of the author.

sympathies, but for the offence it would have given to huge swathes of the global audience, at home and abroad.

Other institutions, persons and events, for which, given their place in national life, a strong case for inclusion could have been made, were similarly omitted from 'Isles of Wonder'. There was, for instance, no procession of **bankers** or representation of the **City of London**, although the previous year UK Prime Minister David Cameron had described them as a 'key national interest' and insisted that the City of London financial markets must be protected from 'constant attack through Brussels [i.e. European Union] directives'.[51] However, as previously observed, a huge protest had taken place outside the London Stock Exchange in 2011 and a section of professional and public opinion blamed the banks for the global financial crisis of the preceding four years. Nor was there reference to the **Second World War**; nor to national political icon **Sir Winston Churchill** (except when, during the James Bond sequence, his statue in London's Parliament Square comes to life and waves at the helicopter carrying Bond and the Queen, rendering him another object for 'quirky' British humour); nor, the appearance of the Suffragists and the Jarrow Marchers notwithstanding, to the biggest political demonstration in British history – against British participation in the **invasion of Iraq in 2003**; nor, despite her domination of the Western political stage during the 1980s, was mention made of **Margaret Thatcher**. All these signifiers would have been divisive of the huge audience, both locally and globally, that the Boyle team was planning to address. The latter point was brought home neatly by a subsequent joke on the *Huffington Post* website. Following Mrs Thatcher's death in the spring of 2013, the *Post*'s UK Comedy page told of rumours that Danny Boyle was to direct her funeral:

> The staged numbers will include hundreds of coal mines being erected only to be dismantled, and a million candles being lit to finally reveal the word 'GOTCHA'.[52] Tightly choreographed dance routines, meanwhile, will see hundreds of private hospital nurses dancing on the grave of the NHS, a thousand bankers jumping up

---

[51] 'David Cameron: EU "constant attacks" on city of London', *BBC News*, 28 October 2011, http://www.bbc.co.uk/news/uk-politics-15487674; accessed 16 November 2014.

[52] A reference to the headline on the front of the British right wing tabloid the *Sun*, on 4 May 1982, following the Royal Navy's sinking of the Argentine cruiser *General Belgrano*.

and down on piles of cash, and a re-enactment of the poll tax riots set to Mike Oldfield's 'Tubular Bells'. [...] 'We think there's something for everyone – pomp and circumstance for the Thatcherites and subversive messages for the lefties,' a St Paul's insider told us. 'It will be a celebration of all that made Britain great. And terrible.'[53]

On her death, Cottrell Boyce, somewhat unconvincingly, argued in a newspaper article that her neoliberalism had made Margaret Thatcher 'un-British':[54] 'Although she draped herself in the union flag, Thatcher never seemed really to like or understand this country'. This brought an equally implausible response from right wing blogger Toby Young – 'Aidan Burley [a Conservative MP] was right about the Olympics opening ceremony being "Leftie crap" – and here's the proof' – who argued that 'the principle of limited government' was 'arguably our greatest export' and reminded *Telegraph* readers that Scottish philosopher Adam Smith, whose *Wealth of Nations* (1776) was widely regarded as the bible of economic liberals, had been British.[55]

Two things, then, seem important to say. First, in a society (like Britain) increasingly divided by **social class**, there are (often severe) limits to what can be achieved by deploying the concept of 'social inclusion'. Second, despite the best of intentions, the Boyle team had simply done what the International Olympic Committee always requires of such occasions – that the politics of the time be suspended in favour of something more palatable to a mass audience. The politics of the time soon returned to normal. I will now expand on these points.

'Isles of Wonder' necessarily, given Boyle's remit and his commitment to the notion of 'social inclusion', underplayed social class as a theme in British history. As one commentator observed: 'What does not quite fit, however, is the non-antagonistic nature of the relationship between the industrialists and the workers. The performance depicts it as one of

---

[53] Andrea Mann, 'Danny Boyle "To Direct Margaret Thatcher's funeral"', http://www.huffingtonpost.co.uk/2013/04/10/danny-boyle-margaret-thatcher-funeral-spoof-news_n_3051382.html, posted 10 April 2013; accessed 17 November 2014.
[54] Frank Cottrell Boyce, 'Margaret Thatcher never liked her country', *Observer*, 14 April 2014, http://www.theguardian.com/commentisfree/2013/apr/14/thatcher-never-liked-her-country; accessed 18 November 2014
[55] Toby Young, 'Aidan Burley was right about the Olympics opening ceremony being "Leftie crap" – and here's the proof', *Telegraph*, 15 April 2014, http://blogs.telegraph.co.uk/news/tobyyoung/100212168/aidan-burley-was-right-about-the-olympics-opening-ceremony-being-leftie-crap-and-heres-the-proof/;   accessed 18 November 2014.

a partnership, an archaic corporatism assiduously intent on increasing the productive capabilities of the nation, of capital and of the human species. What of worker resistance – Luddism, the Captain Swing riots of the 1830s...?'[56] As we saw earlier, the term 'social exclusion' gained wide political currency in the 1990s. It was immediately associated with the 'New' Labour government of Tony Blair, which set up a Social Exclusion Unit in 1997, the year it took office. It is also a term widely used in the European Union. It is held variously to refer to social integration, to the need for greater access of social groups (women, ethnic minorities...) to particular institutions (politics, banking...) and to the need to fight poverty, but it can be seen as a catch-all term, with no consensually agreed definition.[57] Academic commentators recognised right away that the adoption of the concept of 'social inclusion' signalled a decreasing concern with equality in a more and more market-oriented society, and an emphasis instead upon social cohesion and equality of opportunity.[58] 'Isles of Wonder', with its 'good sport' Queen, its suffragists, its rags-to-riches pop stars, its multi-ethnic nurses and its texting teenagers, was certainly a motif of social cohesion and equality of opportunity. But, by the time of the Olympics, Britain was a far more unequal society than it had been in the 1960s, when the Beatles and the Rolling Stones had first entered the charts. Less than two years after London 2012, Oxfam reported that since 'the mid-1990s the incomes of the top 0.1 per cent have grown almost four times faster than the incomes of the bottom 90 per cent of the population' and that the five richest families in the UK were now wealthier than the bottom 20% of the entire population (12.6 million people) put together.[59] London, moreover, was home to

---

[56] Aaron Bastani, 'Olympic Britishness and the crisis of identity', *Open Democracy*, 3 August 2012, https://www.opendemocracy.net/ourkingdom/aaron-peters/olympic-britishness-and-crisis-of-identity; accessed 18 November 2014.

[57] A key writer here is Ruth Levitas. See, for example, Ruth Levitas, 'Defining and measuring social exclusion: a critical overview of current proposals', http://www.radstats.org.uk/no071/article2.htm; accessed 17 November 2014; Ruth Levitas, 'The concept and measurement of social exclusion', in C. Pantazis et al. (eds.), *Poverty and Social Exclusion in Britain* (Bristol: Policy Press, 2006), pp. 123–160, http://www.open.ac.uk/poverty/pdf/poverty-and-social-exclusion_chap5.pdf; accessed 17 November 2014; and Ruth Levitas, 'The idea of social exclusion', http://socialpolicyframework.alberta.ca/files/documents/2003_social_inclusion_research_conference.pdf; accessed 17 November 2014.

[58] See, for instance, Ruth Lister, 'From equality to social inclusion: New Labour and the welfare state', *Critical Social Policy*, Vol. 18, No. 55 (May 1998), pp. 215–225.

[59] PSE (Poverty and Social Exclusion), http://www.poverty.ac.uk/editorial/five-families-worth-more-poorest-20-cent, posted 17 March 2014; accessed 17 November 2014.

more billionaires than any other city in the world.[60] They certainly would have been among the comparatively small number of people able to afford the best seats for 'Isles of Wonder', priced at £2,012 each.[61]

The neoliberal arguments and policies (privatisation, continuing cuts in public spending, increased recourse to 'immigration' and 'multiculturalism', rather than the market, as the cause of the growing impoverishment of many Britons...) that had helped to heighten inequality were put on hold for the duration of the Games. The chief proponents of these policies were supportive of the opening ceremony, acted as cheerleaders for the Games and otherwise kept a low profile, the advisability of this latter strategy being underlined in early September when Chancellor of the Exchequer George Osborne, the chief architect of the government's 'austerity' programme, stepped forward to present the medals for the men's 400 metres at the Paralympics and was booed by a crowd of 60,000 people.[62] Indeed, when the Conservative MP Aiden Burley referred to the opening ceremony in a widely circulated tweet as 'leftie multicultural crap', the Conservative Party hierarchy disowned him. London mayor Boris Johnson, prone to disguise his free market politics behind a carefully cultivated naughty boarding schoolboy persona, insisted: 'The thing I loved was the heavy political stuff. I loved the emergence of the urban proletariat and the rise of the chimneys and the forging of the rings',[63] adding

> We have just stunned the world with what was the best opening ceremony ever produced – and by quite a margin. Danny Boyle's filmic mixture of Blake, Dickens, Tolkien, JK Rowling etc etc has confirmed London's status as the global capital of art and culture. [...] James Bond and the Monarchy – not to mention The Eton Boating Song... How can anyone call that Lefty propaganda?[64]

---

[60] See therichest.com, http://www.therichest.com/rich-list/nation/britains-10-richest-billionaires-in-2014/; accessed 17 November 2014.

[61] '2012 London Olympic Games ticket prices released', *BBC News*, 15 October 2010, http://www.bbc.co.uk/news/uk-england-london-11546228; accessed 17 November 2014.

[62] http://www.youtube.com/watch?v=v0nMtSJDrGc; accessed 17 November 2014.

[63] ' "Nonsense": Boris Johnson scoffs at London 2012 opening ceremony "leftie" accusations as he admits to crying "hot tears of patriotic pride" ', *Mirror*, 28 July 2012, http://www.mirror.co.uk/news/uk-news/boris-johnson-dismisses-olympic-opening-1179600; accessed 17 November 2014.

[64] *Telegraph*, 30 July 2012, http://www.telegraph.co.uk/comment/columnists/borisjohnson/9437495/London-Olympics-2012-heres-20-jolly-good-reasons-to-feel-cheerful-about-the-Games.html; accessed 17 November 2014.

And Prime Minister David Cameron told Burley it was 'an idiotic thing to say', adding that the ceremony was 'not about politics. We all celebrate the NHS. We all think James Bond is fantastic. We all revere the Queen'.[65] But, outside of the Games, the inclusiveness flagged up by Boyle had been, and would soon again be, bitterly contested in the political arena. Cameron himself, in a speech in Munich in February 2011, had denounced 'state multiculturalism' and argued 'We have even tolerated segregated communities behaving in ways that run counter to our values. All this leaves some young Muslims feeling rootless. And the search for something to belong to and believe in can lead them to extremist ideology'.[66] A variety of opinion polls taken during 2012 showed a steady rise in support (from around 5% to roughly 15%) for the right wing UK Independence Party (UKIP),[67] whose principal platforms consisted of British withdrawal from the European Union and anti-immigrant racism. UKIP's leader, Nigel Farage, had growing access to the mainstream media[68] and in March 2014 he told his party's annual conference about passing through London on the train:

> It was rush hour, from Charing Cross, it was the stopper going out. We stopped at London Bridge, New Cross, Hither Green. It wasn't until after we got past Grove Park that I could actually hear English being audibly spoken in the carriage. Does that make me feel slightly awkward? Yes. I wonder what's really going on. And I'm sure that's a view that will be reflected by three quarters of the population, perhaps even more.

With the major political parties all pledging to cut immigration ('David Cameron pledges further action on EU immigration',[69] 'Ed Miliband:

---

[65] *BBC News*, 30 July 2012, http://www.bbc.co.uk/news/uk-politics-19046448; accessed 17 November 2014.

[66] Oliver Wright and Jerome Taylor, 'Cameron: my war on multiculturalism', *Independent*, 5 February 2011, http://www.independent.co.uk/news/uk/politics/cameron-my-war-on-multiculturalism-2205074.html; accessed 17 November 2014.

[67] http://en.wikipedia.org/wiki/Opinion_polling_for_the_next_United_Kingdom _general_election#2012; accessed 17 November 2014.

[68] Matthew Goodwin and Robert Ford, 'Just how much media coverage does UKIP get?', *New Statesman*, 11 November 2013, http://www.newstatesman.com/politics/2013/11/just-how-much-media-coverage-does-ukip-get;   accessed 17 November 2014.

[69] Christopher Hope and Bruno Waterfield, 'David Cameron pledges further action on EU immigration', *Telegraph*, 16 October 2014, http://www.telegraph.

immigration is at top of Labour's agenda'[70]), public discourse in Britain soon seemed to have travelled some distance from the notion of London as the city of 200 nationalities celebrated in the Coe team's original bid for the Olympic Games.

Moreover, outside of local and national political leadership, important aspects of 'Isles of Wonder', notably **the interpretation of history** and **the National Health Service**, soon became re-established as matters for contention.

The historian Catherine Baker analysed 'Isles of Wonder' from the standpoint of public history and identified the Marxist historian Raphael Samuel, an advocate of 'history from below', and the documentary film maker and founder of Mass Observation social research unit Humphrey Jennings as influences. Cottrell Boyce, she pointed out, had been familiar with Samuel's work. This, she noted, put Boyle's team in a position that ran strongly counter to the current politicking over History at the British Department of Education, under the then minister Michael Gove.[71] The right wing *Daily Mail* reported that Gove had been among several ministers who 'were yesterday reported to have voiced concerns privately' after seeing a rehearsal of 'Isles of Wonder'.[72] (Gove is said to have objected to the exclusion of Sir Winston Churchill.[73]) In October 2010 Gove had told the Conservative Party Conference: 'One of the under-appreciated tragedies of our time has been the sundering of our society from its past. Children are growing up ignorant of one of the

co.uk/news/uknews/immigration/11168526/David-Cameron-pledges-further-action-on-EU-immigration.html; accessed 17 November 2014.

[70] Rowena Mason, 'Ed Miliband: immigration is at top of Labour's agenda', *The Guardian*, 23 October 2014, http://www.theguardian.com/politics/2014/oct/23/labour-immigration-reform-bill-voter-concerns; accessed 17 November 2014.

[71] Catherine Baker, 'Beyond the island story?: the opening ceremony of the London 2012 Olympic Games as public history', *Rethinking History*, published online 2014, http://www.academia.edu/6839567/Beyond_the_island_story_The_opening_ceremony_of_the_London_2012_Olympic_Games_as_public_history; accessed 17 November 2014.

[72] Jason Groves, 'Labour glee over its "best advert in years": party delighted at games "socialist" opening ceremony', *Daily Mail*, 30 July 2012, http://www.dailymail.co.uk/news/article-2180863/London-2012-Olympics-Labour-Party-delighted-Games-socialist-opening-ceremony.html; accessed 17 November 2014.

[73] Paul Kelso and Patrick Hennessy, 'Ministers "pushed for changes" to opening ceremony', *Telegraph*, 29 July 2012, http://www.telegraph.co.uk/sport/olympics/london-2012/9435509/Ministers-pushed-for-changes-to-opening-ceremony.html; accessed 18 November 2014.

most inspiring stories I know – the history of our United Kingdom'.[74] The task of devising a new approach to the teaching of history was later given to Simon Schama, Professor of Art History and History at Columbia University in the United States. Richard J. Evans, Professor of History at Cambridge University, had seen a grim prospect for the sort of history from below now being associated with 'Isles of Wonder' in the proposals for school history submitted by Gove's advisors, the 'Better History' group:

> The demand, really, is for a celebratory history: how otherwise could it serve as the cement of national identity? Sample exam questions proposed by the Better History group for the new curriculum have included: 'Why did Nelson and Wellington become national heroes?'; 'What liberties did English people enjoy by the end of the 17th century that they hadn't had at the start?'; and 'How dangerous was the Spanish Armada?' – the examinee, it's presumed, isn't going to answer from the point of view of the Spanish.[75]

Among the several facets of the ceremony that caused grumbling on the political right, particularly in Britain and the United States, was the segment featuring the National Health Service and acted out by over 600 nurses and health care workers from the NHS itself. In a press conference after the ceremony, Boyle said:

> One of the reasons we put the NHS in the show is that everyone is aware of how important the NHS is to everybody in this country. We believe, as a nation, in universal healthcare. It doesn't matter how poor you are, how rich you are, you will get treated. One of the core values of our society is that it doesn't matter who you are, you will get treated the same in terms of healthcare. We all end up there. You can be in all these private hospitals – if anything serious happens to you,

---

[74] The speech can be read in full at: http://centrallobby.politicshome. com/latestnews/article-detail/newsarticle/speech-in-full-michael-gove/; accessed 17 November 2014.

[75] Richard J. Evans, 'The wonderfulness of us (the Tory interpretation of history)', *London Review of Books*, Vol. 33, No. 6 (17 March 2011), pp. 9–12, http://www.lrb. co.uk/v33/n06/richard-j-evans/the-wonderfulness-of-us; accessed 17 November 2014.

you are in the NHS. And that felt like something that we thought was a great thing to celebrate.[76]

There was, expectably, some adverse comment in the American media about this section of the ceremony[77] and there was similar grumbling in the UK. Indeed, while public support for the National Health Service had remained high in Britain throughout its existence and it had been established, to use Allyson Pollock's phrase, as 'a right of citizenship',[78] for some years the NHS had been privatised from within, with successive governments deploying the Private Finance Initiative in hospital building and contracting services out to private healthcare companies.[79] This pattern had been established by the 'New' Labour governments of 1997–2010 and open opposition to state-funded health care was beginning to flourish in the Conservative Party. So, while the service, its basic tenets and dedicated staff were heavily supported by the British public, the same could not be said for British politicians, despite their frequent recourse to the phrase 'free at the point of delivery'. This truth was underscored by the news that the Secretary of State for Health, Jeremy Hunt, had tried to have the NHS tribute removed from the ceremony.[80] Private health companies, which by now had become leading donors to the Conservative Party,[81] are unlikely to have been pleased by this part of the ceremony. 'Cameron and his gang', wrote Richard Williams

---

[76] 'Director's tribute to "amazing" NHS', Orange website (undated), http://web.orange.co.uk/article/news/director_s_tribute_to_amazing_nhs;      accessed 19 November 2014.

[77] A number of US responses were collected by the Moral Low Ground website. See Brett Wilkins, 'Inclusion of NHS in London Olympic opening ceremony angers UK conservatives, vexes US media', 28 July 2012, http://morallowground.com/2012/07/28/inclusion-of-nhs-in-london-olympic-opening-ceremony-angers-uk-conservatives-vexes-us-media/; accessed 19 November 2014.

[78] Allyson M. Pollock et al., *NHS plc The Privatisation of Our Health Care* (London: Verso, 2005), p. 34.

[79] See Pollock et al., *NHS plc The Privatisation of Our Health Care.*

[80] Denis Campbell, 'Jeremy Hunt under fire for stance on NHS tribute, homeopathy and abortion', *The Guardian*, 4 September 2012, http://www.theguardian.com/politics/2012/sep/04/jeremy-hunt-nhs-tribute-homeopathy;      accessed 19 November 2014.

[81] See, for example, James Lyons, 'NHS reform leaves Tory backers with links to private healthcare firms set for bonanza', *Mirror*, 19 January 2011, http://www.mirror.co.uk/news/uk-news/nhs-reform-leaves-tory-backers-105302;      accessed 19 November 2014.

in *The Guardian*, 'will surely not dare to continue the dismemberment of the NHS after this'.[82] Williams' hope was the fear of the (thriving) privatisation lobby. Ian Birrell in the right wing *Mail on Sunday* suggested:

> the last time the World Health Organisation ranked countries' health systems, Britain came in below Greece, Malta, Oman and Portugal. More recent studies found we had the worst patient care among seven leading industrialised nations and among the lowest cancer survival rates in the Western world. This may seem harsh, but I believe Britain's sentimentality over its health system – which will intensify now Boyle has decreed it to be an official strand of our island story – is preventing real reform, a damaging and ultimately self-defeating national tragedy.[83]

Political disquiet over the NHS tribute, however, appeared specifically to do with Boyle's stress on the NHS *as a free public service*; the coalition government, on the other hand, preferred to see the NHS *as a business* and the following month urged NHS hospitals to consider setting up clinics abroad, deploying the 'famous NHS brand' – a process already in train: for instance, Great Ormond Street Hospital for Children, prominently featured in 'Isles of Wonder', had signed a contract with the Kuwaiti government three years earlier.[84]

Coe had helped Danny Boyle procure an internationally attractive presentation of Britain. This had necessarily involved the celebration of aspects of British life that had strong public support, both at home and abroad. These aspects had, for many, run counter to dominant ideology and government policy, the principal proponents of which agreed a truce for the duration of the Games. Despite an apparent international triumph, Boyle remained defensive. Pressed

---

[82] Williams, 'Boyle's inventive ceremony grabs the licence... and thrills', http://www.theguardian.com/sport/2012/jul/28/richard-williams-olympic-opening-ceremony; accessed 18 November 2014.

[83] Ian Birrell, 'The London 2012 opening ceremony, and a night that set NHS reform back years', *Mail on Sunday*, 3 August 2012, http://www.dailymail.co.uk/debate/article-2183440/London-2012-opening-ceremony-The-night-set-NHS-reform-years.html; accessed 19 November 2014.

[84] See Sarah Boseley, 'NHS "brand" could be sold abroad to generate income, says government', *The Guardian*, 21 August 2012, p. 1, pp. 4–5, http://www.theguardian.com/society/2012/aug/21/nhs-brand-sold-overseas-hospitals; accessed 19 November 2014.

by writer Amy Raphael to comment on the view that 'Isles' had 'flicked a V sign at' the coalition government and expressed 'a Marxist view of history', he (perhaps unconsciously) avoided the question: 'Not at all. Isambard Kingdom Brunel wasn't a Marxist. Nor is Tim Berners-Lee'.[85]

## Reflection: opening the Olympics in the twenty-first century – 'Isles of Wonder' in perspective

To a degree Boyle's task had been prescribed for him. Since the 1980s certain elements in the Games' opening ceremony had become virtually mandatory. First, the ceremony had now to be a striking spectacle featuring a myriad of actors moving in formation – a phenomenon first seen in the modern era in the Soviet Union's spartakiads of the 1920s and the 'Nazi Olympics' in Berlin in 1936, with its nationalistic pageantry and appropriation of the Olympic flame.[86] (The opening of the previous Olympics, in Los Angeles in 1932, was comparatively low-key and the organisers had largely contented themselves with a march-past of the competitors. The President, Herbert Hoover, did not bother to attend, leaving his Vice President, Charles Curtis, to declare the Games open.) With the growing involvement of television in the Olympics, the expectation of an extravagant spectacle has grown, with the organisers of each ceremony called upon to outdo the preceding one. Special effects have been part of this expectation since the Los Angeles Olympics of 1984, when Bill Suitor (Sean Connery's stunt double in several James Bond films) flew into the stadium using a jet pack (equipment normally employed by astronauts for extra-vehicular activity). By 2012, as the writer Rafil Kroll-Zaidi sardonically observed, those devising Olympic ceremonies were availing themselves of an established model:

> Olympic opening ceremonies, so it is written, present a vision of the host country, which lately (Atlanta, Sydney, Athens) has meant Cirque du Soleil–ified stage shows of varying national specificity but considerable stylistic consistency: LED [light emitting diode] and

---

[85] Amy Raphael, *Danny Boyle: Creating Wonder* (London: Faber, 2013), pp. 411–412.
[86] See David Clay Large, 'The Nazi Olympics: Berlin 1936', in Helen Jefferson Lenskyj and Stephen Wagg (eds.), *The Palgrave Handbook of Olympic Studies* (Basingstoke: Palgrave Macmillan, 2012), pp. 60–72, at pp. 62–64.

fibre-optic light effects, elaborate and ethereal costumes, colossal puppetry, acrobatics and wirework – most of it slow and graceful. Beijing transformed these elements with a performance of globally lauded and metonymically freighted military precision. The London organizers' appointment of Boyle signalled a wholesale departure from Beijing: in place of faceless Politburo pyrotechnics, British officials promised a demonstration of British character, and in place of British might, wry understatement and mellow self-confidence.[87]

But the departure wasn't as wholesale as all that. Most Olympic opening ceremonies of recent vintage, including Boyle's, have had two other important features: first, the identification of the host country by its popular culture and popular cultural figures and, second, a depiction of ethnic harmony which often flew in the face of prevailing political realities. (These two features had often amounted to the same thing.) At Los Angeles in 1984 84 pianists had played George Gershwin's *Rhapsody in Blue* and the African American blues singer Etta James (born in the city) had sung *When the Saints Go Marching In*. The Barcelona Games had begun with an operatic performance by the Spanish singers Giacomo Aragall, Jose Carreras and Placido Domingo (tenors), Juan Pons (baritone) and Teresa Berganza and Montserrat Caballe (sopranos). There followed a procession of popular vocalists in the opening ceremonies of successive Games: Georgia-born Gladys Knight sang Hoagy Carmichael's *Georgia on My Mind* at the opening of the Atlanta Olympics in 1996; Oliver Newton-John and John Farnham (who had both grown up in Melbourne) duetted at Sydney; rapper R. Kelly and country singer Leann Rimes sang at the Salt Lake Winter Games in 2002; Luciano Pavarotti sang *Nessun Dorma* at the opening of the next Winter Games in Turin in 2006; and k.d.lang, along with local residents Bryan Adams, Sarah McLachlan and the Portuguese Canadian singer Nelly Furtado, performed to three billion television viewers at the opening of the Winter Games of 2010 in Vancouver. The popular musical heritage of London, once styled as 'Swinging London' and home at one time or another to a host of influential bands and singers – The Beatles, the Rolling Stones, David Bowie, the Sex Pistols, Led Zeppelin . . . – was a theme that Boyle could scarcely have ignored.

---

[87] Rafil Kroll-Zaidi, 'Hacks Britannica: Reviving an Olympic tradition of crapness', http://www.theparisreview.org/blog/2012/07/31/hacks-britannica-reviving-an-olympic-tradition-of-crapness/, posted 31 July 2012; accessed 4 February 2015.

Similarly *Isles'* multi-ethnic character. As I observed, most Olympic opening ceremonies of the last 20 years have depicted racial or ethnic harmony in the host locality. While Etta James was singing in 1984, LA's black communities were being harassed by a police force widely regarded as racist: race riots would erupt there eight years later following the beating (captured on film) of an African American man called Rodney King by four white police officers who were subsequently exonerated.[88] In Atlanta the key moment in the opening segment was the lighting of the Olympic flame by a now-ailing Muhammad Ali. Ali, as Cassius Clay, had won the Olympic light heavyweight gold medal in Rome in 1960, but had thrown his medal away soon afterwards after being refused service in a restaurant which ran a colour bar. He had relinquished his birth name in 1964, espoused the (black separatist) Nation of Islam and declined to serve in the US army in Vietnam, famously stating 'Ain't no Viet Cong ever called me "Nigger"'.[89] Asking Ali to light the flame was an act of reconciliation on the part both of the Olympic committee and of white America, but life in Atlanta remained largely racially segregated. A report four years later by the Brookings Institution Centre on Urban and Metropolitan Policy reported the city to be 'starkly divided by race. The numbers speak for themselves: African-Americans tend to live in Fulton and DeKalb counties and the City of Atlanta. By contrast, the northern and far southern suburban counties – Gwinnett, Cherokee, Cobb, Henry, and Fayette – are overwhelmingly white'.[90] In Sydney in 2000, in a similar gesture of apparent reconciliation, the Olympic flame was lit by Cathy Freeman, an Australian Aborigine athlete who had done a lap of honour draped in the aborigine flag after winning the 400 metres in the 1994 Commonwealth Games in Canada,[91] and Aboriginals in traditional costume had featured strongly in the Sydney opening pageant. Some saw this as evidence of improved inter-communal relations in Australia and as an indication

---

[88] See, for example, Playthell Benjamin, 'From the archive, 1 May 1992: Rodney King verdict sparks LA riots', http://www.theguardian.com/theguardian/2013/may/01/la-riots-rodney-king-race, posted 1 May 2013; accessed 4 February 2015.

[89] For a full account of Ali's politics, see Mike Marqusee, *Redemption Song: Muhammad Ali and the Spirit of the Sixties* (London: Verso, 2000).

[90] The Brookings Institution Centre on Urban and Metropolitan Policy, *Moving Beyond Sprawl: The Challenge for Metropolitan Atlanta* (Washington, DC: The Brookings Institution, 2000), p. 16, http://www.brookings.edu/~/media/research/files/reports/2000/3/atlanta/atlanta.pdf; accessed 4 February 2015.

[91] See   http://nga.gov.au/federation/Detail.cfm?WorkID=27708;   accessed   4 February 2015.

that Australia had freed itself of 'cultural cringe' – its mythical cultural-national inferiority complex.[92] However, as Lenskyj pointed out, 'while Aboriginal dancers were performing for mostly White audiences, Black men continued to die in police custody'.[93] Moreover, as Toni Bruce and Emma Wensing observed,[94] the year after the Olympics Prime Minister John Howard's right wing Liberal-National coalition was re-elected on the back of a manifesto composed of apparently 'hard-line and xeno-phobic policies': this manifesto was dominated by the 'One Australia Policy' which called for an end to multiculturalism and was opposed to a treaty with Aboriginal Australians.

Similar contradictions were present in Vancouver in 2010. 'With the opening of its third Olympics, Canada tried to prove to the world that it is about more than just maple leaves', wrote Geoffrey A. Fowler and Phred Dvorak in the *Wall Street Journal*.

> To be sure, there were maple leaves at the opening ceremony of the Vancouver Games, including paper ones falling from the ceiling and a giant one made out of torches. But there was also an homage to Canada's aboriginal peoples, a journey through the country's land-scapes from east to west and an extended paean to the new Canada by slam poet Shane Koyczan. 'We are more than genteel or civilized, we are an idea in the process of being realized,' recited Mr. Koyczan.

However, as Charles Taylor of McGill University suggested to Fowler and Dvorak: 'We run around the world telling people we have been a success. In this context, the situation of the aboriginals doesn't fit well'.[95] (As we saw in Chapter 1, First Nation Canadians had protested that the Sea-to-Sky highway, built for the Games, would run through land stolen from them.) Another commentator argued that, 'Vancouver won their bid on the argument that Vancouver is the most diverse place on earth, with the highest rate of mixed-race marriage in North America' but had failed

---

[92] See Helen Jefferson Lenskyj, *The Best Olympics Ever? Social Impacts of Sydney 2000* (Albany: State University of New York Press, 2002), p. 220.

[93] Ibid.

[94] Toni Bruce and Emma Wensing, 'The Olympics and indigenous peoples: Australia', in Lenskyj and Wagg (eds.), *The Palgrave Handbook of Olympic Studies*, pp. 487–504, at p. 495.

[95] Geoffrey A. Fowler and Phred Dvorak, 'Canada redefines itself in Olympic opening ceremony', http://www.wsj.com/articles/SB100014240527487 03525704575062463944286380, posted 13 February 2010; accessed 4 February 2015.

to represent that fact in its pageant, omitting any sign of the city's large Chinese and South Asian populations and thus producing the 'whitest opening ceremony ever'.[96]

So, once again, Danny Boyle, his good will and optimism notwithstanding, was not mining a wholly new seam in fashioning what disgruntled right wing politicians denounced as 'multicultural crap'; it was, in effect, part of his job description. Similarly, Boyle could not be held responsible for the rising tide of anti-immigrant rhetoric and denunciation of multiculturalism (of which latter London's mayor Boris Johnson was a leading exponent) in British politics: 'I think that we should have a culture in this country that if you come here, you do as the Romans do, you learn English and you speak English', said Johnson on LBC Radio in 2015. 'You go to Tower Hamlets, places like that, you can find people who have been there for several generations who still don't speak English'.[97]

---

[96] Alden E. Habacon, 'Vancouver 2010 Olympic Winter Games: whitest opening ceremony ever?', http://www.straight.com/blogra/vancouver-2010-olympic-winter-games-whitest-opening-ceremony-ever, posted 13 February 2010; accessed 4 February 2015.

[97] Rebecca Perring, 'Boris Johnson: all public service workers "should speak English"', *Daily Express*, 6 January 2015, http://www.express.co.uk/news/uk/550502/Boris-Johnson-public-service-workers-speak-English; accessed 4 February 2015.

# 6

# 'Just Put Down the Pepsi...':
# London 2012 and the Corporations

As has by now been well established by critical accounts of the Olympic movement, the Games have become increasingly corporate in nature over the last 30 years. In relation to London 2012, two anecdotes, among many, evoke the restrictions imposed on behalf of Olympic 'partner' corporations, not only on the Games themselves but on the civil liberties of citizens of the host city. The first occurred while Danny Boyle's 'Isles of Wonder' was still being performed. Members of Critical Mass, a group that promotes cycling and takes a monthly cycle ride around London, were prevented by Metropolitan Police from riding their bikes north across Thames bridges and detained under Section 12 of the Public Order Act of 1986. They were then 'kettled' – that is, herded into, and confined within, a specific space for a prolonged period. There were 182 arrests.[1] The contradictions here were numerous and inescapable: a British cyclist (Bradley Wiggins, the winner of the recent Tour de France) had just rung the bell to open the Olympic ceremony and, according to the promotional template established by the Coe team, could become an 'inspiration' to would-be cyclists across the nation; cyclists were among the most fancied to win medals in the British contingent; the

---

[1] See Alexandra Topping, 'Critical mass cyclists arrested near Olympic stadium', *The Guardian*, 28 July 2012, http://www.theguardian.com/lifeandstyle/2012/jul/28/critical-mass-cyclists-arrested; accessed 19 November 2014; Tom Richards, 'Cycling arrests raise questions about legacy Olympic organisers want to leave', http://www.theguardian.com/environment/bike-blog/2012/jul/30/critical-mass-arrest-olympic-games; accessed 19 November 2014; and Kerry-Anne Mendoza, 'Mass arrests outside London's Olympic opening ceremony: an eyewitness account', *Open Democracy*, 31 July 2012, https://www.opendemocracy.net/ourkingdom/kerry-anne-mendoza/mass-arrests-outside-londons-olympic-opening-ceremony-eye-witness-acco; accessed 19 November 2014.

ceremony itself celebrated the history and tradition of political demonstration in Britain; cycling, as opposed to motor transport, might have been applauded as ecologically sensible, amid a 'sustainable' Olympics; and, most importantly, the Games had been awarded on the basis of a promise to promote sports participation and physical fitness. Moreover, Shami Chakrabarti, Director of Liberty (formerly the National Council for Civil Liberties), was one of eight Olympic Flag carriers at the Games opening ceremony, then taking place. Two weeks earlier, powers allowing police officers to move on groups of two or more people found in the vicinity of the Olympic Park had come into force.[2]

Second, in an expression of the British humour celebrated in the opening ceremony, the issue of the satirical magazine *Private Eye* published on 27 July featured on its cover a photograph, captioned 'OLYMPIC ALERT', of two heavily armed policemen patrolling the Olympic Park. One says 'Just put down the Pepsi can and no one will get hurt'. This joke, which gained wide currency, took for granted *Eye* readers' knowledge of the now apparently pervasive restrictions placed on Olympic spectators, consumers and businesses in the cause of protecting the IOC's corporate partners: cans of Pepsi Cola, it need hardly be added, were banned from the Olympic Park, Coca Cola being a (long standing) sponsor of the Olympic Games. This chapter discusses corporate involvement in London 2012 and its implications. The principal themes of the chapter will be: the relationship between the Games and the construction companies; the influence of the security industry in promoting 'Fortress London'; the aforementioned controversy over the 'brand police' assigned to protect the commercial interests of Olympic 'partners'; and the campaigns to expose and tackle the exploitation of workers by firms with Olympic contracts.

## The contemporary Olympics: reconstruction and construction

It's now an axiom of Olympic discussions that the Games of 1984 in Los Angeles represented a watershed in the commercialisation of the Olympics, but, as the Canadian scholar Rick Gruneau noted at the time, Olympic costs had been rising steeply since the early 1970s. The cost of staging the Winter Games in Sapporo, Japan, in 1972 had been almost seven times the $100 million bill for the corresponding event

---

[2] Kevin Rawlinson, 'Meeting a friend by the Olympic park? Police have other ideas...', *The Independent*, 9 July 2012, p. 13.

held in Innsbruck in 1964; the Summer Games of 1972, in Munich, cost
$850 million and four years later the Summer Olympics in Montreal had
left that city with a debt of around £1.5 billion[3] – a debt, as we saw, not
cleared until 2006. Since Los Angeles, in the end the only candidate to
host the Games of 1984,[4] was situated in a US state (California) known
for popular hostility to public spending, the Games were turned over to
a private company, which, under the leadership of travel entrepreneur
Peter Uberroth, established exclusive sponsorship deals with a number
of leading corporations, which, in return, agreed to provide facilities for
the Games. So, for example, in return for being designated the 'Official
Food Supplier' to LA84, McDonalds agreed to finance the building of an
Olympic swimming pool[5] – originally called the McDonald's Olympic
Swim Stadium. Since 1984, the trend has been toward purpose-built,
'state-of-the-art' facilities for the Olympics – Seoul in 1988, Atlanta in
1996, Sydney in 2000 and Beijing in 2008 had all provided new Olympic
stadia, for example – and these have been financed extensively out
of the now-familiar partnership of private sponsor and public purse:
South Korean government expenditure on the Olympic Park in Seoul
and other infrastructure, for instance, is estimated at $1.5 billion[6] and
the Beijing National Stadium (or 'Birds Nest') was financed by a com-
bination of the CITIC group (a state-owned investment company) and
the Beijing municipal government.[7] The notion that the Games cannot
now survive without corporate funding, and the curtailment of civil and
commercial liberties that that entails, is therefore at the centre of public
debate about the relationship between the corporations and the IOC.

---

[3] Rick Gruneau, 'The chocolate Olympics', *New Socialist*, May/June 1984,
pp. 56–59, p. 57. See also Rick Gruneau, 'Commercialism and the modern
Olympics', in Alan Tomlinson and Garry Whannel (eds.), *Five Ring Circus: Money,
Power and Politics at the Olympic Games* (London: Pluto Press, 1984), pp. 1–15 and
Rick Gruneau and Robert Neubauer, 'A gold medal for the market: the 1984 Los
Angeles Olympics, the Reagan Era and the politics of neoliberalism', in Helen
Jefferson Lenskyj and Stephen Wagg (eds.), *The Palgrave Handbook of Olympic
Studies* (Basingstoke: Palgrave Macmillan, 2012), pp. 134–162.
[4] Tehran withdrew its bid in 1978. Iran was still governed by the Shah but,
following mounting unrest, the monarchy was overthrown the following year.
[5] Gruneau, 'The chocolate Olympics', pp. 57–58.
[6] Andrew Blackman, 'The economics of the Olympics: does it pay to host?', *Wall
Street Survivor*, 4 January 2014, Blog 13, http://blog.wallstreetsurvivor.com/2014/
01/13/the-economics-of-the-olympics-some-fun-facts/; accessed 26 November
2014.
[7] http://www.designbuild-network.com/projects/national_stadium/;      accessed
26 November 2014.

Accounts of the construction of the Olympic site for London 2012 were written against the now-familiar narratives of Olympic preparation – in particular the 'ticking clock' cited by Helen Lenskyj and alluded to in Chapter 2 – the issue of whether the facilities will be ready in time[8] – and the cost to human life – specifically the lives of construction workers. The latter is, of course, conditional on the former. In Atlanta in 1995 a building worker had died when a steel lighting tower in the Olympic Stadium collapsed, whereupon

[c]onstruction officials said that there was 'a significant amount of cushion' in the building schedule and that the stadium was likely to be completed in time for the opening ceremonies on July 19, 1996. 'But we're not concerned about the schedule now,' said A. D. Frazier, the chief operating officer of the Atlanta Committee on the Olympic Games, organizers of the event. 'We're now concerned about these men and their families.'[9]

Just prior to the Games of 2004 George Theodorou, general secretary of the Greek Construction Workers' Union, had told the BBC that 14 of his members had died on Olympic building sites around Athens, although he believed that, taking into account the supporting infrastructure for the Games, such as Athens' new roads, tram lines and metro, the figure was more like 40: 'Men are being forced to work long shifts, up to 14 hours a day every day, in very hot temperatures and under constant pressure to complete construction work in time for the Olympics. Most have no hard hats or safety boots and if they complain, they're sacked'.[10] Ten building workers had died during the construction of Olympic sites in Beijing prior to the Games of 2008.[11] In the UK the building industry accounted for 5% of the workforce but a quarter of deaths at work; in 2012, 39 construction workers died on sites in Britain. In principle, the

---

[8] Helen Jefferson Lenskyj, *Olympic Industry Resistance: Challenging Olympic Power and Propaganda* (Albany: State University of New York Press, 2008), p. 18.
[9] Ronald Smothers, 'Olympic stadium tower falls, killing worker', *New York Times*, 21 March 1995, http://www.nytimes.com/1995/03/21/us/olympic-stadium-tower-falls-killing-worker.html; accessed 28 November 2014.
[10] 'Workers in peril at Athens sites', *BBC News*, 23 July 2004, http://news.bbc.co.uk/1/hi/world/europe/3920919.stm; accessed 28 November 2014.
[11] Sophie McBain, '400 Nepalese construction workers have died since Qatar won the World Cup bid', *New Statesman*, 17 February 2014, http://www.news tatesman.com/global-issues/2014/02/400-nepalese-construction-workers-have-died-qatar-won-world-cup-bid; accessed 29 November 2014.

'ticking clock' of the Olympic schedule does not enhance the prospect of a safe working environment for building workers. All the more reason, then, for the Olympic Delivery Authority (ODA) appointed ahead of London 2012 to be pleased with the manner of the completion of the Olympic site, which took place ahead of the deadline and without casualties.

Indeed, sections of the British press applauded the project as the ideal showcase for the country's building industry. A year ahead of the Games, John Armitt announced that 98% of the facilities for the Olympics had been built by British companies and that the project had generated £6 billion worth of business and 1,400 contracts: 'I think our message is, "Look at what British companies can do. Look at the quality, the imagination and their capability to manage"'.[12] Armitt also informed reporters that 'a detailed vetting process' had preceded the award of contracts and that a number of companies had been rejected 'after they failed to grasp the ODA's values' – those of 'legacy, sustainability, safety, employment and training and equality'.[13] Armitt added that the global recession of 2008–2009 had benefited the ODA: 'It would be wrong to deny the recession has helped. It was good in the sense that it clearly kept down prices – and labour availability, which we saw as a risk a few years ago, has not really been an issue'.[14]

But 'labour availability' had not been the whole story. Several weeks earlier, in March and April 2011, trade unionists had blocked the entrance to the Olympic site on Pudding Mill Lane following the sacking of Frank Morris, an electrician who'd been working on the site's media centre. Morris had been dismissed for making public the fact that construction firms on the site had been operating a blacklist of building workers.[15] Several months after the Games it was established that labour on the other Olympic sites had indeed also been vetted: Balfour Beatty, Carillion and Sir Robert McAlpine, the three lead construction firms on

---

[12] Graham Ruddick, 'London 2012 Olympics: the Olympic stadium made in Britain', *The Telegraph*, 16 July 2011, http://www.telegraph.co.uk/finance/london-olympics-business/8641977/London-2012-Olympics-The-Olympic-Stadium-made-in-Britain.html; accessed 29 November 2014.

[13] Ibid.

[14] Ibid.

[15] Rory [no surname], 'Olympic site blockaded in blacklist protest', *Blacklist Blog*, 13 April 2011, http://www.hazards.org/blacklistblog/2011/04/13/olympic-site-blockaded-in-blacklist-protest/; accessed 30 November 2014. See also http://www.tuc.org.uk/workplace-issues/construction/anti-blacklist-demo-targets-olympic-site; accessed 30 November 2014.

the Olympic project, had all used a consulting agency (established in 1993 and closed down by the Information Commissioner's Office in 2009 for breaches of the Data Protection Act) to 'screen out trouble-some left wing workers'.[16] Steve Murphy, the general secretary of the construction workers' union UCATT, told a parliamentary committee in late October 2012 that during the second quarter of the financial year 2008–2009 (July to September)

> Sir Robert McAlpine was invoiced a record £12,839.20 for blacklist-ing checks. A total of 5,836 individual checks were carried out during this quarter, according to Murphy. He added: 'In March 2008, the Olympic Delivery Authority (ODA) announced that work would start early on the Olympic stadium ... with work starting in late May 2008. Therefore [Sir] Robert McAlpine's surge in blacklisting checks cor-responds with the large scale recruitment on the building of the Olympic stadium. I would therefore suggest ... that taxpayers' money meant to be spent on the building of the Olympic stadium was instead spent on blacklisting construction workers.'[17]

(In 2008 the Labour government had agreed to put a further £5.9 billion into the Olympic construction budget. The House of Commons Public Accounts Committee later confirmed that less than 2% of the project had been financed by private capital.[18]) Questioned by the same par-liamentary committee several months later, Balfour Beatty's UK chief executive Mike Peasland said repeatedly that information about how his company had used data supplied by the now-defunct blacklist-ing agency was 'legally privileged';[19] this diminished the chances of compensation for the workers concerned. The committee heard also

---

[16] Phil Chamberlain, 'Man who compiled industrial blacklist comes out of the dark', *The Independent*, 28 November 2012, p. 25; see also '200 GMB members on construction blacklist', http://www.gmb-southern.org.uk/200-gmb-members-on-construction-blacklist/; accessed 30 November 2014.

[17] Will Hurst, 'Ucatt: taxpayers' cash spent on Olympic blacklist checks', *Building.co.uk*, 31 October 2012, http://www.building.co.uk/ucatt-taxpayers%E2%80%99-cash-spent-on-olympic-blacklist-checks/5045250.article; accessed 30 November 2014.

[18] Anna Minton, *Ground Control: Fear and Happiness in the Twenty-First Century City* (London: Penguin, 2012), p. xvii.

[19] Pete Murray, 'Balfour Beatty boss "hiding behind lawyer" over blacklisting', *Union-News.co.uk*, 13 March 2013, http://union-news.co.uk/2013/03/balfour-beatty-boss-hiding-behind-lawyer-over-blacklisting/; accessed 30 November 2014.

that McAlpine had paid the £5,000 fine incurred by Ian Kerr, compiler of the blacklist (which comprised 3,213 names), for breaching the Data Protection Act.[20] Inclusion on the 'troublemaker' database seemed in some cases to have been provoked by expression of the mildest liberal sentiment – one worker, it was reported, had been put on the list for writing a letter, which mentioned Nelson Mandela, to his local newspaper.[21] But it was widely reported (and universally assumed) that, generally speaking, the blacklisted construction workers had been labelled 'troublesome' and/or 'left wing' largely because of a history of 'raising health and safety concerns'.[22]

The onset of the recession appears to have coincided with Balfour Beatty's availing itself of this blacklist and it may be that the company calculated that it could now be selective in its recruitment of site workers. In any event, it seems incontestable that the major construction companies were anxious to prevent any dialogue with the workforce on the issue of health and safety. The fact that (publically funded) private capital did not want to sit down with labour to discuss the matter does not imply confidence on their part in the site safety regime – one of the five key ODA values proclaimed by John Armitt. So, although there were no deaths among the workers constructing the venues for London 2012, this seems to have been despite unnecessary risks taken by management.

## The Shadow of Munich? The homeland security industry and London 2012

Using the previous three Olympic Games as precedents, London 2012 also promised huge benefits to corporations providing 'security', be it in the form of weaponry, 'systems' or personnel. There were two principal political issues here: first, the militarisation of this area of the East End (and much of London besides) and the corresponding curtailment of civil liberties and, second, the outsourcing of much of

---

[20] Nigel Nelson, 'Rob the builder: thousands of construction workers were denied jobs as they were put on a sinister blacklist', *Mirror*, website 2 December 2012, http://www.mirror.co.uk/news/uk-news/blacklist-thousands-of-construction-workers-denied-1469233; accessed 30 November 2014.

[21] Simon Basketter, 'Blacklist bosses forced out of the shadows', *Socialist Worker*, 8 December 2012, pp. 10–11, p. 10.

[22] Andrew Clark and Will Hurst, 'Games stadium builder "bought worker blacklist"', *The Times*, 1 November 2012, http://www.thetimes.co.uk/tto/business/industries/construction-property/article3586143.ece; accessed 30 November 2014.

the Olympic security provision to the global private security firm G4S, which, briefly, brought the company's typical employment practices to public prominence.

On 23 July 2012, a ceremony took place in the Olympic athletes' village to commemorate the 11 Israeli athletes killed at the Munich Olympics of 1972 by the Palestinian Black September group. It was attended by Jacques Rogge, President of the IOC, Lord Coe, London mayor Boris Johnson and Jeremy Hunt, now the Secretary of State for Culture, Media and Sport.[23] On 27 July *The Times of Israel* website, while praising the Games' opening ceremony, noted that it had included 'no Munich tribute', adding that Ankie Spitzer, the widow of one of the Israeli athletes killed, had been campaigning for 40 years for a permanent memorial to the 11.[24] Coupled with the frequent reference to 'terrorism' in British political discourse, following the attack on New York's World Trade Center in September 2001 and President George W. Bush's subsequent declaration of a 'global war on terror', these re-visitations of the grotesque Olympic events of 1972 inevitably lent force to arguments for tight security at London 2012. For instance, a few days earlier, on 15 July, the *Independent on Sunday* had published an article entitled 'Dark day in Munich still casts shadow over London' by the strongly pro-Olympic writer Alan Hubbard. The article entailed a lengthy recounting of the murders in Munich and noted that a series of bombings had taken place in London 'a day after the 2012 Olympics had been won in Singapore'.[25] Referring to the 'more than £1 billion' expended 'to protect this summer's Games', the article concluded: 'Black September is the grim reminder that it has to be worth it'.[26]

As the Games approached, the phrase 'Welcome to fortress London' worked either as straight-faced reassurance or as ironic reflection, according to the commentator using it. For example, an article with that title published on the *International Business Times* website constituted an approving catalogue of the weaponry that would be deployed

[23] Press Association, 'London 2012: silence held for 1972 Munich victims at athletes village', *theguardian.com*, 23 July 2012, http://www.theguardian.com/sport/2012/jul/23/london-2012-olympics-minutes-silence-munich; accessed 1 December 2014.

[24] 'No Munich tribute as Olympics open with dazzling ceremony', *Times of Israel*, 27 July 2012, http://www.timesofisrael.com/2012-olympics-opening-ceremony-live-from-an-israeli-point-of-view/; accessed 1 December 2014.

[25] Alan Hubbard, 'Dark day in Munich still casts shadow over London', *Independent on Sunday*, 15 July 2012, pp. 8–9, p. 9.

[26] Ibid.

in London with a clear message that it would therefore be safe for readers to go there:

> Enjoy your time in London for the 2012 Olympics. The organizers have taken all measures to ensure that your stay will be a safe one – perhaps the safest in Olympic history. In what is likely to be the most security-conscious Olympics in memory, British authorities are leaving nothing to chance to provide security for the capital. Eleven miles of electric fencing, charged with 5,000 volts of electricity and topped with razor wire for good measure, cordon off the Olympic site. The entrances to the major venues are guarded by soldiers, the streets outside patrolled by heavily armed police carrying automatic weapons – a rare sight in Britain, where police often do not carry firearms.[27]

A Royal Navy warship, the 21,500 ton helicopter carrier HMS *Ocean*, would be moored on the Thames, six missile sites and four Eurofighter Typhoon fighter jets were on standby and any aircraft not pre-authorised or on a commercial flight would 'find itself squarely within the sights of numerous air, water, and ground-based systems'.[28] But this wasn't all –

> the forces protecting civilians, athletes and visitors to London will also be smart. E-3D Sentry aircraft, which house powerful electronic sensor suites, will be used to coordinate forces from the sky. Unmanned drones will be flying around the city to provide surveillance for security forces. Helicopters with powerful imaging equipment will be able to peek down and identify faces, clothes, even the color of the shoelaces on any suspect individuals. And down in the streets thousands of cameras will feed data to face-recognition software used to pick out any known hostiles from the crowds.[29]

For commentators of a more critical disposition, these same observations were severely disquieting and formed the basis of a critique, not only of London 2012, nor even of the Olympics in general, but of new (disturbing) trends in policing and urban governance and the

---

[27] IB Times Reporter, 'Welcome to fortress London, your destination for the 2012 Summer Olympics', *International Business Times*, 26 July 2012, http://www.ibtimes.com/welcome-fortress-london-your-destination-2012-summer-olympics-hold-am-review-731891; accessed 1 December 2014.
[28] Ibid.
[29] Ibid.

(corresponding) growth of a surveillance society.[30] These trends were disquieting to sections of the political right – particularly libertarians – as well as the left. Thus, another article bearing the title 'Welcome to fortress London' (amended to 'Olympics 2012 security: welcome to lockdown London' on the paper's Olympic web page) had appeared in *The Guardian* the previous March. Written by Stephen Graham, Professor of Cities and Society at Newcastle University in the UK, it spelled out the political economy and Orwellian implications of the wide-ranging security measures taken for the London Games.

Graham drew on a growing academic literature on surveillance in relation to the Olympics, to mega-events more generally and to the governing of contemporary urban spaces.[31] Prominent contributors to this literature include the Canadian sociologists Philip Boyle and Philip Haggerty,[32] who have closely documented and sought to explain the convergence, in the twenty-first century, of sport mega-events and regimes of blanket, hi-tech surveillance.

In an essay of 2012, Boyle pointed out that Olympic security budgets had been rising steeply since the turn of the century:

> the estimated $180 million US spent on security for the 2000 Sydney Games is a suitable point of comparison as this figure was, up to that time, unprecedented. Four years later, and after 9/11 [the attack on the World Trade Centre], the Greek government is reported to have spent an estimated $1.5 billion US on security for the 2004 Athens Games. Chinese officials state that $350 million USD was spent on security for the 2008 Games, but this is widely regarded to be an extremely conservative figure.[33]

There were, he suggested, several interconnected reasons for this.

---

[30] See http://www.surveillance-studies.net/?page_id=5; accessed 1 December 2014.
[31] Stephen Graham, 'Welcome to fortress London', *The Guardian*, 13 March 2012; see also Stephen Graham, 'Olympics 2012 security: welcome to lockdown London', http://www.theguardian.com/sport/2012/mar/12/london-olympics-security-lockdown-london, posted 12 March 2012; accessed 1 December 2014.
[32] See, for example, Philip Boyle and Kevin Haggerty, 'Spectacular security: mega-events and the security complex', *International Political Sociology*, No. 3 (2009), pp. 257–274, http://geeksandglobaljustice.com/wp-content/Boyle-Haggarty.pdf; accessed 2 December 2014.
[33] Philip Boyle, 'Securing the Olympic games: exemplifications of global governance', in Lenskyj and Wagg (eds.), *The Palgrave Handbook of Olympic Studies*, pp. 394–409.

First, there has been a drive to 'cleanse' areas of the city, particularly in preparation for some big happening such as a political convention or, of course, the Olympics. This 'cleansing' has entailed the elimination of any signs of poverty, homelessness, drug taking, begging (known as 'panhandling' in North America) and anything else that might deter or displease tourists. In Atlanta, Georgia, this pattern was observed as early as 1988, when, several days before the Democratic Convention there, police began hassling and arresting the city's homeless.[34] Eight years later, as Atlanta prepared for the Olympics, researcher Mary Beadnell 'reported that in the eight months leading up to the Games, 9,000 people were arrested for begging and loitering, and others were moved more than a hundred miles away from the city'.[35] With the next Olympics in 2000 a few months away, Beadnell revealed that

> Sydney City Council Rangers and private security guards employed by various local and Olympics authorities have been handed new powers to remove 'by reasonable force' anyone deemed a nuisance. 'Offences' ranging from drinking alcohol to demonstrating, begging, or camping in The Rocks, Circular Quay, Darling Harbour and Olympics sites will be subject to the new measures.[36]

This was scarcely the half of it. In her comprehensive study of these Olympics, Helen Lenskyj details how, in the absence of identifiable terrorist threats to the Games, the Australian Security Intelligence Organisation (ASIO) had warned instead of the need to deal with 'amateur terrorists' – a catch-all term for protesters of various political persuasions.[37] These and other Olympic 'undesirables' (the young, the homeless, Aborigines, sex workers...) were then subject to an escalating and disquieting range of powers, passed into law during the late 1990s. Under the *Homebush Bay Operations Regulation* of 1999, for example, both police and other authorised personnel (i.e. private security

---

[34] See P.J. O'Rourke, *Parliament of Whores* (New York: The Atlantic Monthly Press, 1991), p. 22.

[35] Pat Hartman, 'Vancouver Olympics aftermath studied', *House the Homeless*, 17 February 2011, http://www.housethehomeless.org/tag/police/; accessed 3 December 2014.

[36] Mary Beadnell, 'Sydney's homeless to be removed for Olympics', http://www.wsws.org/en/articles/2000/02/olymp-f03.html, posted 3 February 2000; accessed 3 December 2014.

[37] Helen Jefferson Lenskyj, *The Best Olympics Ever? Social Impacts of Sydney 2000* (Albany: State University of New York Press, 2002), pp. 43–44.

guards) were given the right to remove people deemed to be causing 'annoyance or inconvenience' with 'reasonable force'.[38]

In 2006 a similar but wider-ranging regime called Project Civil City was initiated in Vancouver, ahead of the Winter Olympics of 2010.[39] Not surprisingly, perhaps, this pattern was repeated at, and prior to, London 2012.

In the summer of 2011, *The Argus*, the local paper in the coastal towns of Brighton and Hove, fifty miles south of London, reported that:

> Homeless people are heading to Brighton and Hove to escape a purge of London's streets ahead of the Olympics. Charities have reported 'harassment' of rough sleepers in the capital as London mayor Boris Johnson looks to eradicate homelessness before the 2012 Games. [...] Hove MP Mike Weatherley [a Conservative] said: 'If there has been some sort of drive to reduce homelessness in London, I can only hope that it has been carried out in a responsible manner'.[40]

The paper added that the campaign to banish rough sleepers from London had begun in 2005, soon after the capital had been named as host of the 2012 Olympic Games,[41] meaning that it had originated under the mayoralty of Ken Livingstone. Many of the allegations of harassment were directed at a joint police and council initiative called Operation Poncho, begun in 2008; Operation Poncho 'partners' employed the tactic of waking sleepers in the early hours of the morning, telling them to move on and then hosing down the places where they'd been sleeping – a practice known as 'wetting down', which had been suspended and then reinstated in September of 2008.[42]

The second reason for escalating Olympic security measures identified by Boyle is the trend toward a surveillance society more generally,

---

[38] Ibid., pp. 54–55. For a full account of these measures, See Lenskyj, *The Best Olympics Ever?*, pp. 43–65.

[39] Boyle, 'Securing the Olympic games', pp. 396–398.

[40] 'Olympic homeless on Brighton and Hove Streets', *The Argus*, 19 July 2011, http://www.theargus.co.uk/news/9147052.Olympic_homeless_on_Brighton_ and_Hove_Streets/; accessed 3 December 2014.

[41] Ibid.

[42] Alison Benjamin, 'Cleaned out', *The Guardian*, 24 September 2008, http://www. theguardian.com/society/2008/sep/24/homelessness.rough.sleepers; accessed 3 December 2014.

which the Olympic Games provide an opportunity to accelerate. He quotes Peter Ryan, British-born policeman and now 'security consultant' to the IOC: 'The preparations for the Games and the investment in security infrastructure will be an enormous legacy for the country and its national security capability after the Games are over. This opportunity should not be wasted'.[43] For example, the Homebush Bay Operations Regulation of 1999 remained in force until 2002, two years after the conclusion of the Sydney Olympics. By this time it had simply been renamed and its powers to control public behaviour (a clear breach, in the view of many, of civil liberties) transferred to the Sydney Olympic Park Authority, which now ran the site.[44] Technological innovation at both the Athens and Beijing Games greatly enhanced the surveillance capabilities of the state in the respective countries, authorities in the latter having deployed an 'estimated 300,000 fully networked CCTV cameras, mandatory residential ID cards for all inhabitants, and a host of rumoured monitoring capabilities such as facial recognition software, long-range RFID detection capabilities (to scan the mandatory ID cards from a distance), and wiretaps in taxies and hotels frequented by foreigners'.[45] As previously noted, China is a command economy run by the Communist Party and is therefore more readily rendered as prone to 'Big Brother'-style surveillance strategies. However, even before the Beijing Games, in early 2007 the journalists at the right wing *Daily Telegraph* had written with foreboding of powers now being contemplated by government for the 'security' of the London Olympics in 2012: a leaked document

> drawn up by officials at the Home Office and sent to 10 Downing Street, paves the way for a much wider use of the police's DNA database to identify suspects through their relatives. Police are also to be empowered to scan postal packages to find drugs and to monitor an individual's progress in even greater detail than they can today, by using advances in CCTV technology as well as electronic travel passes such as the Oyster [travel] cards in use in London. The Conservatives

---

[43] Boyle, 'Securing the Olympic games', p. 398; taken from Peter Ryan, *Olympic Security: The Relevance to Homeland Security* (Salt Lake City: The Oquirrh Institute, 2002).

[44] See Kristine Toohey, 'Is Sydney still an Olympic city?', p. 11, https://doc.rero.ch/record/22122/files/2010_-_Toohey.pdf, posted 2010; accessed 5 February 2015.

[45] Boyle, 'Securing the Olympic games', p. 399.

and civil liberties campaigners are leading protests against the pro-posals, with Shami Chakrabarti, director of Liberty, accusing John Reid, the Home Secretary, of presiding over a 'make liberty history' campaign.[46]

As Stephen Graham wrote later:

London is also being wired up with a new range of scanners, bio-metric ID cards, number-plate and facial-recognition CCTV systems, disease tracking systems, new police control centres and checkpoints. These will intensify the sense of lockdown in a city which is already a byword across the world for remarkably intensive surveillance. Many such systems, deliberately installed to exploit unparalleled security budgets and relatively little scrutiny or protest, have been designed to linger long after the athletes and VIPs have left. Already, the Dorset police are proudly boasting that their new number-plate recognition cameras, built for sailing events, are allowing them to catch criminals more effectively.[47]

And in *The Guardian* reporter Robin Tudge observed:

Random security screening has been carried out on cars parked at Stratford City's Westfield shopping centre, by officers from the staggering 23,700-strong private security contingent of the London Organising Committee of the Olympic and Paralympic Games (LOCOG) and G4S. Westfield isn't even in the Olympic park, itself a hotbed of embedded biometric scanners and CCTV with automatic facial and behaviour recognition technologies, amid which LOCOG's forces can search anyone and use 'all available powers' to dispose of troublemakers, particularly anyone caught with anything that could be used...in a tent. Who LOCOG's bouncers are accountable to is not clear, but they are backed by 13,500 military reservists, apart from countless police deployments, and international contingents such as up to 1,000 US agents, possibly armed.[48]

---

[46] Patrick Hennessy and Ben Leapman, 'Ministers plan "Big Brother" police powers', http://www.telegraph.co.uk/news/uknews/1541513/Ministers-plan-Big-Brother-police-powers.html, posted 4 February 2007; accessed 3 December 2014.
[47] Graham, 'Welcome to lockdown London'.
[48] Robin Tudge, 'Every movement of London's Olympics will be monitored – including yours', *The Guardian*, 22 February 2012, http://www.theguardian.

Writing on the *Counter Olympics Network* website, Mike Wells suggested: 'Enhanced by new technology Britain seems to be sleep walking towards a big-brother state, which is camouflaging itself as means of protecting ordinary "hard working families"'; the telling headline to Wells' article was 'London 2012: one big party or one big prison?'[49]

The third factor cited by Boyle is the growing state-to-state dialogue, and resulting international consensus, on 'best practice' in tackling an array of often unspecified threats to the Games. This has resulted in a loose international agglomeration of politicians, ex-police personnel, think tanks, security consultancies and 'risk management' companies. At the heart of this agglomeration are the corporations which produce and market an array of 'security systems'. Inhabitants of this social and political world enthusiastically talk up the security threats to sport mega-events. A *Daily Mail* sports writer interviewed Peter Ryan some months before the Sydney Olympics, for which Ryan was coordinating security, and stated later: 'Peter Ryan's concern is that some Islamic maniac or Irish Republican dropout might call in here to earn headlines around the world during the Olympics. He's pretty cool about the challenge. An amalgam of calm and bloody-mindedness helps and Ryan has them both'.[50] More recently, Leo Gleser, president of International Security and Defense Systems (ISDS), an Israeli security company founded by ex-Mossad [Israeli secret service] agents, has spoken of 'growing tsunamis of violence, criminal acts, and global insecurity triggered by the 9/11 events' which made the 'the western world finally understand that measures had to be taken'.[51] Israel – not wholly by coincidence the main site of media memorialising of the Munich massacre – is the heartland of the security and counter insurgency industry and ISDS, having since its founding in 1948 on land previously occupied by Palestinians been subject to what is generally seen in the Arab world as Palestinian reprisal. Such reprisal has taken the form of comparatively small scale bombings, often involving the suicide of the bomber,

---

com/commentisfree/libertycentral/2012/feb/22/london-olympics-security-surveillance; accessed 3 December 2014.
[49] http://www.gamesmonitor.org.uk/node/938, posted 12 April 2010; accessed 3 December 2014.
[50] Ian Wooldridge, 'How a bloody Pom police chief struck gold in his bid to clean up Sydney', *Mail Online*, 9 January 1999, http://www.dailymail.co.uk/columnists/article-302047/how-bloody-pom-police-chief-struck-gold-bid-clean-sydney.html; accessed 3 December 2014.
[51] Graham, 'Welcome to lockdown London'.

and they have become more frequent in Europe since the invasion of Iraq by the United States, Britain and their allies in 2003. These attacks are part of a pattern of what is now referred to as 'asymmetrical warfare', wherein a nation militarily powerful in the conventional sense is purportedly menaced by a spectral enemy, operating through networks and small cells. The invocation of asymmetrical warfare, greatly strengthened in the instance of London 2012 by the bombings in the city in July 2005, forms a key part of the case for mammoth security precaution presented by companies such as ISDS. In this regard, the nexus of corporations, consultancies and security services that constitute the international surveillance elite produces a sealed discourse of mutually affirming voices, in which threats are invoked, counter measures prescribed and huge sums of public money expended on them. For example, in September 2010 Jonathan Evans, head of Britain's security service MI5, gave a speech to the Worshipful Company of Security Professionals in which he spoke of (inevitably) unspecified terrorist threats to Britain, noting that

> we are now less than two years from the London Olympics. The eyes of the world will be on London during the Olympic period and the run up to it. We have to assume that those eyes will include some malign ones that will see an opportunity to gain notoriety and to inflict damage on the UK and on some other participating nations.[52]

Two years later researchers at the right wing Heritage Foundation in Washington, DC, fashioned a rationale for high security at the London Olympics using Evans' vague allusion and adding reference to Munich, the London bombings of 2005 and other incidents, along with the security measures taken at recent Olympics. They asserted that the Games were 'an obvious target for attacks by radical Islamist terrorists, as well as anti-capitalist anarchists, supporters of various national causes, and other groups' and called for the United States to support the British authorities in meeting these 'security threats'.[53] Philip Hammond,

[52] 'Jonathan Evans' terrorism speech', http://www.telegraph.co.uk/news/uknews/terrorism-in-the-uk/8008252/Jonathan-Evans-terrorism-speech.html,    posted 17 September 2010; accessed 5 December 2014.
[53] Theodore R. Bromund, Steven P. Bucci, Luke Coffey, Jessica Zuckerman and Robin Simcox, 'U.S. should assist Britain in meeting security threats to the 2012 London Olympic Games', *Heritage Foundation*, 16 July 2012, http://www.heritage.org/research/reports/2012/07/us-should-assist-britain-in-meeting-security-threats-to-the-2012-london-olympic-games#_ftn3; accessed 5 December 2014.

Secretary of State for Defence in Britain's Conservative–Liberal Democrat coalition government, told the BBC that the Games were 'the biggest security challenge this country has faced for decades', while simultaneously suggesting that military deployment for the Olympic Games had been routine since the 1996 Atlanta Games.[54]

Amid this unrelenting talk of threats and the need to counter them, the writer David Cronin noted in the summer of 2011 that

> Heathrow Airport will have shiny new equipment for screening passengers installed with the help of several Israeli firms as part of preparations for next year's Olympic Games. The sporting event affords an opportunity to run a 'live test' on the Total Airport Security System (TASS), a 14.5 million euro ($21 million) project mainly financed by the European Union. The system would use 'real-time sensors' and various other tools to monitor aircraft, people, cargo, and restaurant areas in an airport separately and then blend all the resulting data in a 'multisource labyrinth'. The project is being coordinated by Verint, an Israeli supplier of surveillance equipment [...] Another participant in the consortium is Elbit, which made many of the pilotless drones that Israel used to devastate Gaza during 2008 and 2009. Elbit also helped install an electronic spying system into the annexation wall that Israel is building in the West Bank (illegally, according to a 2004 ruling of the International Court of Justice).[55]

Elbit systems are well established in Brazil, host nation of the 2016 Olympics, for which ISDS were appointed chief security consultants and suppliers on a $2.2 billion contract in 2014. Gleser suggested that state-of-the-art 'Homeland Security' (HLS) was now, like 'legacy', a vital credential for an aspiring host city: 'The people managing the Olympic Games today [...] know that proper management of the event would lead them to manage other events – like the 2020 Olympic Games in Japan and other mega sports events all over the world'.[56] ISDS had

[54] 'London 2012: 13,500 troops to provide Olympic security', *BBC News*, 15 December 2011, http://www.bbc.co.uk/news/uk-16195861; accessed 5 December 2014.

[55] David Cronin, 'London is turning into Israel's laboratory in preparation for 2012 Summer Olympics'; see http://mondoweiss.net/2011/06/london-is-turning-into-israel's-laboratory-in-preparation-for-2012-summer-olympics#sthash.gzSXUSh2.dpuf; accessed 5 December 2014.

[56] Amir Rapaport, 'The Olympic Games are a showcase for technologies', *Israel Defense*, http://webcache.googleusercontent.com/search?q=cache:

security contracts at the 1992 Summer Olympics in Barcelona, the 2000 Summer Olympics in Sydney, the 2008 Summer Olympics in Beijing, and the 2010 FIFA World Cup in South Africa.[57] They became an official Olympic partner in 2014.

Of opposition to this unprecedented militarisation of the city of London there was little sign in mainstream British politics, but residents of the Fred Wigg tower block in Leytonstone, East London, went to the High Court to try to prevent Starstreak ground-to-air missiles being sited on their roof during the Games. (The Wigg tower was one of two sites for these missiles, the other being the Lexington Building in Tower Hamlets. Rapier missiles were deployed in Blackheath and in Oxleas Wood, Eltham, South East London, at William Girling Reservoir, Enfield, in North London and at Barn Hill, Netherstone Farm, near Epping Forest.) The judge ruled against residents' application for judicial review. David Enright of Howe & Co., human rights solicitors in West London, who represented the residents, said afterwards that the verdict implied that even in the absence of war or a state of emergency

the MoD now has power to militarise the private homes of any person. They do not need to ask you, do not need to consult you, but can take over your home and put a missile on the roof, a tank on the lawn and soldiers in the front living room, exercising powers under the royal prerogative. Parliament has not been consulted on this dramatic change in the English way of life.[58]

Thus, to borrow the apposite phrase of Nick Pickles, spokespeople for the burgeoning 'Homeland Security' complex had once again been able to 'hide empire-building behind warnings of the sky falling in'.[59]

---

SHo2aSQTAh8J; http://www.israeldefense.com/?CategoryID%3D475%26Article ID%3D3232%2BISDS+Israel+security+London+2012&hl=en-GB&gbv=2&nfpr& spell=1&&ct=clnk; accessed 5 December 2014.

[57] 'Israeli firm to guarantee Rio Olympics security in 2016 in $2.2 billion deal', *Israel and Stuff*, http://www.israelandstuff.com/israeli-firm-to-guarantee-rio-olympics-security-in-2016-in-2-2-billion-deal; accessed 5 December 2014.

[58] See Richard Norton-Taylor, 'London tower block residents lose bid to challenge Olympic missiles', *The Guardian*, 10 July 2012, http://www.theguardian.com/sport/2012/jul/10/residents-tower-government-olympic-missiles; accessed 5 December 2014.

[59] Nick Pickles, 'Security industry has politicians in its thrall', *Independent on Sunday*, 15 July 2012, p. 40.

## Mr Buckles regrets ... : G4S and pauper management at London 2012

However, ultimately, public discussion of security at the London Olympics 2012 was not primarily concerned with missiles or the military, but with the multinational company G4S. G4S became the official 'security services provider' for the Games in March 2011, but partially defaulted on their contract shortly before the Olympics were about to begin. This default led to parliamentary and media criticism but this criticism concentrated on the company and its chief executive Nick Buckles, who faced an uncomfortable interrogation by the House of Commons Public Accounts Committee just prior to the Games and stood down the following May. Importantly, the criticism in general did not extend to the process by which contracts such as this one were awarded to companies such as G4S, nor to the controversial services rendered by the firm in other parts of the world. Moreover, the Minister of Defence's decision to send in troops to replace the security marshals that G4S had been unable to provide, cast the British army in a more benevolent light: rather than a hostile and problematic presence on the roof of a London council block (or, for that matter in Iraq or Afghanistan), they could now be seen simply as a bunch of British squaddies[60] cheerfully helping out at the world's festival of sport.

In November 2013, G4S was the third largest employer in the world with an estimated global workforce of 620,500 staff spread across 115 countries.[61] The growth of the company, and companies like it such as Atos (a 'Technology Partner' to the IOC and provider of IT services at London 2012) and Serco, lies in the British Local Government Act of 1988, passed during the last administration of Margaret Thatcher. This Act imposed 'compulsory competitive tendering' (CCT) on local authorities for blue collar services such as refuse collection. The practice of contracting out services grew steadily, along with the Private Finance Initiative, and, possibly to mitigate the notion that this was merely a cost-cutting exercise, the first Blair government passed a further Local Government Act in 1999 which imposed the concept of 'best value' – that's to say there would have to be continuous improvement in the quality of the service, along with the assumed economic

---

[60] A colloquialism for a British soldier of low rank.
[61] Andrew Hill and Gill Plimmer, 'G4S: the inside story', http://www.ft.com/cms/s/2/a6b46fc0-4cc0-11e3-958f-00144feabdc0.html, posted 14 November 2013; accessed 6 December 2014.

efficiency. G4S have been awarded a range of contracts around the world in the broad security field, including extensive work for the Israeli government in the Occupied Territories taken by Israel after the Six Day War of 1967.[62] Their main market was the UK[63] and much of their work entailed providing guards for commercial and residential properties and for events. But by the time of the London Olympics, they had begun to be awarded lucrative contracts for work previously done by the police, immigration officials, probation officers and the prison service: in 2011 British government contracts accounted for 27% of the company's (prodigious) overall revenue.[64] To some observers this was a very disturbing trend. Stephen Graham commented in 2012: 'With virtually no public debate or democratic scrutiny, crucial pieces of our criminal justice and public security systems are being taken over by private security corporations. The long-term implications for public justice, accountability, transparency and equality are likely to be very grave indeed'.[65] The writer Jeremy Seabrook recently characterised the outsourcing of these matters to companies such as G4S as a return to the Benthamite 'pauper management' of the eighteenth century.[66]

Given the parliamentary consensus broadly in favour of this outsourcing, and given also that LOCOG and the ODA were financed largely by public funds, in itself the award of the security contract for the London Olympics of 2012 to G4S provoked little public comment. Rising costs, however, did. In December 2011, according to the right wing *Daily Telegraph*, G4S's initial contract with LOCOG to provide 2,000 security staff was adjusted to accommodate 10,400 personnel, with the firm's contract now worth £284 million. The paper claimed also to have seen confidential documents showing that G4S's management fee had gone up from £7.3 million to £60 million. Nearly £34 million of the increase was said to be for the 'G4S "programme management office" overseeing the security operation, compared to an increase of just £2.8 million in the firm's

[62] See http://www.corporatewatch.org.uk/company-profiles/g4s-palestine; accessed 7 December 2014.

[63] Matthew Taylor, 'How G4S is "securing your world" ', http://www.theguardian.com/uk/2012/jun/20/g4s-securing-your-world-policing, posted 20 June 2012; accessed 7 December 2014.

[64] Ibid.

[65] Ibid.

[66] Jeremy Seabrook, 'Pauper management by G4S, Serco and Atos is inspired by a punitive past', *The Guardian*, 25 November 2013, http://www.theguardian.com/commentisfree/2013/nov/25/pauper-management-g4s-serco-atos-poor-laws; accessed 13 February 2015.

recruitment spending'.[67] The hourly rate paid to G4S security guards was said to be a meagre £6 an hour.[68] In early March 2012 the House of Commons Public Accounts Committee published a report on Olympic preparations and expressed disquiet that 'the £9.3 billion Public Sector Funding Package is close to being used up'; they were specifically concerned about the deal with G4S, which, they held, LOCOG had renegotiated from a position of weakness.[69] On 11 July it was announced that G4S would not, after all, be able to provide the extra security guards and the following day the Secretary of State for Defence allocated 3,500 British soldiers to fill the breach. Home Secretary Theresa May announced that Olympic security would not be compromised by this new arrangement.[70]

To most of the many critics of this pattern of outsourcing it was significant that G4S had renegotiated a huge increase in its management fee, as against a modest one to cover what was a dramatic upward adjustment of the number of required security guards. Nor was the failure to recruit this complement of guards entirely unforeseeable. Readers of the liberal press in Britain had some intimation of the financial dynamics of these outsourced security deals earlier in the summer of 2012 when *The Guardian* reported that Close Protection UK, a company hired to provide security for the river pageant that formed part of the British Queen's Diamond Jubilee had used up to 30 unpaid staff (unemployed job seekers) and 50 apprentices, who were paid £2.80 an hour, and told them to sleep rough under London Bridge the night before the event. The press was told that the unpaid work 'was a trial for paid roles at the Olympics'.[71] This was wholly consistent with government policy: the previous November Prime Minister Cameron had announced that

[67] Szu Ping Chan, and agencies, 'Timeline: how G4S's bungled Olympics security contract unfolded', http://www.telegraph.co.uk/finance/newsbysector/support services/10070425/Timeline-how-G4Ss-bungled-Olympics-security-contract-unfolded.html, posted 21 May 2013; accessed 7 December 2014.
[68] Chris Youett, 'G4S paying staff only £6 an hour', *The Independent*, 23 July 2012, p. 16.
[69] See http://www.parliament.uk/business/committees/committees-a-z/commons-select/public-accounts-committee/news/olympics-report/, posted 9 March 2012; accessed 7 December 2014.
[70] Chan, and agencies, 'Timeline...'.
[71] Shiv Malik, 'Unemployed bussed in to steward river pageant', http://www.theguardian.com/uk/2012/jun/04/jubilee-pageant-unemployed, posted 4 June 2012; accessed 7 December 2014; see also Kevin Rawlinson, Martin Hickman and Tom Peck, 'Firm in row over unpaid stewards for Jubilee to have Olympic fire safety role', *The Guardian*, 7 June 2012, pp. 1–2.

those who had been 'through the work programme' but were still unable to find work would be required to undertake a community work programme of 30 hours a week for 26 weeks. 'That', he had said, 'will help many people to get back in touch with the world of work'.[72] What the river pageant incident appeared to reveal was a pattern wherein expensive government or government-related contracts were discharged via the use of cheap or unpaid, sparsely trained and provisioned labour, generating considerable profits for security companies and their investors. Moreover, despite the bulk of G4S's fee being attributed to management costs, the company was assuring their investors that such costs were minimal: 'The company has been using a team of less than 10 permanent staff alongside a 700-strong force of so-called managers to run the £284 m [Olympic] contract', reported the *Daily Telegraph*. 'Less than two months ago, G4S boasted to investors that this overall reliance on temporary managers on fixed-term contracts would keep costs down and simply be aided "with a bit of expertise from elsewhere in the group"'.[73] It was also clear that the guards that G4S were supposed to have recruited would have lost their jobs after the Games: Buckles said in mid-July that he'd 'learnt from previous companies' experiences [that] the legacy costs of having a workforce laying idle after the Olympics almost does away with the benefits of doing it'.[74] The likelihood is that G4S left it too late to recruit the number of guards they had specified because they were trying to avoid paying them for more than a few weeks. It's worth noting, in this regard, that, when he appeared before the House of Commons Home Affairs Committee on 17 July, Buckles regretted taking on the Olympic contract and admitted that it had resulted in a 'humiliating shambles', but said that he would nevertheless be claiming the £57 million 'management fee'.[75]

---

[72] Prime Minister's Office, 'Compulsory placements will "get people back in touch with the world of work," says David Cameron', https://www.gov.uk/government/news/community-work-for-job-seekers, posted 8 November 2011; accessed 7 December 2014.

[73] Emma Rowley and Graham Ruddick, 'Olympic security: G4S relies on army of temporary managers', http://www.telegraph.co.uk/finance/newsbysector/supportservices/9401943/Olympic-security-G4S-relies-on-army-of-temporary-managers.html, posted 15 July 2012; accessed 7 December 2014.

[74] Telegraph Staff, 'Olympic security: G4S shares plunge, future of chief Nick Buckles in doubt', http://www.telegraph.co.uk/finance/newsbysector/supportservices/9402497/Olympic-security-G4S-shares-plunge-future-of-chief-Nick-Buckles-in-doubt.html, posted 16 July 2012; accessed 9 December 2014.

[75] Nigel Morris, 'G4S chief stuns MPs with intention to claim £57m management fee', *The Independent*, 18 July 2012, p. 7.

A minor moral panic developed in the media over this affair, in which politicians were briefly held to account for a lack of vigilance, G4S were depicted as a rogue company and, given the 'ticking clock' paradigm that framed the whole controversy, the public were reassured that the army was now in control. On 13 July Prime Minister David Cameron issued a vague assurance that G4S would face 'consequences' for their failure to provide enough security guards at the Olympics;[76] the next day it was reported that Home Secretary Theresa May had been warned of the 'Olympics security fiasco' ten months earlier;[77] and on 15 July Secretary of State for Culture, Media and Sport Jeremy Hunt appeared on BBC1's politics programme *The Andrew Marr Show* to play down the seriousness of the situation:

> G4S have been quite honourable. They have put their hands up. Nick Buckles, the chief executive, has said they got it wrong, they have apologised, they are going to cover all the costs, he has apologised to the troops who are going to be drafted in at the last moment.[78]

Meanwhile sections of the British press launched further investigations of G4S and similar companies. David Randall and Jonathan Owen raised an obvious question in the *Independent on Sunday*:

> As of today, there are 12 days to go to the opening ceremony; or, in other words, it is seven years and nine days since the Games were awarded to London – ample time, you might think, to recruit, train and establish the security staff. In 2010, it was calculated that the Games would need 10,000 security personnel. G4S was contracted to provide 2,000 of these. The Home Office, having overall responsibility both for security in Britain and specifically for the Olympics, would have been involved in calculating these numbers.[79]

A week later news came of 'leaked documents' revealing that 40% of the guards that G4S *had* recruited for Olympic security had not showed

---

[76] Tom Peck, 'Cameron says G4S will be penalised for its failings', *The Independent*, 14 July 2012, p. 6.

[77] Jane Merrick, Matt Chorley, Mark Leftly and Brian Brady, 'May "was told 10 months ago of G4S failings"', *Independent on Sunday*, 15 July 2012, pp. 2–3.

[78] See Press Association, 'Hunt defends security giant G4S', http://www. thisislocallondon.co.uk/uk_national_news/9818137.Hunt_defends_security_ giant_G4S/?ref=nt, posted 15 July 2012; accessed 8 December 2014.

[79] David Randall and Jonathan Owen, 'Blame Games', *Independent on Sunday*, 15 July 2012, pp. 16–17, p. 16.

up for work, that the company had tried to plug the gap by taking on young women under twenty and that senior police officers were shocked at the lack of training given to G4S staff.[80] Two weeks on and: 'New and damaging allegations against G4S staff – ranging from a rape accusation to claims of theft, drug-taking and a major security breach – emerged yesterday, prompting renewed calls for a full investigation into the company's performance'.[81] In early November the government cancelled G4S's contract to run Wolds Prison in East Yorkshire – a contract which had been signed in 1992 when the prison opened; shares in the company dropped by 3%.[82] In March 2013, G4S – now styled as 'the controversial security firm' – was said to be 'struggling' to honour a contract to house asylum seekers.[83] Later that year, the *Independent on Sunday* announced that:

> Executives from scandal-hit corporate giants Serco and G4S face a public grilling from a powerful group of MPs, who are determined to 'lance the boils' of failing government contractors. A source on the Public Accounts Committee said the two companies, which have seen their shares battered this year, will be questioned on Wednesday about 'suspicions that they cheated on contracts'. The Serious Fraud Office (SFO) has launched a criminal investigation into G4S and Serco, following allegations they had billed the Ministry of Justice for monitoring 3,000 non-existent offenders on a lucrative electronic tagging contract. The companies could potentially have made tens of millions of pounds for claiming that they had tagged offenders who were already in custody, had left the country, or had died. Serco, which runs the Docklands Light Railway in London, schools inspections, and the Atomic Weapons Establishment in Reading, has struggled since the scandal, issuing profit warnings for both 2013 and 2014 last week. Staff have also been referred to the City of London police over irregularities in a prisoner escort contract.[84]

[80] Terri Judd, 'G4S shambles revealed in internal report', *The Independent*, 23 July 2012, p. 12.

[81] Jonathan Owen and Mark Leftly, 'New claims about G4S prompt calls for inquiry', *Independent on Sunday*, 2 September 2012, p. 14.

[82] Andrew Grice, 'G4S pays price for Olympics shambles as Government cancels prison contract', *Independent*, 9 November 2012, p. 10.

[83] Kevin Rawlinson, 'G4S chief admits it is struggling to find homes for asylum seekers', *The Independent*, 20 March 2013, p. 27.

[84] Mark Leftly, ' "Cheats" Serco and G4S forced to face a grilling from powerful group of MPs', *Independent on Sunday*, 17 November 2013, p. 10.

During the course of this escalating controversy, three leading G4S executives resigned. David Taylor-Smith and Ian Horseman Sewell departed in September 2012, with the Olympic 'shambles' still fresh in the public memory. (Sewell had a typical twenty-first century 'security' background, having worked at the British Foreign Office, where he had 'looked at the Arab world and counterterrorism'.[85]) Buckles stepped down in May 2013.

During this apparent security crisis the British press welcomed the army, which, understandably, was depicted as riding to the rescue of the Games, and the press reassured readers that security and stability had been restored. 'What is the role of our armed forces if it's not to defend us?' asked columnist Mary Dejevsky.[86] 'Olympic security: now the army is giving the orders' said the front page of *The Independent* on 17 July; 'As foreign athletes start to arrive, military sends officers to G4S HQ to tackle security shambles'.[87] Soldiers smiled for myriad press cameras and senior officers stressed the sacrifices that their men might be making:

> Hundreds of British soldiers face being stuck in Afghanistan for weeks longer than they had expected as a result of the G4S scandal, which has seen 3,500 troops drafted in to provide security during the Olympic Games. Commanding officers have warned that the additional demands, including delays to training and holidays, could have a knock-on effect on operations and require servicemen and women to extend their six-month tours of duty by up to a month.[88]

In 2013, when much of the political dust had settled and three of the company's top managers had resigned, business pages turned to discussing the task G4S's new CEO, Ashley Almanza, now faced in steadying the corporate ship. For this branch of the outsourced security industry, business returned to normal and, in this regard, the Olympics seemed to many observers on a number of counts to have been a huge pretext on which to put large amounts of public money into corporate pockets. It's also important to note that this transfer took place at a time

---

[85] Randall and Owen, 'Blame Games', p. 17.

[86] Mary Dejevsky, 'What is the role of our armed forces if it's not to defend us?', *The Independent*, 13 July 2012, pp. 16–17.

[87] See Kim Sengupta and Nigel Morris, 'Olympic security: now the army is giving the orders', *The Independent*, 17 July 2012, p. 1, pp. 6–7.

[88] Brian Brady and Jonathan Owen, 'G4S fiasco could lead to longer Afghan tours for troops, officers warn', *Independent on Sunday*, 15 July 2012, p. 3.

of unprecedented 'austerity measures' – what writers on the *Financial Times* called 'the most drastic budget cuts in living memory, outstripping measures taken by other advanced economies'[89] – instituted by the Conservative-Liberal Democrat coalition government in October 2010. In February 2012 Len McCluskey, general secretary of Unite, Britain's biggest trade union, suggested that workers should consider strikes and acts of civil disobedience during the Olympics in protest at the austerity programme:

> The attacks that are being launched on public sector workers at the moment are so deep and ideological that the idea the world should arrive in London and have these wonderful Olympic Games as though everything is nice and rosy in the garden is unthinkable. The unions, and the general community, have got every right to be out protesting. If the Olympics provide us with an opportunity, then that's exactly one that we should be looking at.[90]

However, regardless of what level of support these suggestions might have had at grass roots level, they were quickly repudiated by party leaders. Prime Minister Cameron, through a spokesman, said 'The Olympics are a great opportunity for this country to show everything that is great about the United Kingdom and advertise ourselves to the world. It is completely unacceptable and unpatriotic what he is proposing'.[91] Perhaps a little more disconcertingly for trade unionists, Ed Miliband, leader of the (part-union funded) Labour Party, agreed: 'Any threat to the Olympics is totally unacceptable and wrong. This is a celebration for the whole country and must not be disrupted'.[92] As we have seen, it was the prospect of such protests that formed part of the rationale for the massive security measures recommended for London 2012 by the international 'Homeland Security' complex.

---

[89] See Daniel Pimlott, Chris Giles and Robin Harding, 'UK unveils dramatic austerity measures', http://www.ft.com/cms/s/0/53fe06e2-dc98-11df-84f5-00144feabdc0.html#axzz3LJqrMYI4, posted 20 October 2010; accessed 8 December 2014.

[90] Andrew Sparrow, 'Len McCluskey: unions should consider disrupting London Olympics', http://www.theguardian.com/politics/2012/feb/28/len-mccluskey-unions-london-olympics, posted 28 February 2012; accessed 8 December 2014.

[91] Len McCluskey, 'Strike threat attacked by David Cameron as "unacceptable and unpatriotic"', http://www.huffingtonpost.co.uk/2012/02/29/len-mccluskey-strike-unpatriotic-david-cameron_n_1309287.html, posted 29 February 2012; accessed 8 December 2014.

[92] Ibid.

## 'Sausages "exploit" Olympic logo': London 2012, the sponsors and the brand police

As we saw at the beginning of this chapter, corporate sponsorship of the Olympic Games and Olympic athletes became established in the 1980s and the protection of sponsors' interests formed another major part of the rationale for the blanket security measures taken at London 2012. But these sponsorships have never gone uncontested and, one way and another, they were contested at the London Games. The final section of this chapter considers the ways in which the politics of sponsorship at London 2012 were negotiated.

Olympic teams at London 2012 invariably had sponsors, it being virtually impossible by then to reach Olympic standard in any sport without a training regime that was sustained, rigorous and generously funded: the main sponsors of the British Olympic athletics team, for example, was the insurance company Aviva, which had first financed British athletic endeavours in 1999. When British athletes gained a slew of gold medals at the Games, Aviva responded with a full page advertisement in the press featuring several of these athletes and the caption 'We gave them our backing. They gave it their all'.[93] Aside from team sponsorship, a number of athletes were contracted by Olympic partners as 'brand ambassadors'. For instance, Procter and Gamble (P&G), the US consumer goods multinational corporation, which signed a ten year partnership deal with the IOC in 2010, recruited 11 athletes participating in the London Games and allocated each to a brand within the company's portfolio as follows: Mark Cavendish, road cycling, *Head & Shoulders* shampoo; Jessica Ennis, athletics, *Olay* skin care products; Sir Chris Hoy, track cycling, *Gillette* shaving products; Jeanette Kwakye, athletics, *Ariel* washing products; Keri-Anne Payne, swimming, *Max Factor* cosmetics and *Oral B* oral hygiene products; Victoria Pendleton, track cycling, *Pantene* hair care products; Paula Radcliffe, athletics, *Fairy* washing up liquid and *Pampers* baby products; Jenna Randall, synchronised swimming, *Braun Female* hair products; Liam Tancock, swimming, Gillette; and Ben Rushgrove and Sophia Warner, Paralympic athletics, the P&G brand.[94] In December 2011, synchronised swimmer Jenna

---

[93] See, for instance, *The Independent*, 16 August 2012, p. 28.
[94] Loulla-Mae Eleftheriou-Smith, 'P&G picks Olympic athletes for brand ambassadors', http://www.marketingmagazine.co.uk/article/1106879/p-g-picks-olympic-athletes-brand-ambassadors, posted 30 November 2011; accessed 8 December 2014.

Randall, water polo players Vicki Hawkins and Frankie Snell, and triathlete Hollie Avil modelled expensive lingerie by the British designer Nichole de Carle for the charity Wellbeing of Women.[95] The cause was worthy but, as Helen Lenskyj argued, the sexual availability implied in the poses placed them in the 'soft porn' category and did little to 'empower' female athletes.[96]

For much of its history the International Olympic Committee abhorred, and severely punished, advertising on the part of Olympic competitors,[97] but since the 1980s many of these competitors have become, to paraphrase the French sociologist and critic of sport Jean-Marie Brohm, human sandwich boards.[98] Their status as such was affirmed when, in 2010, and following the marital infidelities of American golfer Tiger Woods and English footballer Wayne Rooney, there was a reported boom in insurance policies taken out by multinational companies on the reputations of the sportspeople they sponsored. At the same time the British athlete Jessica Ennis, an apparently unaffected 'girl next door'[99] with a blameless private life, began to attract advertisers in some numbers; there was talk in sport-media-advertising circles of the 'Jess Effect'.[100]

Outside of the individual athletes' feelings about their ambassadorial roles and assigned products, London 2012 threw up clear conflicts with regard to the sponsorship of Olympic sportspeople. For example, the performance of the Great Britain swimming team (Team GB) at London 2012 (a silver medal and two bronzes) was deemed disappointing and a lengthy review recommended that the team should

---

[95] Telegraph Staff, 'London 2012 Olympics: Team GB hopefuls model lingerie for charity calendar', http://www.telegraph.co.uk/sport/olympics/8973017/London-2012-Olympics-Team-GB-hopefuls-model-lingerie-for-charity-calendar.html, posted 22 December 2011; accessed 5 February 2015.

[96] Helen Jefferson Lenskyj, *Gender Politics and the Olympic Industry* (Basingstoke: Palgrave Macmillan, 2013), p. 28.

[97] For a discussion of this, see Stephen Wagg, 'Tilting at windmills? Olympic politics and the spectre of amateurism', in Lenskyj and Wagg (eds.), *The Palgrave Handbook of Olympic Studies*, pp. 321–336.

[98] See Jean-Marie Brohm, *Sport: A Prison of Measured Time* (London: Ink Links, 1978), p. 176. Brohm's original phrase was 'advertising "sandwich-board" men'.

[99] See Stephen Wagg, 'If you want the girl next door: Olympic sport and the popular press in early cold war Britain', in Stephen Wagg and David L. Andrews (eds.), *East Plays West: Sport and the Cold War* (London: Routledge, 2007), pp. 100–122.

[100] Andrew Johnson and Charlie Cooper, 'Sponsors seeking a Jess effect take out "disgrace" insurance', *Independent on Sunday*, 14 November 2010, p. 14.

in future avoid 'commercial distractions'.[101] However, the dependence of many competitors on sponsorship income was underscored during the Games when American track and field athletes staged a protest against the IOC's 'Rule 40', which banned the representation of any brand other than those of the Olympic partners.[102] Some appeared with duct tape over their mouths with the words 'Rule 40' written on it. Jamaican American 400 metres runner Sanya Richards-Ross argued that many of her colleagues were being priced out of athletics by these IOC restrictions:

> I've been very fortunate to do very well around the Olympics [she had deals with BMW, an Olympic partner, and Nike], but so many of my peers struggle in this sport and I just think it's unjust. People see the Olympics, they see the two weeks when athletes are at their best. It's the most glorious time in their lives, but they don't see the three or four years leading up to the Olympic Games when a lot of my peers are struggling to stay in the sport. The majority of track and field athletes don't have sponsors and don't have support to stay in the sport. A lot have second and third jobs to do this.[103]

Richards-Ross estimated that only 2% of Team USA's athletes were contracted to official Olympic sponsors; a number of them had been told to take photos down from Facebook accounts promoting non-official brands.[104] (Occasionally, Olympic athletes have railed against Olympic sponsorship itself and the attendant notion of being turned into a commodity by an interested corporation. In a powerful article in 2014 the US luge [one- or two-person sled] specialist Samantha Retrosi, who competed in the Winter Games of 2006 in Turin, wrote:

> There's a lot of money to be made in Olympic sports, a huge global media event that rolls around every two years. Corporate-sponsor bottom lines are merely one indicator of the vast sums involved. To see just who is generating this wealth, one has to look no further than the act of sponsorship itself, with individual athletes and

[101] Liz Byrnes, 'British team told to cut commercial links after London failure', *The Independent*, 3 December 2012, p. 21.
[102] Jerome Taylor, 'American stars in protest at "unjust" ban on their sponsors', *The Independent*, 31 July 2012, p. 8.
[103] Ibid.
[104] Ibid.

entire teams purchased and traded among the corporate elite like valuable additions to bursting stock portfolios. As an athlete in a sport as insignificant in the United States as luge, I could never hope to see my face plastered on a Wheaties box. However, I wasn't too obscure to escape the eye of the masterminds of gender commodification at Maxim [the leading men's lifestyle magazine]. Apparently, spandex uniforms make the women of USA Luge hot commodities. Lucky me).[105]

Needless to say, these athletes were not alone. In the matter of 'brand protection', London 2012 became a theatre for the severe, and occasionally self-parodic, infringement of civil and commercial liberties, the full force of which had first been witnessed at the Sydney Olympics, when the *Olympic Arrangements Act* of 2000 had given wide-ranging powers to confiscate unauthorised merchandise and protest materials within 3 kilometres of the Games – a measure aimed both at 'ambush marketers' (peddling rival brands), small time traders and political dissidents, such as Aboriginal groups.[106]

Two years before the London Games, Coe was, in effect, issuing a renewed warning that this would be the case. Deploying the familiar arguments that without the sponsors there would be no Olympics and that there was a real danger from the 'ambush marketing' of rival brands, Coe told the press in the summer of 2010:

> The approach has been to educate before you litigate. By the time we get to the Games, we will effectively have £1.5 billion in sponsorship sitting around the table. Without that, we don't have a Games. It is always about proportionality, but we will fearlessly defend our major partners who are making all this happen.[107]

This process of education with the threat of litigation was already in play following the passing of the *London Olympic Games and Paralympic Games Act* the previous year. This act strengthened and extended the provisions of the *Olympic Symbol etc. (Protection) Act* of 1995 and

---

[105] Samantha Retrosi, 'Why the Olympics are a lot like "the hunger games"', *The Nation*, 10 February 2014, http://www.thenation.com/article/178048/why-olympics-are-lot-hunger-games; accessed 5 February 2015.
[106] Helen Jefferson Lenskyj, *The Best Olympics Ever?*, pp. 56–61.
[107] Robin Scott-Elliot, ' "Education then litigation": Coe will follow Fifa's example to protect Olympic sponsors', *The Independent*, 24 July 2010, pp. 10–11, p. 10.

gave the IOC exclusive use of a range of Olympic-related vocabulary and symbols.[108] The zealousness with which this legislation might be enforced was glimpsed in August 2007 when Dennis Spurr, a butcher in Weymouth, Dorset, venue for the Olympic sailing events of London 2012, was told to take down a sign showing five sausage rings in the shape of the Olympic logo. The BBC deadpanned the headline 'Sausages "exploit" Olympic logo' on their news website.[109] Incidents such as this, while raising smiles of incredulity in some quarters and rightful indignation in others, appear to have acted as a template for other authorities: in mid-July a café owner in Camberwell, south London, was told by Southwark Borough Council to take down five bagels in the shape of the Olympic rings hanging in his window.[110] The council's action coincided with the intervention of nearly 300 enforcement officers:

> Wearing purple caps and tops, the experts in trading and advertising working for the Olympic Delivery Authority (ODA) are heading the biggest brand protection operation staged in the UK. Under legislation specially introduced for the London Games, they have the right to enter shops and offices and bring court action with fines of up to £20,000. Olympics organisers have warned businesses that during London 2012 their advertising should not include a list of banned words, including 'gold', 'silver' and 'bronze', 'summer', 'sponsors' and 'London', if they give the impression of a formal connection to the Olympics. Publicans have been advised that blackboards advertising live TV coverage must not refer to beer brands or brewers without an Olympics deal, while caterers and restaurateurs have been told not to advertise dishes that could be construed as having an association with the event. At the 40 Olympics venues, 800 retailers have been banned from serving chips to avoid infringing fast-food rights secured by McDonald's.[111]

---

[108] See Mark James and Guy Osborn, 'London 2012 and the impact of the UK's Olympic and Paralympic legislation: protecting commerce or preserving culture?', *Modern Law Review*, Vol. 74, No. 3 (2011), pp. 410–429.

[109] http://news.bbc.co.uk/1/hi/england/dorset/6972224.stm, posted 31 August 2007; accessed 9 December 2014.

[110] Sam Greenhill, 'Dough! Olympic ring bagels banned from cafe window…despite the Government saying bakers should NOT be prosecuted', *Daily Mail*, 19 July 2012, http://www.dailymail.co.uk/news/article-2175817/Bakers-churches-use-Olympics-rings-NOT-prosecuted-says-minister.html; accessed 9 December 2014.

[111] Martin Hickman, 'Britain flooded with "brand police" to protect sponsors', *The Independent*, 16 July 2012, pp. 1 and 4.

There was already evidence, however, that competitor brands to those of the Olympic partners were neither deterred nor necessarily disadvantaged commercially by this policing. Two months earlier Jerome Taylor had reported:

> The latest analysis by the Global Language Monitor, a company that assesses which brands are linked in the public's imagination with various events, shows more than half of the top 50 companies associated with the Olympics are not official sponsors. A new campaign by the fast food chain Subway, a major rival to the official Olympic sponsor McDonald's, has raised eyebrows for using four British athletes to advertise sandwiches under the strap-line 'Train hard. Eat fresh'. Meanwhile FedEx, the main competitor to the official logistics supplier UPS, will unveil a new campaign later this month [...] to sponsor awards of £1,000 to 25 'future Olympians and Paralympians' who will feature in the campaign.[112]

It seems sensible to argue, then, that this purported brand protection was less to do with the deterrence of 'ambush marketing' by major rivals than is generally claimed. Certainly 'ambush marketing' has been known – notably at the FIFA World Cup Finals of 2010 when a Dutch brewing company arranged a stunt involving a group of glamorous women in orange dresses, who attracted camera attention during a televised match[113] – but, as Taylor shows, rival corporations have the media access and other resources to circumvent Olympic brand protections. These protections work more centrally to affirm the corporate governance of sporting events – as the columnist Yasmin Alibhai-Brown wrote, 'The Games are here, but they don't belong to us'.[114] Beyond that, recalling the arguments of the French philosopher Michel Foucault, they are to do with securing the self-policing[115] of Olympic subjects – the consumers at the Olympic sites and other (otherwise crucial) social actors, such as the athletes, and the general public. To a degree, this was

---

[112] Jerome Taylor, 'Want to strike gold at the Olympics? Don't be an official sponsor', *The Independent*, 11 May 2012, p. 10.

[113] Martin Evans, 'World Cup 2010: Bavaria beer stunt organisers arrested', http://www.telegraph.co.uk/sport/football/world-cup/7832413/World-Cup-2010-Bavaria-beer-stunt-organisers-arrested.html, posted 16 June 2010; accessed 9 December 2014.

[114] *The Independent*, 23 July 2012, p. 17.

[115] Explored in his *Discipline and Punish: The Birth of the Prison* (London: Penguin, 1979).

recognised by Michael Payne, former marketing director of the IOC and chief architect of these arrangements, who was an observer at London 2012: 'The public do get it. They do understand that Coca-Cola has paid, Pepsi hasn't, so Coca-Cola should be entitled to provide the soft drinks…'[116] Payne now, however, took the view that brand policing was over-zealous. He insisted that the restrictions were

> never intended to shut down the flower shop that put its flowers in Olympic rings in the window, or the local butcher who has put out his meat in an Olympic display. [ … ] There is no question in my view that the controls and protections have gone too far when it is starting to suffocate local street traders and I don't think that is necessarily what the Olympic sponsors are looking for.[117]

But this seems a mistaken view of the situation Payne himself had helped to create. The restrictions were now also such as to assert the primacy of big business over small business – precisely those street traders, pork butchers and café proprietors who thought they could take small commercial advantage of a big public event, only to find that it wasn't public at all. Big brands, on the whole, don't menace each other (for instance, Coca Cola and Pepsi Cola's market share and relatively peaceful coexistence is taken for granted); they menace the smaller fry.

Indeed, it's possible to argue that this pattern of heavy policing is not so much to eliminate competition as to draw attention to the sponsorship itself. After all, every apparently petty restriction became a news story and provoked an airing, usually via Lord Coe, of the 'Without the Sponsors, No Games' argument. Thus, at the risk of their seeming small-minded to some, Olympic partners were nevertheless reaffirmed as the facilitators of this prestigious, global sporting event. As the sociologist Alan Tomlinson has put it: 'The halo effect continues to work for the sponsoring corporation on one of the biggest stages in human history'.[118] Moreover, there was little doubt of the need for many of the

---

[116] Tom Peck, 'I have said to the organisers, I think you're scoring an own goal here', *The Independent*, 21 July 2012, p. 10. Republished as Tom Peck, 'Father of Olympic branding: my rules are being abused', http://www.independent.co.uk/sport/olympics/news/father-of-olympic-branding-my-rules-are-being-abused-7962593.html, posted 21 July 2012; accessed 9 December 2014.
[117] Ibid.
[118] Alan Tomlinson, 'The making – and unmaking? – of the Olympic corporate class', in Lenskyj and Wagg (eds.), *The Palgrave Handbook of Olympic Studies*, pp. 233–247, p. 243.

corporations engaged at London 2012 to avail themselves of this 'halo effect', as the following examples suggest.

Atos, a French multinational IT corporation, had been the IOC's 'official IT partner' since 2001. Atos Healthcare, a division of the company, had been contracted in 2008 by the Labour government of Gordon Brown to conduct a Work Capability Assessment programme for the Department of Work and Pensions. The firm had caused uproar among the disabled by deeming a large number of apparently severely handicapped people to be fit for work and therefore not eligible for disability benefits. Although estimates differed, it was widely accepted that large numbers of disabled people assessed to be fit for work had died soon afterwards. Many saw Atos as the instrument whereby the government, as part of its policy of reducing welfare spending, sought to reduce the number of people claiming Employment Support Allowance (ESA).[119]

Dow Chemical Company of the US paid for a £7 million art work 'wrap' around the main Olympic stadium at the London Games. They had taken over the Union Carbide Corporation (UCC), which in 1984 had been responsible for exposing over 500,000 people in the town of Bhopal in Madhya Pradesh in central India to methyl isocyanate (MIC) gas and other chemicals. Some 10,000 people died at the time and a further 15,000 had died since from exposure to the gases. A high rate of cancers and congenital abnormalities was (and is still) reported in the Bhopal area. Some compensation was paid in 1991, but Dow, which had bought Union Carbide in 2001, denied liability for UCC's previous actions.[120] In November 2011, Indian athletes threatened to boycott London 2012[121] and the following February it was made known that Dow had circumvented a trade ban by using intermediaries.[122] Moreover, Dow had manufactured the napalm and Agent Orange defoliant used by the US Army in Vietnam in the 1960s.[123] The company were

---

[119] See, for example, Nick Sommerlad, '32 die a week after failing test for new incapacity benefit', http://blogs.mirror.co.uk/investigations/2012/04/32-die-a-week-after-failing-in.html, posted 4 April 2012; accessed 1 January 2015.

[120] See Nina Lakhani, 'Olympic chiefs under fire over sponsor's links to Bhopal disaster', *The Independent*, 24 October 2011.

[121] See Nina Lakhani, 'London Olympics in crisis as India threatens boycott', *The Independent*, 26 November 2011, pp. 1–2.

[122] See Nina Lakhani, 'Olympic sponsor row fuelled by new Bhopal controversy', *The Independent*, 13 February 2012, p. 2.

[123] See Nina Lakhani, 'Dow, Bhopal and the $1bn push for damages', *The Independent*, 26 November 2011, p. 3.

now permitted to advertise on 336 panels on the new stadium wrap.[124] Amnesty International's Meredith Alexander, the Games' 'ethics commissioner', resigned over this issue in January 2012.[125] (Alexander had been a member of the 'Commission for a Sustainable London 2012', which had been asked to look into the suitability of Dow for this Olympic 'partnership'.) She explained her resignation to *The Guardian*:

> I was shocked to see that the result of our investigation was a public statement from the commission that essentially portrays Dow as a responsible company. I had been providing information about Bhopal to commission members and I was stunned that it publicly repeated Dow's line that it bears no responsibility for Bhopal. I did everything I could to get the statement corrected or retracted. When it became apparent that this would not happen, I realised that the only way to ensure that my name was not used to justify Dow's position was to resign. And the only way to ensure that the victims' side of the story was told was to do so in public'.[126]

BP were named a 'sustainability partner' for London 2012. In 2010 their Deepwater Horizon oil rig had exploded, killing 11 workers and creating the worst oil spill in US history in the Gulf of Mexico.

Since the 1990s there has been an international campaign against the production practices of Coca Cola, known as 'Killer Coke' among human rights and international labour organisations. Lawsuits have been brought in the United States alleging company complicity in the murder of trade unionists at their bottling plants in Columbia and Guatemala and there have been widespread claims of the brutal exploitation of labour (including child labour) and the arbitrary dismissal of trade unionists.[127] The Latin America Bureau issued a book

---

[124] 'London 2012: Coe backs chemical firm Dow's connection', http://www.bbc.co.uk/news/business-15745449, posted 15 November 2011; accessed 9 December 2014.

[125] 'Olympics ethics chief: London 2012 committee "apologists" for Dow chemicals', http://www.amnesty.org/en/news/olympics-ethics-chief-london-2012-committee-apologists-dow-chemicals-2012-01-26; accessed 10 December 2014.

[126] Meredith Alexander, 'Why I resigned over Bhopal', *The Guardian*, 26 January 2012, http://www.theguardian.com/commentisfree/2012/jan/26/why-meredith-alexander-resigned-bhopal-olympic; accessed 5 February 2015. See also: https://www.youtube.com/watch?v=obyLJ8ojHWA; accessed 5 February 2015.

[127] See 'Killer Coke', http://killercoke.org/; accessed 9 December 2014.

called *Soft Drink, Hard Labour: Guatemalan Workers Take on Coca-Cola* in 1987.[128]

During the Games themselves it was reported that toys representing the official London 2012 mascots, Wenlock and Mandeville, had been manufactured in China by workers being paid only £6 per day: workers at the Yancheng Rainbow Arts & Crafts in Dafeng city worked 11.5 hour days for 26 p per hour.[129] Similarly Emily Dugan reported in May 2012 that

> Official Olympic clothing sold by Next is claimed to have been produced in sweatshop conditions in Sri Lanka. The allegation comes days after the high street chain unveiled the formal outfits that Team GB will wear at the opening ceremony. [...] The claims emerged in a wider investigation into Olympic brands that found 'widespread abuse of the human rights of workers' in eight factories around the world. Research by the Playfair 2012 campaign also cited allegations of mistreatment of staff working for the sportswear manufacturer Adidas [Olympic partner and supplier of apparel to the British Olympic athletics team] in the Philippines and China.[130]

Like Coca Cola, the global fast food chain McDonalds, an IOC partner at London 2012, had faced numerous lawsuits in the United States brought by parents and/or health campaigners accusing them of causing childhood obesity. These had failed (although in a Brazilian court in 2010 a man won damages from McDonalds for making him obese[131]), largely because of the difficulty, in law, of tracing obesity to the products of one specific company. Moreover, as Wilensky and O'Dell observe, 'nearly

---

[128] Mike Gatehouse and Miguel Angel Reyes, *Soft Drink, Hard Labour: Guatemalan Workers Take on Coca-Cola* (London: Latin America Bureau, 1987).

[129] Chris Parsons, 'Revealed: the Chinese sweatshop where workers are paid just £6 a day to make Wenlock and Mandeville Olympic mascot toys', *Mail Online*, 24 July 2012, http://www.dailymail.co.uk/news/article-2178133/Revealed-The-Chinese-sweatshop-workers-paid-just-6-day-make-Wenlock-Mandeville-Olympic-mascot-toys.html; accessed 10 December 2014.

[130] Emily Dugan, 'Forced labour claims dent image of London 2012', *Independent on Sunday*, 6 May 2012, http://www.independent.co.uk/sport/olympics/forced-labour-claims-dent-image-of-london-2012-7717615.html; accessed 10 December 2014.

[131] 'Obese worker wins McDonald's lawsuit', *Columbia Daily Tribune*, 29 October 2010, http://www.columbiatribune.com/wire/obese-worker-wins-mcdonald-s-lawsuit/article_f95d271b-c845-57ea-a90c-d95c3a55d9b9.html; accessed 10 December 2014.

half of the states [in the US] enacted "cheeseburger bills" to immunize food and beverage companies from liability arising from obesity and related injuries. Similar federal legislation was supported by the Bush administration, but failed to pass both houses of Congress'.[132] However the defence of McDonalds, and companies like them, has been based largely on notions of choice and personal responsibility; it has seldom rested on claims for the nutritious nature of their fast food and in 2010 the Washington-based Centre for Science in the Public Interest accused the company of 'unfairly and deceptively' marketing their 'Happy Meals' to children.[133] The engagement of McDonalds with London 2012 (announced by Gordon Brown in Beijing in 2008 as a theatre for the banishing of obesity) and childhood (the generation to be 'inspired' by these Games) was self-evidently problematic. McDonalds, of course, tried to reconcile the apparently irreconcilable: 'In the week that the British medical profession united behind a campaign to fight obesity', wrote Charlie Cooper three months before the Games,

> McDonald's, a sponsor of the Olympics, has come up with its own recipe to improve children's health: nine million free toys, two one-eyed mascots and a mysterious force called 'Rainbow Power'. In the wake of criticism from nutritionists over the global fast food brand's involvement with the Olympics, McDonald's is giving away free exercise toys with Happy Meals as part of a national campaign to make children more active ahead of the Games.[134]

Professor Terence Stephenson, Vice Chair of the Academy of Medical Royal Colleges and President of the Royal College of Paediatrics and Child Health, responded that toys were, of course, a good thing because they encouraged children to be active. 'But having them once you've bought a fairly unhealthy meal just doesn't stack up.'[135]

---

[132] Saul Wilensky and Kerry C. O'Dell, 'Where's the beef? The challenges of obesity lawsuits', http://www.bna.com/wheres-the-beef-the-challenges-of-obesity-lawsuits/, posted 18 July 2013; accessed 10 December 2014.

[133] Mary Clare Jalonick, 'Consumer group threatens to sue McDonald's for "unfairly and deceptively" marketing Happy Meals to children', http://www.huffingtonpost.com/2010/06/22/mcdonalds-happy-meal-lawsuit_n_621946.html, posted 22 June 2010; accessed 10 December 2014.

[134] Charlie Cooper, 'Would you like a relay baton with that Happy Meal? McDonald's goes for Olympic gold', *The Independent*, 19 April 2012, p. 17.

[135] Ibid.

Former Prime Minister Tony Blair stepped into the breach to issue the now-standard reminder of the corporations' benefaction. 'We, as a country, have obesity problems as we all know', he told the press.

> Sport and diet are an important part of that. But I think, everything in its proper place and everything in moderation. I have no problem with McDonald's and Coke being sponsors here. On the contrary I'm very pleased. They would say they are encouraging young people to do sport. People have to be realistic about this. Businesses exist to make a profit for shareholders. [ ... ] But it is about giving something back. People are cynical. But I say to them, 'Of course companies are doing it because it helps their business and it is good they do that. Don't worry about being cynical about it. The fact they are doing it at all is good'.[136]

## Conclusion: the 'Greed Olympics' or the most ethical Games ever?

As we have seen, London 2012 was the latest stage in the process of corporatising the Olympics. Despite his professed misgivings, it had become, in the words of ex-IOC marketing director Michael Payne 'the world's longest commercial'.[137] As was now customary – and ironically, given the widespread invocation of, and commitment to, neoliberal economic philosophies in the Western world – corporate sponsors had successfully demanded the elimination of all competition. Similarly, as part of the now-routine IOC contract, they had been given tax exemption for the duration of the Games. For corporate partners, dignitaries and other official guests the IOC had required at least 40,000 hotel rooms for the duration of the Games.[138] The biggest proportion of the much-invoked 'Olympic family', estimated to be 80,000 people in

---

[136] Richard Gillis, 'McDonald's? They're great for youth sport, says Blair', *The Independent*, 27 July 2012, p. 5.

[137] Quoted by Jules Boykoff and Alan Tomlinson in their article, 'Olympic arrogance', for *The New York Times*, 4 July 2012, http://www.nytimes.com/2012/07/05/opinion/no-medal-for-the-international-olympic-committee.html?_r=0; accessed 10 December 2014.

[138] Andrew Gilligan, 'London's secret Olympic contracts: the full download', http://blogs.telegraph.co.uk/news/andrewgilligan/100067813/londons-secret-olympic-contracts-the-full-download/, posted 10 December 2010; accessed 10 December 2014.

number, was made up of sponsors.[139] Coca Cola had hired the entire 380 room Langham Hotel in Portland Place for the Games and its public bars were closed; at the time of writing the cheapest room at the Langham cost around £400 per night.[140] A fleet of 4,000 BMW cars had been made available to the 'Olympic family', while green campaigners pointed out that the public had been urged to travel to Olympic events by bus or train.[141] An Olympic Route Network had been established in and around London, providing 30 miles of lanes to which only accredited vehicles had access; by the second week in August 2012 nearly 2,500 unaccredited drivers had been fined for entering these lanes.[142]

Liberal media commentary oscillated between playing to the understandable public anger at these VIP provisions (mitigated, on occasion, by tributes to the 70,000 Olympic volunteers who helped out at the Games and thus provided an antidote to 'the Olympic greed and hype'[143]) and the rehearsal of conventional government wisdom (in the UK and elsewhere) that the Olympics would boost the economy and put their host at centre stage in the global arena. 'Consumer spending will soar by £750m during London's Olympic Games next summer', said *The Guardian* in July 2011, 'according to a new economic study [commissioned by the debit card company Visa, an Olympic partner] which also forecasts a sustained boost to the British economy of a total £5.1 bn over the next four years'.[144] In this alternative narration the presence of so many VIPs became a virtue and London welled up with

---

[139] Tom Peck, 'VIP treatment: life is golden in the Olympic fast lane', *The Independent*, 24 May 2012, p. 14.

[140] https://gc.synxis.com/rez.aspx?Hotel=27406&Chain=10316&adult=1& Rooms=1&Child=0&arrive=11/12/2014&depart=12/12/2014&start=availresults; accessed 10 December 2014.

[141] Martin Delgado, 'The Olympic lane BMWs: first picture of the high-powered cars that will ferry VIPs across the capital', *Mail on Sunday*, http://www.dailymail. co.uk/news/article-2129809/London-2012-Olympics-First-picture-BMW-cars-ferry-VIPs-capital.html, first posted 14 April 2012; accessed 10 December 2014.

[142] Kevin Rawlinson, 'London 2012: nearly 2,500 drivers slapped with Olympic Games lanes fines', *The Independent*, 9 August 2012, http://www.independent. co.uk/sport/olympics/news/london-2012-nearly-2500-drivers-slapped-with-olympic-games-lanes-fines-8022681.html; accessed 10 December 2014.

[143] See, for example, Poppy McPherson, 'Here come the volunteers', *The Independent*, 19 July 2012, pp. 16–17.

[144] Rebecca Smithers, 'London Olympics to lift consumer spending by £750m, report predicts', 11 July 2011, http://www.theguardian.com/business/2011/jul/ 11/london-olympics-consumer-spending; accessed 11 December 2014.

business possibilities and free-spending tourists. The panhandlers and pork butchers were forgotten as on the eve of the Games the *Independent on Sunday* emblazoned its front page with: 'WELCOME TO THE CAPITAL OF THE WORLD'; 'As 100 heads of state, 3,000 business leaders and millions more descend, UK plc is open for business. Can we take advantage?' Overleaf, Matt Chorley and Emily Dugan wrote:

> London, capital of England. Capital of the United Kingdom. And, for the next seven weeks at least, capital of the world. The 2012 Olympic and Paralympic Games are no mere sporting event. They are the catalyst for a foreign invasion by the worlds of business, politics, finance and the arts which, it is hoped, will showcase the very best of UK plc and attract investment for decades to come. Deals will be done, billions will be spent, poses will be struck and the eyes of the world will, everyone hopes, witness Britain at its finest.[145]

Two days later news came that:

> Senior ministers are using the Olympics as the backdrop for a carefully choreographed diplomatic and commercial charm offensive which Downing Street today said will be centred on 17 separate business summits for 3,000 foreign investors and business partners, starting with a 'global investment conference' being held at Lancaster House from Thursday. Prince Charles will then host a drinks reception at Clarence House.[146]

Twelve months later the government was claiming that this charm offensive had worked:

> Lavish hospitality laid on for foreign dignitaries and businessmen during the London Olympics has helped British companies secure contracts and agreements abroad worth £1.5bn in areas including oil drilling in Brazil and nuclear power in Jordan. A government report into the economic legacy of the 2012 Games published today estimates that the sporting extravaganza has garnered a £9.9 bn windfall

---

[145] Matt Chorley and Emily Dugan, 'Marketing of UK plc goes into Olympic overdrive', *Independent on Sunday*, 22 July 2012, pp. 2–3, p. 2.

[146] Cahal Milmo and Jerome Taylor, 'Let the power games begin: VIP invasion fires pistol on super-summit', *Independent*, 24 July 2012, p. 4.

in trade and investment for the battered economy, potentially rising to £41 bn by 2020.[147]

For London traders this anticipated commercial 'windfall' of the Olympics seemed to have been negligible. In early August Culture Secretary Jeremy Hunt had stated that 'Anyone who has a business anywhere in London is frankly quids in'.[148] However, Ufi Ibrahim of the British Hospitality Association countered:

> Our postcode research shows an average decline in takings of 40 per cent in central London restaurants compared with a year ago. One is down by 61 per cent. The problem is that the authorities were making so much noise about fears of gridlock. People were told not to drive into London and to work from home.[149]

Richard Bradford of the Restaurant Association described Hunt as 'an idiot' – 'This is total rubbish. There has been a serious fall in trade. They encouraged the British to stay out of London, which removed the regular trade we rely on'.[150]

There's little doubt, then, that corporate greed dictated many of the arrangements for London 2012 or that these arrangements were greatly to the ideological and commercial benefit of the major sponsors. But it's also important to note that the corporations' attempts to dictate Olympic realities on their own terms were never either total or without significant challenge. In January 2012, comedian and columnist Mark Steel probably spoke for many across the political spectrum when he openly mocked Prime Minister Cameron's plans for a pre-Olympic business summit thus:

> we're missing out, because this conference shouldn't be before the Games, it should be an event in them, with commentators whispering, 'What an atmosphere as we approach the final of the Freestyle Tax-Dodging. Can anyone challenge the mighty Vodafone, dominant

---

[147] Cahal Milmo, 'Games have given UK £10bn windfall already, say ministers', *Independent*, 19 July 2013, p. 30.

[148] Sean Poulter, ' "You idiot"! London traders react with anger after Olympics minister Jeremy Hunt insists they're "quids in" ', *Daily Mail*, 3 August 2012, http://www.dailymail.co.uk/news/article-2182945/You-idiot-London-traders-react-anger-Olympics-minister-Jeremy-Hunt-insists-theyre-quids-in.html?ITO=1490; accessed 11 December 2014.

[149] Ibid.

[150] Ibid.

in this field for so long? Oh, it's a false start, Goldman Sachs transferred two billion dollars to the Seychelles before the gun went off.'[151]

Indeed, the week before the Games, London mayor Boris Johnson had
felt moved to tell Londoners to 'stop whining' about the Olympics
'despite draconian rules over brand usage and continued security and
strike threats'.[152] 'The comment came as Olympic organiser Seb Coe was
mocked online for saying people could not go to the Games wearing
a Pepsi T-shirt, because of Coca-Cola's sponsorship of the Olympics'.[153]
Johnson said in the right wing tabloid the *Sun*: 'Cut out the whining.
And as for you whingers, put a sock in it, fast. We've got an advanced
case of Olympo-funk'.[154]

Moreover, although marginalised (or excluded) by the mainstream
media and (in some cases) mollified by British success at the Games,
political critique of the Olympic corporations was maintained. For
example, campaigns by bodies such as the Tax Justice Network successfully confronted the Olympics as tax haven. McDonalds agreed to forgo
their tax exemptions for London 2012 in mid-July 2012.[155] And, following an online petition which rapidly gathered 160,000 signatures,[156] GE
(General Electric), Coca Cola and Visa did likewise.[157]

And, as we have seen, other political campaigners had been monitoring the working conditions in factories where Olympic products are
manufactured. Pre-eminent here is the Play Fair campaign,[158] which has

---

[151] Mark Steel, 'Let's hand out the gold medals to big business', *The Independent*,
11 January 2012, p. 13.
[152] Ian Dunt, 'Boris tells Londoners to "stop whining" as Olympic chaos
continues', http://www.politics.co.uk/news/2012/07/20/boris-tells-londoners-to-
stop-whining-as-olympic-chaos-conti, posted 20 July; accessed 11 December
2014.
[153] Ibid.
[154] Ibid.
[155] 'The Olympic tax swindle: McDonalds breaks from the pack?', http://
taxjustice.blogspot.ch/2012/07/mcdonalds-clarification-of-olympics-tax.html;
accessed 11 December 2014.
[156] Cahal Milmo, 'Sponsors urged to waive Olympic tax breaks worth tens of
millions', *The Independent*, 19 July 2012, p. 4.
[157] Simon Goodley, Josephine Moulds and Simon Rogers, 'London 2012:
Olympic sponsors waive tax break', http://www.theguardian.com/sport/2012/jul/
18/london-2012-visa-olympic-tax; accessed 11 December 2014.
[158] For a detailed study of this campaign, see Jill Timms, 'The Olympics as a platform for protest: a case study of the London 2012 "ethical" Games and the Play
Fair campaign for workers' rights', *Leisure Studies*, Vol. 31, No. 3, pp. 355–372,
http://dx.doi.org/10.1080/02614367.2012.667821.

been conducted by a global alliance of international trade union federations and non-governmental organisations (NGOs) since before the Athens Olympics of 2004. In Britain it was supported by the Trades Union Congress and the Bristol-based campaigners Labour Behind the Label. In January 2012 it published a report called *Toying With Workers' Rights* based on an investigation of conditions in two factories in China producing official merchandise bearing the London 2012 Olympic Games logo: one producing pin badges and the second the stuffed toys of the Olympic mascots Wenlock and Mandeville. The workers were paid well below a liveable wage, obliged to work long (sometimes 24 hour) shifts and faced fines for minor infractions; some of them, in contravention of Chinese law, were children.[159] The report was presented to LOCOG and, in February, Coe responded:

> We place a high priority on environmental, social and ethical issues when securing goods and services. As soon as we were made aware of the Play Fair 2012 report, we instructed our independent monitor to carry out a comprehensive investigation and review. The outcome of this will be made public as soon as it is concluded.[160]

LOCOG subsequently 'signed a ground-breaking agreement with the Playfair 2012 campaign to take further steps to protect workers' rights in China and the UK'.[161] In May the campaign issued a further report called *Fair Games?*, detailing the oppressive work regimes (low wages, long hours, fines and punishments, neglect of safety, casualisation and the banning of union membership) in factories in China, the Philippines and Sri Lanka that made Olympic goods for such brands as Adidas, Next, Nike and Speedo, and urging LOCOG (and the IOC) to do more in this regard.[162] In October 2012, the TUC announced the conclusion

---

[159] Labour Behind the Label, *Toying with Workers' Rights: A Report on Producing Merchandise for the London 2012 Olympic Games*, Play Fair 2012, published by Trades Union Congress, January 2012, http://www.tuc.org.uk/sites/default/files/tucfiles/toying_with_workers_rights.pdf; accessed 11 December 2014.

[160] TUC, http://www.tuc.org.uk/international-issues/playfair-2012/olympics-set-get-fairer-workers-making-goods-london-2012, posted 22 February 2012; accessed 11 December 2014.

[161] International Textile, Garment and Leather Workers' Federation, *Fair Games?*, published by Play Fair 2012 Campaign, the Trades Union Congress and Labour Behind the Label (LBL), May 2012, p. 2, http://www.play-fair.org/media/index.php/2012/05/fair-games/; accessed 11 December 2014.

[162] Ibid.

of the three year Play Fair 2012 project, suggesting that its objective – to raise worker and student awareness of the interdependence of global sportswear supply chains and of how their power to effect change as consumers strengthens the efforts of ethical suppliers and workers in the developing world to alleviate their poverty – had been achieved. There had been 'real advances in the open-ness and worker-friendly nature of the supply chains involved' and Play Fair 2012 had 'achieved significant media coverage and widespread support in the trade union movement'. In this sense, then, the TUC suggested that London 2012 had, after all, been 'the most ethical Olympics ever'.[163] This had been valuable and progressive political work, but the implications of this gesture were bleak: they showed how marginal the trade union movement currently was, both in relation to the Olympics and to the wider transaction of politics since the late 1970s, and, if the London Games had indeed been the most ethical ever, one was compelled to wonder how low, morally, must the bar have been set.

---

[163] http://www.tuc.org.uk/international-issues/international-development/global-economic-justice-campaigns/labour-standards-2; accessed 11 December 2014.

# 7
## How Good Does That Feel? London 2012: Media and Celebrity

With London 2012 about to begin, the Canadian lawyer and former Olympic swimmer Dick Pound (IOC Vice President from 1987 to 1991 and again from 1996 to 2000) was asked by CNN about the financial debacle that had become of his home town Olympics in Montreal back in 1976. Yes, there had been problems, he said, but calling those Games 'the bankrupt Olympics' was 'a bad rap'; after all, they had 'paved the way for a new financial structure and the introduction of lucrative new television rights deals'. He added:

> They were pretty magic. All Olympics are magic but we had [Romanian gymnast Nadia] Comaneci with her first '10' and we had the Spinks brothers and we had Sugar Ray Leonard [Michael and Leon Spinks and Sugar Ray were African American boxers]. I mean we had some magnificent heroes of the modern Olympics.[1]

Pound, in other words, was celebrating the inauguration of the Olympics as a full-blooded television show, with its necessary complement of celebrities – 'heroes' in the preferred Olympic lexicon. This chapter examines London 2012 as a case study in the media handling of Olympic sport, paying due attention to the (often interlocking) themes of celebrity-making; gender and sport; the fluctuating public conversation about nationality; the marginalisation of dissenting voices; and the conceptualisation of sport itself. As in previous chapters, it will argue that the exaltation of sport celebrity-heroes by the media entailed the suspension of – or, at least, posed a challenge to – the fundaments of

---

[1] Paula Newton, 'Olympics worth the price tag? The Montreal Legacy', http://edition.cnn.com/2012/07/19/world/canada-montreal-olympic-legacy/index.html, posted 20 July 2012; accessed 12 December 2014.

mainstream political argument in Britain at the time. It draws, once again, on press coverage in Britain and on the BBC's broadcasting of London 2012. The BBC had supported the formal launch of the British bid in January 2005 and the corporation's Olympic presenter, Sue Barker, had hosted the event.[2] As we've seen, the BBC were named (and proudly proclaimed themselves as) 'the Olympic broadcaster', adding on their website that the Games had brought 'not just some of the greatest sportsmen and women from around the world, but also the best in broadcasting and creative talent from the BBC'.[3] Not only that, but 'BBC Comedy drew inspiration from the Olympics to bring us two series of the critically acclaimed *Twenty Twelve*' and 'the *EastEnders* [TV soap opera] team weaved the Olympics into one of their most exciting story lines this year'.[4] For the journalists covering the Games, this close co-option of the BBC might be thought to have blurred further the already barely perceptible distinction between reporter and publicist, and made the corporation, its status as a public service broadcaster and the *Panorama* documentary of 2004 and David Conn's radio interrogation of Coe's Olympic claims in 2007 notwithstanding, an unlikely outlet for criticism of the event. With regard to London 2012, the implication was that this function had been fulfilled by *Twenty Twelve*, a satirical spoof documentary about a fictitious 'Olympic Deliverance Commission' (ODA), broadcast on various BBC channels in two series between 2011 and 2012. This seemed to have been part of a trend I have identified elsewhere whereby comedy has come to replace, and to be seen as an acceptable substitute for, leftish political comment.[5] The chapter begins with a discussion of this issue.

## 'This could go down as the Games that changed the way the world dries its hands': the politics of *Twenty Twelve*

*Twenty Twelve* was a television programme broadcast by the BBC in two series in 2011 and 2012. The second series concluded three days before

[2] See Mike Lee, with Adrian Warner and David Bond, *The Race for the 2012 Olympics* (London: Virgin Books, 2006), pp. 38–39.

[3] http://www.bbc.co.uk/academy/production/article/art20130702112135235; accessed 12 December 2014.

[4] Ibid.

[5] See Stephen Wagg, 'They can't stop us laughing': politics, leisure and the comedy business', in Peter Bramham and Stephen Wagg (eds.), *The New Politics of Leisure and Pleasure* (Basingstoke: Palgrave Macmillan, 2011), pp. 169–194, pp. 186–187.

the Games themselves began. The first series (of six episodes) went out on BBC4, a channel loosely dedicated to arts and culture, and attracted an audience of around 400,000; for the second series (of seven episodes), *Twenty Twelve* was moved to the longer established BBC2, where its viewing figures built from around one million to nearly two.[6] As previously noted, it was placed within the (by then) familiar media format of the spoof documentary, or 'mockumentary'. This sub-genre of programme-making is virtually as old the broadcasting media themselves – it can certainly be traced back as far as Orson Welles' famously simulated CBS news bulletin announcing a Martian invasion of America in 1938 – and became more commonplace following the success of the film *This is Spinal Tap*, a parody-profile of a fictitious heavy metal band, in 1984.[7] Since then mockumentaries have proliferated, notably with the BBC's highly successful *The Office* (2002–2003, with a 'Christmas Special' in 2004), and indeed by the time *Twenty Twelve* came to be written, there had already been an Olympics mockumentary – *The Games*, which had run for two series on ABC television in Australia prior to the Sydney Olympics of 2000.[8] Moreover, the writers of *The Games* had accused John Morton, creator of *Twenty Twelve*, of plagiarism.[9]

Like all successful mockumentaries, *Twenty Twelve* had a sheen of believability. All its characters spoke and behaved in earnest, their gravitas giving extra edge to the invariably nonsensical things that they said – a device Chris Morris, a leading exponent of this kind of television, once described as 'authenticated bollocks'.[10] Part of *Twenty Twelve*'s comedy is generated outside the Olympics, with running jokes concerning the variously unfortunate single parenthood of ODA team member 'Kay Hope', the disintegrating marriage of the director 'Ian Fletcher', and the evident

---

[6] http://en.wikipedia.org/wiki/Twenty_Twelve; accessed 5 January 2015.

[7] Directed by Rob Reiner, written by Christopher Guest, Michael McKean, Harry Shearer and Rob Reiner.

[8] http://en.wikipedia.org/wiki/The_Games_%28Australian_TV_series%29; accessed 5 January 2015. Discussed in Helen Jefferson Lenskyj, *The Best Olympics Ever? Social Impacts of Sydney 2000* (Albany: State University of New York Press, 2002), pp. 169–172.

[9] Karl Quinn, 'BBC imitation no flattery: Clarke', *The Age*, 16 March 2011, http://www.theage.com.au/entertainment/tv-and-radio/bbc-imitation-no-flattery-clarke-20110315-1bvx4.html; accessed 5 January 2015.

[10] *The Guardian*, 15 January 1994; quoted in Stephen Wagg, 'Everything else is propaganda: the politics of alternative comedy', in George E.C. Paton, Chris Powell and Stephen Wagg (eds.), *The Social Faces of Humour* (Aldershot: Arena, 1996), pp. 321–347, at p. 344.

(but undeclared and unrequited) love for Fletcher harboured by his personal assistant. Similarly, *Twenty Twelve* is a satire at the expense both of the professions of 'impression management' (advertising, public relations, marketing . . .) and of management itself. Many of the characters have vague but portentous titles such as 'Head of Infrastructure' and 'Head of Brand' and, in the second series, two of them aspire to become 'Head of Posterity' after the Games. Inevitably, most of the characters speak a relentlessly promotional vocabulary, putting an optimistic gloss on the most unpromising situation: Fletcher's reflection on any circumstance, however calamitous, is 'So it's all good', and 'Siobhan Sharpe', the 'Head of Brand' seconded from the 'Perfect Curve' PR agency, maintains a semi-euphoric use of language throughout thirteen episodes, supplying a torrent of 'Way cool's, 'I totally get that's and 'OK. Here's the thing's. A candidate for a new post at the ODA says at interview in Episode 5 that she believes in 'underwriting in young people a real commonality of creative purpose through a shared awareness of diversity' and that that is something she has been keen 'to drive forward in Cardiff'; this virtually meaningless statement is met with an approving chorus of 'Absolutely' from the interviewing panel. And, of course, the professional veneer that this vocabulary represents is undermined by the bumbling and ignorance of the speakers: 'Graham Hitchens', the 'Head of Infrastructure', is wholly confused by the workings of London's transport system and, in Episode 3, when a Roman burial ground is unearthed in the (fictionalised) Olympic Park, 'Siobhan' thinks this will be OK because 'didn't the Romans found the Olympics?'

Equally, however, and crucially, much of the satirical comedy in *Twenty Twelve* is aimed at the IOC, the contemporary cultural politics of the Olympics and, by extension, at the London Organising Committee of the Games. There are several points to be made here.

Most importantly, recurrent fun is had with the evasive nature of Olympic values and precepts. A joke running throughout *Twenty Twelve*, for instance, concerns the distinction between 'sustainability' and 'legacy'. 'Kay Hope', as 'Head of Sustainability', continually insists, out of self-evident professional preciousness, that they are not the same thing. In this same preciousness, she becomes consumed by the need to produce a 'Sustainability Audit', contemplates provisions for Olympic toilets that move her to think that 'this could go down as the Games that changed the way the world dries its hands' (Episode 1, Series 2) and, for another plan, makes the (unintelligible) judgement that 'from a sustainability perspective' it 'could be a beacon of inclusiveness for sustainable shared believability post-Games across the whole of the Lower Lea Valley' (Episode 2, Series Two). In Series Two a 'Head of Legacy' is appointed, facilitating a rivalry between the heads of two key, but never-defined and apparently indistinguishable concepts. Indeed, concepts such as 'legacy', 'sustainability', 'inclusivity' and 'multiculturality' are simply incantations, passed off in mission-statement jargon as 'core pledges' and as 'embedded in everything we do, and are'. In Episode 3 of Series 2, in an uncharacteristically plain-speaking moment, 'Siobhan' tells 'Fletcher': 'Legacy and Sustainability – that's your problem, right there'.

> Fletcher: 'Right'.
> Siobhan: 'Who knows what that shit is? Get over it'.
> Fletcher: 'Yes, except that "that shit" is why we got the Games in the first place'.

A similar vacuity attends the notion of 'Olympic values' in general. Episode 4 of Series 1 introduces a touchingly daft ex-athlete called 'Dave Welbeck', who contributes his share of empty phrases ('Raising the bar is what we're about as a brand') and is recruited to enthuse young people about the Games. 'OK', he says to an audience of schoolchildren, in the middle of a chaotic Power Point presentation, 'so what do we mean by Olympic values?' There is a predictable silence in the assembly hall. Similarly, in the final episode, the team agrees to conduct a 'Big Bong' project in which they seek to commission a special peal of bells for 2012; one applicant wants everyone in Britain at an appointed hour to make a noise with any object to hand 'in celebration of Olympic values'.

The point here is this. The argument, widely offered by critical Olympic analysts and others, that 'legacy', 'sustainability' and 'Olympic values' are no more than happy-sounding invocations is an important one. It is part of a wider debate about what the Olympics have, or have not, become. Central to this debate is the notion that these words act as cover for a more baleful political and commercial reality. There is, of course, no obligation on a writer of television satire to facilitate, or even to take part in, these debates. But there is a strong case for saying that, as the public service broadcaster in the host country, the BBC did have this obligation. However, doubtless bruised by the criticism of its *Panorama* critique in 2004 and in any case compromised by its designation as the official Olympic broadcaster, *Twenty Twelve* is very probably the closest the BBC came to an examination of Olympic politics and practices around the time of these London Games.

In effect, then, *Twenty Twelve* can be seen as a token gesture toward what the researcher Konstantinos Zervas and others have called 'democratic lack' – that is, the exclusion (as in Sydney, in Greece in the years preceding the Athens Olympics of 2004 and, it goes without saying, in Beijing coming up to 2008) by state institutions and mainstream media of voices and arguments critical of the Olympic project.[11] This lack gave *Twenty Twelve* an extra importance, bringing, for example, the portrayal of Olympic discontent into sharper focus. In this regard, and quite predictably, *Twenty Twelve* observed what is probably the most important unwritten rule of television satirical comedy – that there should be 'balance' and all political standpoints made open to ridicule.[12] Thus, in *Twenty Twelve* Olympic dissidents are every bit as absurd as the ODA team, being represented principally by an ill-tempered and egotistical veteran film director improbably concerned about the impact of equestrian events on life in Greenwich, an aggressive man obsessed with the preservation of stag beetles (both in Episode 6) and an (unseen) Algerian Olympic delegation threatening boycott because the Olympic 'Shared Belief Centre' does not face Mecca (Episode 1, Series 2). Even 'Nick Jowett', the 'Head of Contracts' and the character installed periodically to puncture the pretensions of the rest of the team, is necessarily a parody, tacking 'I'm from Yorkshire' on to most of his interventions.

*Twenty Twelve* expressed the paradox of satirical comedy. It created a sanctioned space in which things that were unsayable elsewhere could be said; however, in this space they became void politically and no more than harmless mischief. Indeed, contemporary TV satire is so far removed from political critique that it has become common for the purported 'targets' of contemporary satire to relish their portrayal and even to take part in the satire itself.[13] Lord Coe – elsewhere steely in the face of

---

[11] See Konstantinos Zervas, 'Anti-Olympic campaigns', in Helen Jefferson Lenskyj and Stephen Wagg (eds.), *The Palgrave Handbook of Olympic Studies* (Basingstoke: Palgrave Macmillan, 2012), pp. 533–548, particularly pp. 539–541.

[12] I've written elsewhere on the politics of satirical comedy and made this argument. See, in particular, Stephen Wagg, 'You've never had it so silly. The politics of British satirical comedy from *Beyond the Fringe* to *Spitting Image*', in Dominic Strinati and Stephen Wagg (eds.), *Come on Down? Popular Media Culture in Post-War Britain* (London: Routledge, 1992), pp. 254–284; Wagg, 'Everything else is propaganda' – see note 10; and Stephen Wagg, 'Comedy, politics and permissiveness: the "satire boom" and its inheritance', *Contemporary Politics*, Vol. 8, No. 4 (December 2002), pp. 319–334.

[13] The best example of recent times was when Republican Vice Presidential candidate Sarah Palin appeared on the US satirical TV programme *Saturday Night Live* to confront her irreverent doppelganger Tina Fey in October 2008: 'Tina Fey, meet Sarah Palin', http://articles.latimes.com/2008/oct/19/nation/na-palin19, posted 19 October 2008; accessed 6 February 2015.

all Olympic criticism – appeared three times in *Twenty Twelve*; in Episode 2 of Series 2, for example, he assured the Algerian delegation that the Games were 'about multiculturality' – a word which the ODA team were not sure existed.[14] Indeed, at least one critic took all this as a mark of national togetherness – Brian Viner wrote in *The Independent*: 'There is surely no other country in the world that would laugh at itself in this way, even persuading the vast project's principal mover-and-shaker, in our case the Rt Hon Lord Coe KBE, to participate in the joke'.[15] Moreover, in 2013 the BBC commissioned a sequel called *W1A* in which Ian Fletcher moves to the BBC itself to be given the fictitious (and plainly meaningless) title of 'Head of Values'.

The remainder of this chapter deals with media – particularly BBC – coverage of the Games themselves. Here the core concern is with how Olympic athletes – especially British athletes – were portrayed. The principal assumption will be that these athletes were treated for the most part as celebrities and, crucially, as full-time professionals: neither of these designations is escapable, but nor are they wholly compatible with what is still widely understood as the Olympic tradition. Mass media representation, knowingly or not, must work within, and ignore, this contradiction.

## Meet the parents: some thoughts on the media and Olympic celebrity

In early August 2012, with little more than a week of the Games remaining, the British broadsheet press began to publish articles claiming viewer dissatisfaction with the BBC's Olympic coverage. In the *Daily Telegraph* on 3 August Hannah Furness wrote:

> Viewers have condemned some broadcasters for focusing on gold medals to the detriment of everything else, criticising them for making medal winners 'feel bad about their achievements'. One presenter, John Inverdale, was accused of giving 'the most depressing, down beat interviews', after he spoke to silver medal-winning

---

[14] The two series of *Twenty Twelve* were released on DVD by BBC Worldwide in 2012. All quotations are taken from these recordings.

[15] Brian Viner, 'Last Night's TV – Twenty Twelve, BBC4; The Secret War on Terror, BBC2', 15 March 2011, http://www.independent.co.uk/arts-entertainment/tv/reviews/last-nights-tv–twenty-twelve-bbc4-the-secret-war-on-terror-bbc2-2241805.html; accessed 6 January 2015.

Team GB rowers as if they had lost. Chris Hollins, presenting BBC Breakfast this morning, was also rebuked for introducing a segment with cyclist Lizzie Armitstead by saying she had 'sadly' won a silver medal.[16]

The *Daily Mail* (perhaps prompted by this) followed with two similar articles on consecutive days. The main thrust of the first article was that the BBC reporters had been 'insensitive' in their dealings with athletes:

> Referring to interviews where Team GB lost out on medals, Twitter users said BBC interviewers needed to approach the athletes with a little more sensitivity. DNWilkinson wrote: 'BBC are so insensitive? Just after Team GB have come 4th or 5th they say things like you how awful you lost. Give them some respect please. [ ... ] Swimming champion Sharron Davies has come under fire for "commiserating" with Olympian Rebecca Adlington, asking her if she was disappointed with her bronze medal in the 800m race. [ ... ] The interview with triathlete Helen Jenkins, who came fifth, also provoked anger from the audience. One Twitter user, under the name Steven Stokes, said: "BBC's Olympic coverage is superb but tone of Helen Jenkins interview was inappropriate. Made her sound like a failure. Amazing effort by her" '.[17]

The following day the *Mail* raised what seemed to be the opposite objection. 'Britain's victories in the Olympics may have taken the nation's emotions to a new level', it suggested,

> but viewers are unhappy that the BBC's reporters can't seem to keep their own in check. Many have complained about over-excited 'touchy-feely' displays of congratulation or consolation from the corporation's journalists – including rubbing, stroking and patting athletes as they interview them. Most prominent has been athletics trackside reporter Phil Jones, whose tactile interviews with Jessica

---

[16] Hannah Furness, 'London 2012: BBC Olympic interviews "too negative", viewers say', *Telegraph*, 3 August 2012, http://www.telegraph.co.uk/sport/olympics/news/9447297/London-2012-BBC-Olympic-interviews-too-negative-viewers-say.html; accessed 11 January 2015.

[17] 'BBC "lacking sensitivity" in Olympic interviews, say some spectators', *Daily Mail*, 4 August 2012, http://www.dailymail.co.uk/news/article-2183507/BBC-Olympic-coverage-lacking-sensitivity-Olympic-interviews-say-spectators.html; accessed 6 January 2015.

Ennis, Greg Rutherford and Mo Farah raised eyebrows. [...] Others have spotted British contestants being hugged at the side of the swimming pool by Sharron Davies. [...] Another commented: 'Why are some of the BBC Olympic OB presenters so touchy-feely when they interview medal winners, they are practically groping them?'

There was an accompanying photograph of reporter Jones with British athlete Jessica Ennis, captioned 'Shoulder grip: BBC presenter Phil Jones gets a grip on gold medal winner Jessica Ennis'.[18]

While it is widely held that the *Daily Mail* is hostile to the BBC – certainly the view taken by the editor of the *ourBeeb* website[19] – the apparent emotional engagement of BBC commentators with the events they were reporting on did not go unremarked (or unrecorded) elsewhere. The BBC athletics experts, for example, were filmed jumping up and down in their commentary box in celebration of British runner Mo Farah's two gold medals, in the 10,000 metres (4 August) and 5,000 metres (11 August)[20] and rowing commentator John Inverdale famously broke down in tears interviewing Mark Hunter and Zac Purchase after their silver medal in the Men's Lightweight Double Sculls at Eton Dorney on 4 August – they thought they had 'failed' in conceding the gold medal to Denmark and he was anxious to reassure them that they hadn't.[21] The *Mail*'s and other similar observations provide a good starting point for discussing the media, the Olympics and celebrity.

Several, related, factors help to explain the media treatment decried by those quoted in the *Mail*.

First, as I've suggested elsewhere, the Olympic movement has never fully relinquished (and, arguably, can never fully relinquish) the spectre

---

[18] 'BBC's "touch-feely" presenters hit a nerve: viewers unhappy at reporters' methods during post-event interview', *Daily Mail*, 5 August 2012, http://www.dailymail.co.uk/news/article-2184162/London-2012-Olympics-Viewers-unhappy-BBC-reporters-methods-post-event-interview.html, updated 6 August 2012; accessed 6 January 2015.
[19] See Dan Hancox, 'Editor's blog: how the Daily Mail's anti-BBC vitriol stops us talking openly about its future', https://www.opendemocracy.net/ourbeeb/dan-hancox/editors-blog-how-daily-mails-anti-bbc-vitriol-stops-us-talking-openly-about-its-f, posted 26 July 2012; accessed 6 January 2015.
[20] See, for example, https://www.youtube.com/watch?v=Ksmcvv6wmX4; accessed 6 January 2015.
[21] See, for example, http://tvnewsroom.org/sport/john-inverdale-in-tears-as-mark-hunter-and-zac-purchase-win-silver-medal-47595/; accessed 6 January 2015.

of amateurism that the modern Olympic movement has carried for much of its history.[22] The period following the Second World War saw a high tide of the Olympic amateur ethic, with the popular press in Britain eagerly celebrating 'Girl-Next-Door' athletes who stepped briefly out of ordinary life and into the athletic limelight – the Dutch runner and hurdler Fanny Blankers-Koen, who won four gold medals at the London Games of 1948 and was widely styled in the press as 'The Flying Housewife', is perhaps the archetype here – and the IOC still prosecuting competitors for the merest hint of financial gain.[23] By the early 1970s the notion that an Olympic athlete could, in any literal sense, be drawn temporarily from an ordinary life outside of sport was no longer viable and in 1973 the word 'amateur' was dropped from the Olympic Charter. Since the late 1980s the IOC has steadily embraced full-time professionalism and, in part because this professionalism has to be funded, sanctioned the extensive commercialisation of Olympic competitors. For Olympic reportage and boosterism (often indistinguishable in practice) this development has brought two imperatives. On the one hand, Olympic athletes (like all elite athletes, 'mortal engines' in John Hoberman's telling phrase[24]) must in some fashion be rendered homely and 'just like us'; on the other, since many of them have been at the centre of lengthy promotional campaigns leading up to the Games and/or been the recipients of public funding, they must expect questions to be raised if they fail. There were already signs in the early 1970s that the British popular press, in particular, could now speak severely of Olympic athletes who, having been expected to gain a medal, failed to do so: runner David Bedford, for example, was called 'a flop' by the *Daily Express* when he finished down the field in the Men's 10,000 metres at Munich in 1972.[25] Today, in the event of a failure to 'medal' (the word, as a consequence of these ideological changes, now doubles as a verb), not only a primed public and an army of publicists, but, in the British instance, a House of Commons committee, will want to know

[22] See Stephen Wagg, 'Tilting at windmills: Olympic politics and the spectre of amateurism', in Lenskyj and Wagg (eds.), *The Palgrave Handbook of Olympic Studies*, pp. 321–336.
[23] Ibid.; see also Stephen Wagg, 'If you want the girl next door... Olympic sport and the popular press in early Cold War Britain', in Stephen Wagg and David L. Andrews (eds.), *East Plays West: Sport and the Cold War* (London: Routledge, 2007), pp. 100–122.
[24] John Hoberman, *Mortal Engines: The Science of Performance and the Dehumanization of Sport* (New York: The Free Press, 1992).
[25] See Wagg, 'If you want the girl next door....', pp. 119–120.

why. Moreover, after only two days of these London Games, the Mayor of London Boris Johnson remarked that Britain needed 'to step up the medal count a bit'.[26] Political discourse on this issue, especially following *Game Plan*, the government sport strategy document of 2002, now frequently throws up the phrase 'value for money' with regard to the Olympic medal table.

These, and other, factors clearly influenced the BBC representation of London 2012.

As is now widely accepted, the Olympics have, for some time, been primarily a television show, arguably the world's biggest. Sports stars are now central to this – after all, corporate partners, as Olympic commentator Bill Mallon put it back in 1993, won't pay big money 'to watch American college basketball players'.[27] Indeed, as Garry Whannel wrote recently, 'Top sports now are the point of intersection between the global spectacle of the Olympic Games and the celebrity-dominated media culture, and star image has become a promotional tool'.[28] Such stars (the Jamaican sprinter Usain Bolt, the British swimmer and Olympic gold medallist Rebecca Adlington ... ) started appearing in promotional material for the Games well before July 2012, usually accompanied by images of winning – breasting the tape, mounting the podium and so on – and, as we've seen, Olympic sportspeople were widely featured in adverts for a variety of products preceding the Olympics.[29] Moreover, the BBC, which had guaranteed to show every minute of Olympic sport via its various channels, prefaced many of its broadcasts of particular events with a profile of a particular star performer/British medal hope. For example, on Day 1 of the Games (28 July) commentator Matthew Pinsent (who carried the extra validation of being an Olympic gold medallist himself, albeit in rowing) introduced the cycling event, the Men's Road Race, with a brief profile of Britain's Mark Cavendish.

[26] See Rowena Mason, 'Boris Johnson: we need to step up the Olympic medal count', http://www.telegraph.co.uk/sport/olympics/news/9437915/Boris-Johnson-We-need-to-step-up-the-Olympic-medal-count.html, posted 30 July 2012; accessed 13 January 2015.

[27] Bill Mallon, 'Qualification for Olympic games in the 21st century', *Citius, Altius, Fortius*, Vol. 1, No. 2 (Spring 1993), pp. 10–17, p. 10; quoted in Wagg, 'Tilting at windmills? ... ', p. 332.

[28] Garry Whannel, 'The rings and the box: television spectacle and the Olympics', in Lenskyj and Wagg (eds.), *The Palgrave Handbook of Olympic Studies*, pp. 261–273, p. 270.

[29] See, for example, https://www.youtube.com/watch?v=iyOzUf6FPxQ; accessed 7 January 2015.

Cavendish, he said, had returned from the Beijing Games of 2008 'in fury' – the only member of the UK track team not to win a medal: 'Since then he's become [slight pause] King of the Road'. In the event, the gold medal went to the Kazakhstan rider Alexander Vinokourovith, but, with Cavendish established in advance as 'the story', it was inevitable that the microphone would be poked under his chin and he be asked, albeit politely, by interviewer Jill Douglas, what had gone wrong. Many competitors, pleaded Cavendish, had been happy to lose, so long as England didn't win.[30]

As I've suggested, though, there was a corresponding need to present these leading highly paid, full-time professional competitors as in some way 'just like us', in keeping with the enduring Olympic ethos of amateurism. One media trope seemingly designed to meet this imperative was what might be called the 'Meet the Parents' strand in media coverage of London 2012. While there were, arguably, other reasons for it – 'human interest', for example, or the need to fill in time between events – the rush to interview parents of athletes, and to train the camera on them and their children's hometown friends in the crowd, had the effect of humanising the mortal engines of London 2012: after all, while few of us have spent successive years in swimming pools or training camps under the tutelage of specialist coaches[31] and sundry sport scientists, most of us have mums, dads and mates. A good case in point here was swimmer Rebecca Adlington, a double gold medallist in Beijing, who took bronze in the Women's 400 metres freestyle on 30 July. At the finish of the race, the BBC camera switched to a cluster of friends from her home town of Mansfield; after the swim Adlington told poolside interviewer Sharron Davies that she was now tired after 'twelve years of hard work'; later her parents were interviewed by ITN – they told viewers that Beccy was 'a fighter'.[32] The following morning Mr and Mrs Adlington showed up on BBC's *Breakfast* programme, along with the mother and father of British cyclist Lizzie Armitstead, who had won a silver medal in the Women's Road Race the previous day. During the

---

[30] Unless otherwise stated, all quotations from BBC commentary on the Olympics of London 2012 are taken from the DVD *London 2012 Olympic Games*, released by BBC Worldwide in 2012.

[31] Coaches have recently been assimilated into the pantheon of sporting achievement: for instance, the BBC Sports Personality of the Year Awards incorporated a category for coaches in 1999 and Dave Brailsford, coach to the British cycling team, received a knighthood after the London 2012 Games.

[32] https://www.youtube.com/watch?v=03uH_lC_TQk; accessed 7 January 2015.

Olympics interviews were conducted with the parents of, among others, the British triathletes Alistair and Jonathan Brownlee,[33] US swimmer Jessica Hardy,[34] British track and field athlete Jessica Ennis[35] and British winner of the double trap shooting event, Peter Wilson.[36] An interview with Bert Le Clos, the father of American swimmer and Olympic 200 metres butterfly champion Chad Le Clos,[37] led to further media interest and Bert's tongue-in-cheek claim that he was now more famous than his son.[38] Indeed, it can be argued that the parents of Olympic competitors – those ordinary people who have paid for their children's coaching, driven them to training, chivvied them to do their homework and sat in innumerable venues watching them perform – have become the key repository of the myth of Olympic amateurism: in a symbolic way, they shorten the (now considerable) social distance between the elite athlete and a mass audience.

As for the 'touchy feely' approach by interviewer to athletes, this might be interpreted as an expression both of populism and of possession. The Olympics being primarily a television show, the interviewer-commentators – often now ex-competitors – are as much a part of the event as the competitors themselves and, for the latter, being interviewed is as much a part of the job as competing. Olympic television – as witnessed at London 2012 – promotes a kind of *faux* egalitarianism in which athletes and media personnel, the rich, the hereditary and political elite (the camera often picked out Prince Harry, the Duke and Duchess of Cambridge or Prime Minister Cameron, casually dressed, cheering and high-fiving in the crowd) and the ordinary punter merge symbolically into one exuberant national family. In this regard, the reporters sought to appropriate the subjectivities both of the crowd and of the athletes. Thus, when the crowd cheered a home victory (as with Mo Farah's winning performances) so did the commentary team; similarly, when events were concluded interviewers rushed to ask what were, or had been, the competitor's feelings. For example, following

[33] https://www.youtube.com/watch?v=QAKoXGa0ASA; accessed 7 January 2015.
[34] https://www.youtube.com/watch?v=a-JEwLlb1Qk; accessed 7 January 2015.
[35] https://www.youtube.com/watch?v=zPV1dzu24kI; accessed 7 January 2015.
[36] https://www.youtube.com/watch?v=Lf4Vrbtn0G4; accessed 7 January 2015.
[37] https://www.youtube.com/watch?v=sYa0r43Xn-8; accessed 7 January 2015.
[38] Bert Le Clos, 'Bert le Clos says he is now more famous than his Olympic champion son Chad', *Telegraph*, 27 July 2013, http://www.telegraph.co.uk/sport/othersports/athletics/10203182/Bert-le-Clos-says-he-is-now-more-famous-than-his-Olympic-champion-son-Chad.html; accessed 7 January 2015.

the Women's Road Race which finished in front of Buckingham Palace, interviewer Jill Douglas approached the winner, Marianne Vos of the Netherlands: 'Marianne, many congratulations. Just how does it feel to come up the Mall like that?' Jill then moved on to Lizzie Armitstead, who had come in second: 'Lizzie, huge congratulations. Such a thrill for everybody here to see you coming up and taking a silver medal. How good does that feel?' These are questions to which there can only be one answer (winners are invariably thrilled, losers invariably gutted) and, thus, are not really questions at all; they are assertions of the right of television (and therefore of the viewer) to the subjectivity of the athlete.

In concluding this chapter, I now consider as case studies three of the British athletes made celebrities, or brought to greater prominence, by London 2012, examining questions of gender, multiculturalism, national identity and celebrity itself.

## 'Like I was in a boy band'...London 2012 and the politics of Olympic celebrity

As we have seen, since the sea change witnessed at Los Angeles in 1984, commercialism on a grand scale has helped to define successive Olympiads (four-year periods, each beginning on 1 January of a year in which the Summer Olympics are due to take place). Whereas in earlier Olympics a celebrity would emerge, via performance, from a Games – as, for instance with Blankers-Koen in 1948, the Ukrainian distance runner Vladimir Kuts, who won gold in both the 5,000 and 10,000 metres in Melbourne in 1956 or Australian Herb Elliott, who took gold in the 1,500 metres in Rome in 1960 – celebrity is now at the centre of a mutual promotion, with prominent individuals boosting the Games (and, of course, myriad Olympic 'partners') and the Games, subject to performance, enhancing the reputations of individuals. In this regard, one competitor at least could be said almost to transcend the Olympics of 2012: the Jamaican sprinter Usain Bolt had already won three Olympic gold medals in the Beijing Games of 2008 (the 100 metres, 200 metres and 4 by 100 metres relay, each in both an Olympic and a world record time) and by 2012 was widely taken to be the fastest man ever to engage in competitive sport. Bolt was also media-wise, delivering his trademark 'lightning bolt' gesture (an outstretched finger pointing diagonally at the sky) after every victory and becoming the focal point of marketing campaigns for Puma running shoes, Gatorade 'sports drink' and Virgin Media. He would be the star turn at London 2012 and, for those televising London 2012, the Games would have been incomplete without him. However, as we've seen, British athletes also became vehicles for a variety of promotions and considerable media expectation was created around three in particular: Jessica Ennis, Bradley Wiggins and Mo Farah.

Jessica Ennis was 26 at the time of London 2012. If the 'Girl Next Door' of earlier Olympic culture was no longer viable, Ennis was the next best thing. She became the poster girl for the British Olympic effort – in a widely retailed tweet one of her rivals, Canadian pentathlete Jessica Zelinka, remarked that London during the Games was 'like a Jessica Ennis theme park'[39] – and, as observed by David Andrews and Oliver Rick, was central to the BBC narrative of the Games.[40] The columnist Cole Moreton summed up her marketability:

> People warmed to her pluck and skill as well as her beauty, which was cleverly marketed. Like Lewis Hamilton in Formula 1, she had the look the sponsors wanted. Research has shown that the face the majority of people of all ages find most attractive is symmetrical, flawless and mixed race [her mother was white and English, her father an Afro-Caribbean from Jamaica]. Olay used hers to sell moisturiser. Jaguar praised her speed and grace and supplied a black five-litre car. Omega took care of her timekeeping needs. Powerade, BP and Aviva put their money behind her. Adidas gave her a deal said to be the most lucrative of any Team GB athletics competitor, at £320,000.[41]

There was, of course, more to her appeal than that. The media in effect used her subjective ordinariness – the daughter of a social worker and a painter and decorator, she lived with her boyfriend, a construction site manager, in her home town, the northern city of Sheffield – to

---

[39] See, for example, Alison Kervin, 'Sports -Personality 2012: Jessica Ennis – "my feet haven't touched the ground" ', *Radio Times*, 16 December 2012, http://www.radiotimes.com/news/2012-12-16/sports-personality-2012-jessica-ennis—my-feet-havent-touched-the-ground; accessed 11 January 2015.

[40] David L. Andrews and Oliver J.C. Rick, 'Celebrity and the London 2012 spectacle', in Vassil Girginov (ed.), *Handbook of the London Olympic and Paralympic Games Volume One: Making the Games* (Abingdon: Routledge, 2013), pp. 195–211, p. 202.

[41] Cole Moreton, 'Jessica Ennis is queen of the track', *Daily Telegraph*, 5 August 2012, http://www.telegraph.co.uk/news/9453058/Jessica-Ennis-is-queen-of-the-track.html; accessed 11 January 2015.

mitigate her objectively extraordinary existence – she was a full-time athlete and had attended her first athletics training camp at the age of ten.[42] The promotion of Ennis, which began well before the Games, emphasised her modest and unassuming nature. A profile by Emily Dugan, for example, in August 2010, noted that Jessica had 'long been tipped as a golden girl for London's Olympic Games in 2012' but 'has mostly shunned the trappings of the celebrity athlete'.[43] Dugan revisited Jessica two years later and described her once again as 'notoriously modest'.[44]

Paradoxically, of course, modesty (and an apparent diffidence in regard to celebrity) is a highly saleable commodity and, thus, a vital component of celebrity itself. Ennis' modesty, coupled with her commercial responsibilities as a member of the British Olympic team (Dugan's article tagged Jessica as an ambassador for Aviva, the team's sponsors), made for an easy compliance with a range of marketing initiatives. Some of these depicted her in a way that was anything but modest: an earlier profile of the athlete (also by Cole Moreton) was accompanied by a photograph of Ennis with her hair extravagantly styled and wearing a leopard-print silk playsuit, priced at £610, a wrist watch costing £21,300 and a ring tagged at £1,485[45] – a price range well beyond Jessica's friends back in Sheffield, but now cleverly (or cynically) invested with her homeliness. As a celebrity, Jessica Ennis was, to a significant degree, akin to David Beckham – amiable, attractive, vaguely of-the-people and, of course, gifted at sport, but, beyond that, standing for nothing in particular and, thus, an ideal peg on which to hang a range of goods and services.

For the most part Ennis seemed to see all this simply as part of the job and as a symptom of the media complexity of contemporary society.

---

[42] 'Jessica Ennis: I might do *Strictly* one day, but never *I'm a Celebrity*', http://metro.co.uk/2012/11/13/jessica-ennis-i-might-do-strictly-one-day-but-never-im-a-celebrity-get-me-out-of-here-618720/, posted 13 November 2012; accessed 11 January 2015.

[43] Emily Dugan, 'Modest, but with little to be modest about', *Independent on Sunday*, 1 August 2010, p. 22.

[44] Emily Dugan, 'Queen of the five-ring circus', *Independent on Sunday*, 3 June 2012, pp. 32–33, p. 33.

[45] Cole Moreton, 'London 2012 Olympics: how Jessica Ennis became the face of the Olympics', *Daily Telegraph*, 4 August 2012, http://www.telegraph.co.uk/sport/olympics/athletics/9452218/London-2012-Olympics-How-Jessica-Ennis-became-the-face-of-the-Olympics.html; accessed 11 January 2015.

Two months before the Olympics, in another article associated with Aviva, she told Dugan:

> Things have changed so much, with Facebook and Twitter. Everyone is so much more accessible these days: no British athlete has ever experienced what we are experiencing now. It's such a unique situation with the home Olympics. It's not just the sports journalists who want to talk to you and write stories about you, it's all the different journalists from different fields who may not be that interested in what you do, but want to chat about something else – your private life or stuff like that. It's completely different and it's a new situation for all of us ... There was no Twitter in 1948!

Celebrity, in other words, was something outside her control – a process that mobilised her as a text. She herself remained a consumer, rather than a producer, of such texts:

> 'I just find it weird that people get really excited to meet me,' says the 26-year-old, reeling off a list of examples of gifts she has been presented with. The strangest thing, though, which she says she still can't quite get her head around, are the girls who cry at the sight of her. 'Yeah, properly crying!' she says. 'I felt like I was [in] a boy band. I said: "Why are you crying?" And they couldn't even talk. Then I felt like I was going to cry. I was like: "Oh, you're not sad, are you?" [...] Er, I don't feel that I'm a celebrity. [...] Ultimately I'm an athlete. I want to be known for what I do and that's athletics and my performances. All the other things are just nice to dip in and out of. It's really weird being on these chat shows and things, it's very surreal – you know I'm normally at home watching them on TV'.[46]

To another interviewer she said:

> I met Idris Elba, who I'm a big fan of, the other day at an awards event. It was great to meet him. I just said 'Hi' and tried not to be too embarrassing and stalker-ish. I loved his series *Luther* and asked if

[46] Anna Kessel, 'Jessica Ennis: girls cry when they see me, like I was in a boy band', *The Guardian*, 14 December 2012, http://www.theguardian.com/sport/2012/dec/14/jessica-ennis-bbc-sports-personality.

there was going to be more and he said he was doing some. It was a nice little conversation. I got my picture taken with him.[47]

Ennis happily chuckled at the disparity between her celebrity and what she saw as her real self. Bradley Wiggins, by contrast, had an identifiable critique of celebrity, a notion with which he was uncomfortable, but he found himself saddled, in the apt words of Andrews and Rick, with 'a celebrityhood that simply could not be renounced'.[48]

Wiggins turned 32 in the spring of 2012 and was, professionally, at his peak. He came to the Games as the first British winner of the Tour de France, making him, after Bolt, arguably the most accomplished of the competitors at London 2012 and one of its star attractions; as such, he was asked to ring the Olympic bell at the opening ceremony to start the Games. When, as many expected him to, the be-whiskered Wiggins won gold for the cycling time trial at London 2012, the *Daily Mail*, beneath the headline 'Wiggo, king of the road: Tour de France hero routs his rivals and has now won more Olympic medals than any other Briton', trilled: 'He has won more Olympic medals now than Henry VIII had wives. He is the King of Kilburn; the mutton-chopped monarch; the sovereign in the saddle'.[49] But, unlike Ennis, Bradley had a thought-out stance on celebrity and tried to resist it. He told Paul Hayward of the *Daily Telegraph*:

> I've achieved what I've achieved and I accept what I've achieved. But I don't think that makes me better than anyone else. [...] I can't stand the word 'celebrity' and I despise everything about it. It's different from being recognised for being good at something, which I accept in our society, and is nice. I've had people coming up to me and saying, 'You changed my life, I got my bike out of the shed and I've lost five stone'. People say that to me. Brilliant. That's what it's all about. But if people say I saw you on *Big Brother* or in the jungle, it's not something that appeals to me. Our country is fascinated by it as well. It's a disgusting part of our society. It does nothing

---

[47] 'Jessica Ennis: I might do *Strictly* one day, but never *I'm a Celebrity*'.

[48] Andrews and Rick, 'Celebrity and the London 2012 spectacle', p. 208.

[49] David Jones, 'Wiggo, king of the road: Tour de France hero routs his rivals and has now won more Olympic medals than any other Briton', *Daily Mail*, 2 August 2012, http://www.dailymail.co.uk/news/article-2182113/London-2012-Olympics-Bradley-Wiggins-won-Olympic-medals-Briton.html; accessed 12 January 2015.

for our society. This summer did more for our country in terms of inspiring people and having real sporting heroes for people to look up to and kids to be inspired by. Look at the atmosphere around London, the whole country. Then you watch 'In the Jungle' [as he calls *I'm a Celebrity . . . Get Me Out of Here*] and it's pathetic.[50]

Wiggins' rebel streak was expressed in popular culture: some media voices alluding to Wiggins' side-burns and his often-professed love of the music of The Jam, had proclaimed him 'a heart-on-sleeve, practising mod' and 'the counter culture hero of cycling'.[51] This prompts two comments.

First, in his desire to distance himself from the notion of celebrity, Wiggins nevertheless effectively endorsed the official 'Inspire' message propounded by Coe and the Olympic communications team as the ideological backdrop to their bid for the Games. And, indeed, cycling was the area of sporting activity where the strongest case for at least a partial sporting legacy from London 2012 could be made. In 2013, *The Times* reported that:

the number of commuters cycling to work has risen to more than three quarters of a million people in England and Wales, census data shows, as workers choose the bicycle as an affordable and healthy way to travel. The popularity of commuting by bike has increased by 17 per cent to more than 760,000 people in the past ten years, an increase of 110,000 on 2001. Sustained success for British cyclists at the Beijing and London Olympics, as well as a first British Tour de France winner in Bradley Wiggins last year, has pushed Britain to the forefront of the sport of cycling.[52]

Second, Wiggins must at some stage have sensed the political reality of celebrity – which is that it is constructed, and certainly not constructed in circumstances of the individual celebrity's own choosing.

---

[50] Paul Haywood, 'Bradley Wiggins: reluctant hero of the masses', *Daily Telegraph*, 14 December 2012, http://www.telegraph.co.uk/sport/sports-personality-of-the-year/9746833/Bradley-Wiggins-reluctant-hero-of-the-masses.html; accessed 12 January 2015.

[51] See, for example, Patrick Redford, 'Bradley Wiggins: the counter culture hero of cycling', https://sports.vice.com/article/bradley-wiggins-the-counter-culture-hero-of-cycling, posted 26 September 2014; accessed 12 January 2015.

[52] Kaya Burgess, 'Commuting by bike soars by nearly a fifth', *The Times*, 6 March 2013, http://www.thetimes.co.uk/tto/public/cyclesafety/article3706006.ece; accessed 12 January 2015.

Wiggins rode for Team Sky, sponsored by the multinational media conglomerate News Corporation, and, at the Olympics, for Team GB. His
membership of these teams carried with it certain publicity obligations
which were contractual and, beyond that, 'Wiggo' was openly anxious
to use his success to promote cycling. He received the BBC Sports Personality of the Year Award in 2012 and, in December 2012 appeared
at a charity concert given by his musical hero Paul Weller, and he and
Weller made a programme for BBC Radio 6 Music shortly afterwards,[53]
but, unlike Ennis and Farah, he does not appear to have been placed
at the centre of any significant marketing campaigns for products or
services. He accepted a knighthood the following year and, like Ennis,
fell back on personal modesty as the best way to negotiate this process.
'I was just talking to some of the other people getting stuff', he said after
being knighted, 'and asking them what they've been honoured for, and
they're historic things, ground-breaking sciences or whatever. I've won
a bike race, you know, and I feel a little bit inferior to everyone'.[54] But it
may not have escaped Wiggins' notice that celebrity is heavily policed
and the same impression managers who help to create it can equally
move to withdraw it if the celebrity in question does not conform to
expectation. No sooner had Wiggins won his Olympic gold medal than
Piers Morgan, a media commentator on celebrities, tweeted his disap-
pointment that Bradley had not sung the national anthem.[55] And in
September 2013 an article in the same *Daily Mail* that the previous year
had hailed 'the mutton-chopped monarch' announced that 'From great
British hero to gold medallist for selfishness. Sir Bradley Wiggins has
become a . . . KNIGHTMARE'. Wiggins, wrote Jonathan McEvoy,

> was forgiven the odd moment of boorishness because, not unreason-
> ably, we thought his persona represented something that British sport
> lacked. Little less than a year on, we are left to rue the fact that the
> only gold medal he has won in 2013 is for selfishness. The latest
> reminder of Wiggins's unsavoury side came in Florence on Sunday
> when the great master decided not to finish the World Championship

---

[53] 'When Wiggins met Weller', http://www.bbc.co.uk/programmes/p012w946;
accessed 12 January 2015.
[54] Nicole Le Marie, ' "All I did was win a bike race": "Inferior" Bradley Wiggins
knighted by the Queen', http://metro.co.uk/2013/12/10/all-i-did-was-win-a-
bike-race-inferior-bradley-wiggins-knighted-by-the-queen-4225762/, posted
10 December 2013; accessed 12 January 2015.
[55] 'Morgan slammed for Wiggins anthem criticism', https://uk.eurosport.yahoo.
com/news/morgan-slammed-wiggins-anthem-criticism-092950646.html, posted
9 August 2012; accessed 12 January 2015.

road race in the rain. He abandoned compatriot Chris Froome little
more than one lap after the peloton reached the city. He was a sorry,
sodden shadow of the man who had taken silver in the time trial just
four days earlier.

'Good and bad,' the article concluded, 'unreliable and interesting, just
let's not pretend Wiggins is anything like a paragon'.[56] Among other
things, this was a reminder to Wiggins (and others) that the tabloid
press sees itself as the arbiter of matters of celebrity, and not celebrities
themselves.

Mo Farah, the winner, as we've seen, of both the 5,000 and 10,000
metre races at London 2012, had been the recipient of a similar reminder
earlier the same year. Farah, 29 and therefore also around his peak at
London 2012, had been born in Somalia but came to England as a child
and grown up in West London. His father had worked in IT. Unlike
Ennis and Wiggins, Mo Farah had neither qualm nor ironic distance
when it came to the conferring of celebrity: he embraced it, responding
positively to invitations from corporations such as Nike, Lucozade and
Virgin Media to publicise their brands, and in 2011 setting up The Mo
Farah Foundation[57] to support health care projects in Africa. The journalist Simon Hattenstone, who met Mo after the London Games, judged
him to enjoy the limelight: 'Farah is actually Moboting to catch some-
body's attention. It's as if he's convinced nobody will recognise him
unless he pulls his signature pose, hands on head to form an M'.[58] In the
spring of the same year, however, the *Daily Mail* had printed a warning
about 'Mo Farah, his VERY ambitious wife and the dash for cash that
risks tarnishing an Olympic hero'. 'Two weeks ago', reported the *Mail*,

> Team GB hero Mo and his ambitious wife Tania – who helps over-
> see his career – quietly agreed a deal with Connecticut-based global
> sports management firm Octagon that, it is hoped, will propel him
> into the big league. 'Mo is just as much a brand as Virgin,' Octagon's
> UK vice-president Clifford Bloxham told me this week. 'And we have

---

[56] Jonathan McEvoy, 'From great British hero to gold medallist for selfishness.
Sir Bradley Wiggins has become a … KNIGHTMARE', *Daily Mail*, 30 September
2013, http://www.dailymail.co.uk/sport/othersports/article-2439465/Sir-Bradley-
Wiggins-starting-selfish-side.html; accessed 12 January 2015.
[57] http://www.mofarahfoundation.org.uk/.
[58] Simon Hattenstone, 'What drives Mo Farah?', http://www.theguardian.com/
sport/2012/dec/07/what-drives-mo-farah-interview, posted 7 December 2012;
accessed 12 January 2015.

to build that brand'. [...] Suddenly, Farah, who won the nation's hearts with his stunning gold medal achievements in the 5,000 and 10,000 metres at London 2012 and his trademark 'Mobot' celebration, is realising his full commercial worth. Sadly, however, it seems even the 'Mobot', which involves arching the hands over the head to create a letter 'M' – and which was recreated with such innocent glee in the nation's school playgrounds in the wake of his victories – has a price. The runner's aides told me this week that his long-time manager Ricky Simms, who also looks after the career of Olympic sprinter Usain Bolt, has applied to trademark it. 'I am told', wrote Paul Scott, 'behind the scenes in the close-knit world of athletics that there is, among some, unbridled fury over the plan'.[59]

This is the unvarying choreography of celebrity-making: according to circumstance, celebrities are defined either as Inspirational or Grasping and/or Too-Big-For-Their-Boots.

But it was in its implications for nationality and community relations that Farah's Olympic celebrity generated the most significant comment. It was well known that Farah had been born in Somalia, a country largely associated in the British press and political discourse with the negative signifiers of civil war, poverty, piracy and unwelcome (often 'asylum seeking') immigration. Farah was particularly concerned to refute any suggestion that he'd come to Britain as an asylum seeker (his father was born in Hounslow, West London[60]) and to identify himself as a Muslim – 'I think the way I am, the way I'm chilled out, has a lot to do with being a Muslim and having faith', he said before the 10,000 metres.[61] He also, when asked after the 10,000 metres race if he'd have preferred to run for Somalia, asserted his Britishness: 'Look mate, this is my country. This is where I grew up, this is where I started my life ... And when I put on my Great Britain vest I'm proud'.[62] This inspired a widely

---

[59] Paul Scott, 'Mo Farah, his VERY ambitious wife and the dash for cash that risks tarnishing an Olympic hero', *Daily Mail*, 1 March 2013, http://www.dailymail. co.uk/news/article-2286297/Mo-Farah-VERY-ambitious-wife-dash-cash-risks-tarnishing-Olympic-hero.html; accessed 12 January 2015.

[60] See Simon Hattenstone, 'What drives Mo Farah?'.

[61] Cahal Milmo, 'Devout Farah stands on the edge of greatness', *The Independent*, 11 August 2012, p. 5.

[62] Esther Addley, 'Mo Farah also proved that we can cheer without stopping for 14 minutes', *The Guardian*, 11 August 2012, http://www.theguardian.com/sport/blog/2012/aug/11/mo-farah-olympic-stadium-london-2012; accessed 12 January 2015.

quoted article in the *Daily Mirror* by the popular comedian Eddie Izzard, who saw the runner's statement as a token of a united, multicultural Britain: 'What Mo said – in a typically humble, British way – made the whole country cheer. And it must have sent shivers down the spine of any racist in the country'. Noting that Jessica Ennis was mixed race and that Bradley Wiggins had been born in Belgium, he continued:

> This Olympics is the moment we have finally stopped being a nation harking back to the days of the British Empire. We are finally worthy of the title Cool Britannia. The Union Jack has looked very good these past weeks. For too long the far right, the racists, loonies and parties like UKIP have tried to steal it. This summer we ordinary British people fought hard and won it back.[63]

By contrast, for the right, Daniel Hannan was keen to argue that London 2012 had celebrated

> the precise opposite of multiculturalism. The Union flags now flying all over the country are totems of a shared loyalty that supersedes ancestral ties. Wherever our parents were born, we can be patriotic Britons by signing up to a set of common values. And a pretty decent set of values they are: free speech, parliamentary democracy, jury trials, religious toleration, personal liberty, habeas corpus. These are the precepts which make Britain a more agreeable place to live than, say, Somalia.[64]

Farah was also attacked by the far right English Defence League for spending too much time abroad and for raising money for Somali children.[65]

---

[63] Eddie Izzard, 'Cool Britannia: we are finally worthy of the title, says proud Eddie Izzard', *Daily Mirror*, 12 August 2012, http://www.mirror.co.uk/opinion/lifestyle-opinion/eddie-izzard-on-the-london-2012-olympics-1257661; accessed 12 January 2015.

[64] Daniel Hannan, 'Multiculturalism? Nonsense. The Olympics are a victory for patriotism and common British values', *Daily Mail*, 7 August 2012, http://www.dailymail.co.uk/debate/article-2184689/Multiculturalism-Nonsense-The-Olympics-victory-patriotism-common-British-values.html; accessed 12 January 2015.

[65] See http://www.hopenothate.org.uk/blog/insider/edl-attack-olympic-hero-mo-farah-2156; accessed 12 January 2015.

The backdrop to these assertions was a claim, made prior to the Games and floated once again in the *Daily Mail*, pointing out that around 50 of the 550 members of Team GB had been born overseas and suggesting that these 'plastic Brits' were an insult to 'our Games'; others lived abroad – Farah, for example, lived in the United States. The paper took particular exception to the appointment of Tiffany Porter, born Tiffany Ofili in the United States to a Nigerian father and an English mother, as captain of the British women's athletic team; Porter had previously represented the US, but argued 'I have always regarded myself as British, American and Nigerian. I'm all three'.[66] The *Mail* pursued the (Dutch) coach of Team GB on the matter:

> Irked by an enquiry from this newspaper's reporter Jon McEvoy about whether, in keeping with her new captain's role, she could recite a little of *God Save The Queen* on the eve of the World Indoor Championships, [Charles] Van Commenee said: 'I chose the team captain for her leadership skills, her athletic skills and her credibility . . . not her voice'. I defer to his knowledge on all, except credibility. Because it's hard to see how Porter can be a credible British captain ahead of the likes of Jess Ennis.[67]

The *Mail* returned to this theme shortly before the Games, an anonymous reporter insisting that: 'The controversy over "plastic Brits" has been reignited by the revelation that Team GB will have 61 overseasborn athletes competing at this summer's London Olympics' and citing 'the selection of Cuban-born triple jumper Yamile Aldama and wrestler Olga Butkevych, who was born in Ukraine but received her UK passport only a couple of months ago'.[68] This can be read as a jaded piece of populism, aimed at the *Mail* readership's imagined irritability with immigrants and interlopers and directing it toward two countries routinely disparaged in Conservative circles – the nominally communist

---

[66] 'Tiffany Ofili smashes record held by Jess Ennis to take European silver', http://www.mirror.co.uk/sport/other-sports/tiffany-ofili-smashes-record-held-176184, posted 5 March 2011; accessed 12 January 2015.

[67] Des Kelly, 'Plastic Brits insult our Games', *Daily Mail*, 9 March 2012, http://www.dailymail.co.uk/sport/article-2112899/London-2012-Olympics-Plastic-Brits-insult-Games-Des-Kelly.html; accessed 12 January 2015.

[68] Sportsmail Reporter, 'Team GB have 61 "plastic Brits" taking part in London Olympics', *Daily Mail*, 11 July 2012, http://www.dailymail.co.uk/sport/olympics/article-2171923/London-2012-Games-Team-GB-61-plastic-Brits.html; accessed 12 January 2015.

Cuba and Ukraine, which at the time was taken to be part of the Russian sphere of influence.

In *The Independent* Nigel Morris sought to counter the 'plastic Brits' narrative and embrace the Eddie Izzard view, drawing on research by the think-tank British Future showing that more than one third of Britain's medal winners had been born abroad or had had a foreign parent or grandparent. British Future director Sunder Katwala said:

> The record-breaking achievements of Team GB athletes have reflected an inclusive and authentic pride in the shared, multi-ethnic society that we are today. It's a different British Olympic team from the last London Games of 1948. Then, the popular sprinter McDonald Bailey from Trinidad stood out of the team photo as the only black athlete in a sea of white faces. In 2012, Team GB has changed because Britain has changed. Our athletes, selected by fierce meritocratic competition, offer an everyday snapshot of the Britain that we have become, just as the volunteers and the crowds did.[69]

However, as the *Mail* reporters well knew, nationality in the contemporary Olympic movement – as elsewhere in international sport – is (like celebrity) contingent: it comes and goes, according to circumstance. Indeed, early in 1984 the *Daily Mail* had been instrumental in obtaining British citizenship for the white South African runner Zola Budd (who had a British grandfather) in order for her to run for Britain in the Los Angeles Games of that year.[70] Moreover, when one considers the technical support that now lies behind most Olympic performances, then most medals are effectively multinational – or, alternatively, non-national achievements. Farah, for instance, had moved to Portland, Oregon, in order to work with US coach Alberto Salazar, who was based there. Wiggins, despite being described by the *Mail* as 'a quintessential Londoner',[71] had been born in Belgium to an Australian father and, in pursuit of his cycling career, lived for periods in France and Spain. At the time of London 2012 he was based at a training camp in Tenerife. It's arguable, therefore, that Olympic medals today are won via a global

---

[69] Nigel Morris, 'Plastic Brits? They were the secret of our success', *The Independent*, 14 August 2012, pp. 4–5.

[70] For an account of this episode, see the British Athletics website: http://www.britishathletics.org.uk/e-inspire/hall-of-fame-athletes/zola-budd/; accessed 12 January 2015.

[71] Jones, 'Wiggo, king of the road ... '.

sport technocracy – a cadre of coaches, physiologists, biomechanists, nutritionists, psychologists, fitness trainers and various other experts who tend to the contemporary elite athlete which transcends nationality and national culture: in Wiggins' case the close advisors who constituted his 'magic circle' were actually Australians – his coach Shane Sutton and physiologist Tim Kerrison.[72] The athletes are just as much a part of this global sport technocracy as the sport scientists and, to a significant degree, they are only constructed as national flagships – just as they are constructed as Olympic celebrities – to serve a largely promotional and media purpose. As the Conservative columnist Dominic Lawson wrote at the time of this (largely confected) controversy:

> The truth, however, is that the Olympics has for decades been an overt display of whipped-up nationalism disguising the true nature of the event – individuals stopping at nothing to pursue intensely personal ambitions. 'Team GB' could be renamed 'Team BG' and it would make no difference to almost all of those representing it. The public may feel differently – just as football supporters are much more loyal to their team than any of those who actually represent it. For the players, it is all about their careers; as one professional sportsman remarked to me: 'We are much more pragmatic than the fans realise'.[73]

---

[72] William Fotheringham, 'Magic circle turns Wiggins into a winner', *Observer Sport*, 22 July 2012, p. 4.
[73] Dominic Lawson, 'Dominic Lawson: the Olympics are about ambition, not national pride', *The Independent*, 13 March 2012, pp. 16–17, p. 17.

# 8
# Islands of Gentrification? London 2012: Politics and Legacy

This final chapter considers what the Olympic Games of London 2012 left behind. This is, of course, an important issue since it cannot be doubted, as the fictitious 'Ian Fletcher' acknowledged in an episode of the BBC's *Twenty Twelve*, that London would not have been awarded the Games if it had not made extravagant promises as to their 'legacy'. The chapter will be in three parts, dealing successively with: the apparent euphoria that attended the Games and their immediate aftermath, and the political and other claims made in relation to this euphoria; the extent to which the forecast of Lord Coe and his team that the Games would 'inspire a generation' had been, or looked like being, fulfilled, along with the (plainly linked) question of funding and sport provision, in schools and elsewhere; and the destiny of the various Olympic sites, the regeneration of this part of London having been widely seen as the decisive element in the success of the London bid.

## Tears of joy on the sofas of Britain: London 2012, politics and the feel-good factor

Around 8.30 am on the morning of 11 September, two days after the conclusion of the Olympic-Paralympic spectacle of 2012, BBC television's Breakfast programme switched, as was customary, to local BBC studios so that viewers in specific areas could receive regional news bulletins. In the East Midlands, following the news items for the area, BBC Radio Nottingham presenter Mark Dennison was invited to trail his morning programme, which would feature a phone-in. The Trades Union Congress, he announced, had recently given notice of the possibility of a strike against the government's public sector pay freeze. He then alluded to the great success of the summer's Olympics and Paralympics and ended by posing the question to prospective callers:

'A strike – is it madness?' Dennison's implication (that the Games might have brought about a nationwide coming-together in opposition to 'sectional interests') was symptomatic of a widespread, and often highly contentious, rush to a judgement of the national mood and character in the wake of London 2012.

As we've seen, the promotion of a national 'feel-good factor' was an explicit part of the rationale for giving priority to international sport performance set out in *Game Plan*, the British government strategy document of 2002. Section 2.77 of this document stated: 'The feelgood factor is the sense of euphoria in society as a whole due to an event [...] A national sports team or teams/individuals representing a country can bring about the "feelgood factor", generally, from a victory or a better than expected performance'.[1] While London 2012 never enjoyed the universal public approval that the mainstream media implied, there was little doubting the public enthusiasm for these Games, which appeared to be confirmed by an opinion poll taken during the Games themselves. In *The Guardian*, Tom Clark and Owen Gibson reported that 'A new Guardian/ICM poll has revealed that 55% of Britons say the Games are "well worth" the investment because they are doing a valuable job in cheering the country during hard times, outnumbering the 35% who regard them as a costly distraction from serious economic problems'.[2] As to what lay behind this enthusiasm, and what, if anything, it might say about, or presage for, British people in general, opinions abounded in the country's broadsheet newspapers.

With the Games about to begin, *The Guardian* columnist and former editor of *The Times* Simon Jenkins spoke for the 35% in the above poll and poured articulate scorn on the idea that the Olympic Games could promote an authentic sense of well-being in a nation. 'Nowhere outside the communist bloc has power coupled sport so clumsily as in London 2012' declared Jenkins. 'National ecstasy has been declared a duty to the state'.[3]

---

[1] Cabinet Office, 'Game Plan: a strategy for delivering Government's sport and physical activity objectives', December 2002, http://www.gamesmonitor.org.uk/files/game_plan_report.pdf; accessed 13 January 2015.

[2] Tom Clark and Owen Gibson, 'London 2012s Team GB success sparks feelgood factor', *The Guardian*, 10 August 2012, http://www.theguardian.com/sport/2012/aug/10/london-2012-team-gb-success-feelgood-factor; accessed 13 January 2015.

[3] Simon Jenkins, 'London 2012 Olympics: what price fleeting joy? For Britons, it's £9bn', *The Guardian*, 24 July 2012, http://www.theguardian.com/commentisfree/2012/jul/24/london-2012-olympics-what-price-happiness; accessed 14 January 2015.

Watching sport fills a moment of time with a degree of suspense, with outcomes happy or sad according to loyalty. But claiming well-being from the national performance at sport is dangerous. [...] Apart from athletes, few people outside the construction and security industries profit from Olympics. So ministers resort to mendacity. They hype the Games out of all proportion, hiring consultants to claim an implausible 'legacy payback' for the £9bn outlay.[4]

Jenkins' advice, paraphrasing Ralph Waldo Emerson's famous aphorism, was that 'when bidden to mute ecstasy by politicians who have just blown £9 billion on national pride, grown-up citizens have every right to count their spoons'.[5]

Immediately after the Games the columnist Boyd Tonkin offered a thought-provoking, if ultimately elusive, analysis. Comparing the popular euphoria of London 2012 to the outpouring of public emotion 15 years earlier on the death of the Princess of Wales, Tonkin judged both events to have been indications of how British society had become

more expressive, less deferential, adept at marrying a generous humane idealism with rampant celebrity-worship – rather than how it might in the future change. If so, then maybe we should look back at the Olympic and Paralympic summer not as a time when Britain altered, but when we noticed that it had.[6]

'All the intractable divisions of British society remain', he acknowledged.

Still, from the time in May that the Olympic flame began to pass from town to town through always-cheerful crowds, it became clear to any unbigoted observer that most people both wanted to enjoy the show, and were prepared to make it succeed. Moreover, as soon as the competition kicked off, we could see the somewhat camp, music-hall

---

[4] Ibid.

[5] Ibid.; the original phrase was 'We were not deceived by the professions of the private adventurer – the louder he talked of his honour, the faster we counted our spoons...', taken from Emerson's work of 1860, *Conduct of Life: A Philosophical Reading*; see Ralph Waldo Emerson, *Conduct of Life* (London: The Waverley Company Ltd, 1908), p. 203.

[6] Boyd Tonkin, 'The delight has been irresistible. but how will this Olympic euphoria seem to us in 15 years' time?', *The Independent*, 11 September 2012, p. 7.

patriotism that cheered along the British athletes left room for a grudge-free appreciation of everyone else's talent and success.[7]

Whether, quoting Shakespeare's *The Tempest*, this grudge-free enthusiasm would amount to no more than 'fancy's images', or its meaning grow into 'something of great constancy', was unclear. 'That's up to us', Tonkin ended obscurely. 'The play has ended; the work begins'.[8]

Over the weekend of the conclusion of the Olympics there were various expressions of the conviction that London 2012 had revitalised, or the hope that they could in some way re-moralise, the nation, or some important section of it. An editorial announced 'A nation whose sense of itself has been utterly transformed'.[9] Sports correspondent James Lawton suggested that the purported courtesies of the Games would be a lesson to 'our offensive, overpaid footballers'. London 2012, he said, had

> so powerfully reminded us of what sport can be when it is played in a certain spirit. When, for example, it is not irreparably scarred by the cheating and the rancour that have become so deep-seated among many of the multimillionaire and, on important occasions, too-often-mediocre footballers. Some are holding out the hope that these Olympics of Usain Bolt and Jessica Ennis, Michael Phelps and Sir Chris Hoy and Mo Farah may just make some of the plutocrats of the Premier League stop and think about who they are and how they have come to be seen in the eyes of ordinary people.[10]

Alan Hubbard judged that:

> For British sport, this has been a triumph of the human spirit. Not one engineered by backroom boffins built on loads-a-Lottery-money and home advantage, but one built by the endeavours of dedicated athletes in many sports, endeavours that have been unprecedented and received with a pride that has been lacking in the nation of late.

---

[7] Ibid.

[8] Ibid.

[9] *The Independent*, 13 August 2012, p. 42.

[10] James Lawton, 'Let's hope our offensive, overpaid footballers have been watching the Games', *The Independent*, 11 August 2012, http://www.independent.co.uk/voices/commentators/james-lawton-lets-hope-our-offensive-overpaid-footballers-have-been-watching-the-games-8031711.html; accessed 14 January 2015.

'Inspire a Generation' has been the Games' slogan, and the hope is that they already have.[11]

Similarly, writer Tim Lott detected a strong element of national self-discovery:

> The Olympics have been different. It is truly a theatre of the citizens, not the subjects, of the UK and we have surprised ourselves in many different ways. We have discovered that we can make things work: even Swiss newspapers have admired our clockwork efficiency. We have discovered that we are deeply, well, nice. This is a national trait that was identified by Orwell who wrote that 'the gentleness of the English civilisation is perhaps its most marked characteristic'. This was obvious on dozens of occasions but captured most memorably for me in the down-to-earth demeanour of the cyclist Laura Trott and a few days ago, boxing star Nicola Adams saying, bathetically, of her gold medal: 'It made my day.' Compare and contrast with Usain Bolt's 'I am now a living legend'.[12]

And, beneath the headline 'It's not your looks that count, it's giving your heart and soul', the writer Joanna Moorhead expressed the hope that her teenage children would relinquish their trash TV addiction in favour of the worthier ideals of fame held out by Team GB:

> Real fame isn't the nonsense that TV companies serve up for teenage ghettos, conspiring with other commercial interests to promise an unattainable future. Odd that they call it 'reality TV'. But the Olympics, on the other hand, was the genuine article. Every single member of Team GB had only got there because of real grit, real sweat, and real tears. Their stories are of fortitude – like that of the cycling pursuit rider Jo Rowsell who has suffered from alopecia since her teens; or the judo competitor Gemma Gibbons, who, as she finished her match, mouthed 'I love you Mum' up to the mother who died of leukaemia.[13]

---

[11] Alan Hubbard, 'London: A triumph of the human spirit', *Independent on Sunday*, 12 August 2012, p. 6.
[12] Tim Lott, 'We have surprised ourselves – and our potential is unlimited', *Independent on Sunday*, 12 August 2012, p. 42.
[13] Joanna Moorhead, 'It's not your looks that count, it's giving your heart and soul', *Independent on Sunday*, 12 August 2012, p. 39.

These optimistic judgements were, of course, dubious – not simply because they were rendered so close to the Games themselves. It cannot, for instance, be convincingly argued that Jessica Ennis' looks had not been a factor in the prolonged advertising campaigns that had preceded the Games. Nor can a nation's culture be reduced to single behaviour characteristics, such as 'niceness'. Nor can decisive shifts in national culture be brought about by an event lasting a few days. As Howard Jacobson pointed out 'We British are not suddenly such a lovely people on account of all our medals'.[14] Social psychology professor Christine Griffin, interviewed for the *Big Issue*, a magazine supporting the homeless, was similarly sceptical: 'There's a more positive mood in certain areas, but it's not clear how widespread it is. If you're in a bad state economically – you've just lost your job, you face repossession – to see everybody all jolly can make you feel worse'.[15] Expectably, though, politicians moved quickly to avail themselves of London 2012 euphoria. For example, David Cameron's former speechwriter Ian Birrell now published this exhortation:

> If the Government could bottle the Olympic spirit, its problems would be solved. We should note in passing that it was the vision of much-derided politicians that brought the Games here and ensured they were a success. Equally, few have failed to notice the pivotal role played by the 70,000 volunteers, whose friendliness and good humour ensured that they lived up to their moniker as Games Makers. They should inspire Mr Cameron to be bold and true to himself by returning to the themes of the Big Society.[16] The idea was often poorly expressed, badly executed and became ensnared in arguments over whether it was a snake-oil cover for cuts despite originating in happier economic times. But at its heart was a powerful idea of individuals coming together to determine their futures rather than relying on the state.[17]

---

[14] Howard Jacobson, 'We British are not suddenly such a lovely people on account of all our medals', *The Independent*, 14 September 2012, p. 41.

[15] Julian Owen, 'Putting the Great in Britain', *Big Issue*, 13–19 August 2012, pp. 17 and 19, p. 17.

[16] The idea that volunteer groups could run public services such as post offices, libraries, transport and housing projects. It was a theme of the Conservative General Election campaign of 2010 and was reiterated by Cameron in a speech at Liverpool Hope University in July of that year; see http://www.bbc.co.uk/news/uk-10680062, posted 19 July 2010; accessed 14 January 2015.

[17] Ian Birrell, 'Cameron must now embrace the spirit of the Games', *The Independent*, 13 August 2012, pp. 42–43, p. 43.

Conservative MEP (Member of the European Parliament) Daniel Hannan suggested that

> the sight of so many delirious parents watching their now grown-up children [compete in the Olympics] – the children whom they had happily ferried to training session after training session – is a reminder that families are much better than government agencies as providers of education, inspiration, healthcare, social security and discipline.[18]

Defence Minister Philip Hammond artfully exempted the military from his party's concern to roll back the state, claiming that, since the army had stepped in to provide Olympic security following the default of G4S, the Games had 'humanised the face of the armed forces'[19] – recently engaged in unpopular wars in Iraq and Afghanistan. And Conservative Mayor of London Boris Johnson reflected that, through the Olympics, 'Kids around the country are seeing that the more you put in, the more you get out – which is a wonderful Conservative lesson in life'.[20] Johnson, indeed, was the politician to make the most significant political intervention in the immediate aftermath of the Games. His speech at the athletes' Victory Parade in London on 10 September was a tour de force, widely seen as upstaging Prime Minister Cameron (who was standing next to him) and triggering further press talk of a 'Boris bounce' in the direction of the Conservative Party leadership.[21] Johnson's address, playing on his practised 'naughty boy' public persona, was a seductive mix of congratulation, patriotism, Conservative politicking and mildly bawdy humour. He thanked the ancillary staff of the Games – the armed services, the police, the volunteers, the transport operators and even

---

[18] Daniel Hannan, 'Multiculturalism? Nonsense. The Olympics are a victory for patriotism and common British values', *Daily Mail*, 7 August 2012, http://www.dailymail.co.uk/debate/article-2184689/Multiculturalism-Nonsense-The-Olympics-victory-patriotism-common-British-values.html; accessed 14 January 2015.

[19] Oliver Wright, 'The Games humanised the face of the armed forces', *The Independent*, 14 August 2012, pp. 14–15, p. 15.

[20] Daniel Hannan, 'Multiculturalism? Nonsense . . . .'.

[21] See, for example, Telegraph Reporters, 'Boris Johnson as leader would give Tories a six point bounce, says new poll', *Daily Telegraph*, 12 September 2012, http://www.telegraph.co.uk/news/politics/9537477/Boris-Johnson-as-leader-would-give-Tories-a-six-point-bounce-says-new-poll.html; accessed 14 January 2015.

G4S – sensing (and, almost certainly, expecting) the audience's surprise, he insisted 'yes, all the G4S workers'. Having only two weeks earlier expressed anxiety as to the British medal tally, he now, to thunderous applause, paid tribute to 'the greatest team of athletes ever assembled in this country'. He told them that they had 'showed every child in this country that success is not just about talent and luck but about grit and guts and hard work and coming back from defeat' – the familiar right wing invocation of 'self-help'. Fumbling with some sport history, he informed the throng that Team GB had 'brought sport home to a city and country, where by and large, it was invented and codified [and] you brought home the truth about us and about this country – that when we put our minds to it, there is no limit to what Britain can achieve'. For good measure, he threw in some laddish sexual suggestiveness, beginning his remarks by observing that the Olympics had come to a 'final tear-sodden, juddering climax' and later telling the team 'you produced such paroxysms and tears of joy on the sofas of Britain that you probably not only inspired a generation, but helped to create one as well...'[22]

It's difficult to think that any long-term personal or party political advantage could be gained from this speech. Jokily, it exploited the public euphoria to wrap the whole Games, its leading performers, myriad support workers and even some of its more contentious aspects (G4S, the viability of Coe's promise to 'Inspire a Generation'....), in the Union Jack. At that moment any further questions of legacy seemed politically impossible to raise.

## 'If I hear that phrase one more time...': London 2012 and sporting legacy

Perhaps unknowingly, Johnson had affirmed the contemporary politics of sport, wherein national priority and finance were accorded to elite athletes to facilitate their regime of hard work and the remainder of their compatriots sat on their sofas, waiting to have their emotions stirred by a British victory in some televised sporting spectacle. As Owen Gibson observed:

> The most secure aspect of the legacy is that for elite Olympic and Paralympic sport. The heroes of the summer of 2012 have cemented in the public and political mind that the investment of lottery funds

---

[22] The speech can be seen in full at: https://www.youtube.com/watch?v= 57gg2sinGK0; accessed 14 January 2015.

in a competitive team is a worthwhile one. That funding has been guaranteed through to Rio 2016…[23]

This, of course, flew in the face of any undertaking by the London 2012 promotions to inspire a generation to physical activity. After all, as we saw in Chapter 2, back in 2007 Coe had told researcher David Conn: 'I'm not sure that, in any previous Games, there was as much thought given to legacy across all its manifestations as we are giving it here now' and the following year in Beijing then Prime Minister Gordon Brown had promised that the London Games would 'inspire fitness and help tackle obesity. The Olympics can inspire people. More people will give up smoking, less people will become obese'. In December of that year Sport England had announced a government investment of '£480 million to deliver grassroots sporting opportunities and a lasting Olympic legacy of one million people playing more sport'.[24] Secretary of State for Culture, Media and Sport, Andy Burnham MP, had said:

> Ahead of 2012, we have a once-in-a-lifetime opportunity to get more people participating regularly in sport. This will be a tough challenge, but with this huge investment in the broadest range of sports, we believe it can be done. We want a world-leading community sport system in this country driven by the expertise of our national governing bodies, working with Sport England. This will mean excellent sports clubs, quality facilities and more opportunities for people to get involved in sport.[25]

The following year his successor Ben Bradshaw had told the press: 'I wouldn't want to be in a position where we have an array of gold medals at the Olympics and more armchair sports enthusiasts who are not doing it themselves. That would not be a legacy we could be proud of as a nation'.[26] And Lord Coe had maintained this theme well into the

---

[23] Owen Gibson, 'London Olympics triumph gives way to more sober focus on the legacy', *The Guardian*, 6 September 2012, http://www.theguardian.com/sport/2012/sep/06/olympics-legacy-coe; accessed 16 January 2015.

[24] '£480 million investment in 46 sports to deliver sporting opportunities for all', http://archive.sportengland.org/media_centre/press_releases/£480m_investment_in_46_sports.aspx, posted 16 December 2008; accessed 18 January 2015.

[25] Ibid.

[26] Owen Gibson, 'Ben Bradshaw: I do not want array of medals if it means more armchair fans', *The Guardian*, 17 December 2009, http://www.theguardian.com/sport/2009/dec/17/ben-bradshaw-2012-olympics-london; accessed 16 January 2015.

Games themselves, stating in the second week in August 2012: 'We have to recognise that we are likely to be the first generation of parents that are fitter than our kids. [...] Everybody recognises that giving young people a competitive outlet through sport is a very good thing...'[27]

While broken promises long since ceased to raise eyebrows in Western political discourse, the validity of claims of sporting legacy for these, and any other, Olympics remains vitally important to examine. There are, admittedly, real difficulties in doing so. One is the deliberate vagueness of the promises of Olympic legacy, which makes them both open to interpretation and adjustable in retrospect. For example, in 2013 it was made known that:

> In the seven years during which the Games were delivered, at an eventual cost of £8.8 billion to the public purse, a host of other legacy promises were added to the mix. Some of them, such as a promise to get 1 million more people playing sport three or more times a week by 2013, were later dropped. Friday's report will instead trumpet the 1.4m more people playing sport once a week since the bid was won in 2005.[28]

Secondly, in the case of London 2012, the fulfilment of legacy promises (the 'delivery of legacy' in the government lexicon) has been supervised largely by the people who made them – Lord Coe, who stood down as the government's 'Olympic legacy ambassador' in 2013 and ex-Prime Minister Tony Blair, who became an advisor to the British Labour Party on Olympic legacy in 2012. To compound the already considerable a priori difficulty of making any meaningful assessment of the fruits of these Olympics, Blair had made the somewhat enigmatic statement at the outset of London 2012 that the legacy of the Games could not be judged until a decade after they were over.[29]

There's little doubt that London 2012 proved inspirational in some quarters. For example, immediately after the Games two young East Enders – Amber Charles, the basketball player from Bow who had been

---

[27] Robin Scott-Elliot and Richard Garner, 'We risk having children who are less fit than their parents', *The Independent*, 11 August 2012, p. 8.

[28] Owen Gibson, 'Lord Coe: I'm quitting to make sure Olympic legacy is delivered', *The Guardian*, 19 July 2013, http://www.theguardian.com/sport/2013/jul/19/lord-coe-quits-ambassador-olympic-legacy; accessed 15 January 2015.

[29] Owen Gibson, 'Tony Blair tells London 2012 critics to show "a bit of pride"', *The Guardian*, 25 July 2012, http://www.theguardian.com/politics/2012/jul/25/tony-blair-london-2012-critics; accessed 15 January 2015.

a member of the British delegation to Singapore in 2005, and Rumi Begum of Whitechapel, who ran a sports club for local youth – were interviewed on the US radio station NPR about the Games' impact. Both young women testified to the influence of the Games in the multi-ethnic East End. Charles cited:

> Jessica Ennis, the heptathlete. Obviously, she's the poster girl and everyone loves her and, also, she is from that mixed heritage background, so I think she appeals to a lot of people, like, in my area, as well. You got some basketball players like Luol Deng. He grew up here in Brixton,[30] but I think Jessica Ennis is a big poster for a lot of girls trying to compete.[31]

The interviewer, Jacki Lyden, asked Begum how the Games had gone down in the strong Bengali community in East London:

> Lyden: 'Rumi, over 30 percent of the population in your neighbourhood share Bengali heritage, people from Bangladesh, including your own family, and this is Ramadan.'
> Begum: 'Yeah.'
> Lyden: 'Can you tell us a little bit more about the connection between Bengali people and sport?'
> Begum: 'I mean, in my community in general, it's always been something that we don't really think about, especially when it stereotypically is not something that girls get involved with. But that's something that I, myself, want to change. The Olympics has really been able to sort of change views about how it's not – the stereotypes you get about academic careers, going into sort of finance and law and things like that. There's sport, as well, and it's an amazing career to get into and get involved with.'[32]

Indeed, it's in the matter of strengthening the campaign for sporting females that some of the strongest claims for the legacy of London 2012

---

[30] Deng, typically for an Olympic athlete, had lived in several countries. Born in the Sudan in 1985, he moved to Egypt as a child and grew up in South London. He migrated to the United States at the age of 14 and at the time of London 2012 was playing basketball for the Chicago Bulls.

[31] 'Can East London keep the Olympic spirit burning?', http://www.npr.org/2012/08/13/158694545/can-east-london-keep-the-olympic-spirit-burning; accessed 15 January 2015.

[32] Ibid.

can be made. The Games themselves were trailed in some quarters as 'The Women's Games' – *The Independent*,[33] the *Daily Telegraph*,[34] CNN[35] and the British Channel Four News[36] all ran features on this theme and the *Daily Mail* welcomed female competitors from Saudi Arabia, Qatar and Brunei with the headline 'The Muslim women who overcame the odds and the prejudice to make history today on the Olympic stage'.[37] Nicola Adams, a 29 year old, openly bisexual Afro-Caribbean woman from Burmantofts, an inner city district of Leeds, won the first gold medal for women's boxing. The comedian and columnist Mark Steel paid tribute to the growing enthusiasm for women's football, having attended the Olympic semi-final between Japan and France:

> There were 61,000 fans at this game, yet it's only 18 months since two of the most prominent football TV presenters in the country believed women had no place in the sport whatsoever [a reference to the Sky TV football commentators Richard Keys and Andy Gray who had been taken off air in January 2011 for sexist comments about female football officials].[38]

And Maria Miller, who became Secretary of State for Culture, Media and Sport in early September, called immediately for more coverage

---

[33] Robin Scott-Elliot, 'The Women's Games', *The Independent*, 26 July 2012, pp. 6–7.

[34] Paul Kelso, 'London 2012 Olympics: women ushering in a golden age of sporting equality following successes at Games', *Daily Telegraph*, 9 August 2012, http://www.telegraph.co.uk/sport/olympics/9465660/London-2012-Olympics-women-ushering-in-a-golden-age-of-sporting-equality-following-successes-at-Games.html; accessed 15 January 2015.

[35] Sarah Brown, 'London 2012: the women's Olympics?', http://edition.cnn.com/2012/08/10/sport/london-olympics-women/, posted 10 August 2012; accessed 15 January 2015.

[36] 'London 2012: was this the women's Olympics?', http://www.channel4.com/news/london-2012-is-this-the-womens-olympics, posted 12 August 2012; accessed 15 January 2015.

[37] Adam Shergold, 'The Muslim women who overcame the odds and the prejudice to make history today on the Olympic stage', *Daily Mail*, 3 August 2012, http://www.dailymail.co.uk/news/article-2183262/Olympics-2012-The-Muslim-women-overcame-odds-make-London.html; accessed 15 January 2015.

[38] Mark Steel, 'Mark Steel: cyclists, women, refugees – vindicated at last', *The Independent*, 9 August 2012, http://www.independent.co.uk/voices/commentators/mark-steel/mark-steel-cyclists-women-refugees–vindicated-at-last-8022577.html; accessed 15 January 2015.

of women's sport: 'The British media has done a fantastic job championing the achievements of our female athletes at London 2012. But outside the Olympics and Paralympics women's sport has been woefully under-represented on television'.[39]

Beyond this, though, the promised legacy was less in evidence. The month before London 2012 Sport England published once-a-week participation rates for Olympic sports for the period October 2010–October 2011, compared to the same 12 months in 2007–2008. Cycling, as we saw in Chapter 6, had attracted 150,000 new participants and other sports (athletics, football, golf, tennis, hockey...) had prospered more modestly, but the rate of participation among the young had not risen at all. Robin Scott-Elliot wrote:

> In 2005/6, 3.7 million 16- to 25-year-olds played sport once a week; now it's 3.8 million – with the increase in population in this age bracket, this represents an actual decline of 1.6 per cent. Coe's claim that the Games would inspire a generation remains a distant hope as the figures flatline.[40]

A year on and the same reporter was writing of an overall decline in participation:

> Significantly fewer people in England are now playing sport regularly than before the Olympics, prompting accusations that the Government has already squandered the legacy of London 2012. Participation figures published today by Sport England show that nearly a year on from the golden glow of the Games, 20 out of 29 sports recorded a fall in the number of adults taking part between April 2012 and April 2013.[41]

However, this decline could not necessarily be ascribed either to a reluctance to play sport or to a failure to be inspired by London 2012.

---

[39] Oliver Wright, 'New Culture Secretary wants more coverage of women's sports', *The Independent*, 15 September 2012, p. 18.

[40] Robin Scott-Elliot, 'Olympic boost to sporting activity fails to inspire the young', *The Independent*, 23 June 2012, p. 15.

[41] Robin Scott-Elliot, 'Significantly fewer people now playing sport regularly than before last year's Olympic Games', *The Independent*, 14 June 2013, http://www.independent.co.uk/news/uk/politics/significantly-fewer-people-now-playing-sport-regularly-than-before-last-years-olympic-games-8658107.html; accessed 15 January 2015.

It was increasingly being brought home to those who organised sport for the young at grassroots level that inspiration was one thing, but the wherewithal to act upon it quite another: London 2012 was accompanied by swingeing reductions in spending on youth sport. In 2010 the then Minister for Education Michael Gove had abandoned the School Sport Partnership (SSP), which had encompassed 450 projects supporting PE, sport and physical activity in schools. Gove told the BBC that he was concerned about the lack of competitiveness being inculcated in children via sport:

> One of the problems with the existing system that we have had is that we haven't seen the increase in the number of people playing competitive sport. [...] Unlike the situation we have at the moment where the number of people playing rugby, hockey and football has either flat-lined, or gone down in some cases, we'll have a revival of team sports.[42]

(After protests Gove partially reversed his decision, extending SSP until 2013 on a much reduced budget.) During the Olympics health correspondent Denis Campbell wrote:

> At the time of Gove's decision the Youth Sport Trust predicted it would mean 'carnage' for school sport. Two years on the reality is certainly worrying. Only about 30% of local authority areas still have a fully-functioning SSP, and those that survive do so thanks to support from councillors or business people convinced of their value, the trust believes.[43]

On 7 August, with the Games in full swing, the government announced that it would scrap compulsory targets for the minimum number of hours of physical education in British schools. Like Gove, Cameron insisted that this was because of a lack of competitiveness in school sport:

> If the problem is money it would be solved by money. [...] I would like to promote competitive sport – we need more competition, more

---

[42] 'Michael Gove defends school sports funding change', http://www.bbc.co.uk/news/uk-politics-11805413, posted 21 November 2010; accessed 15 January 2015.
[43] Denis Campbell, 'Michael Gove's political own goal on school sports', *The Guardian*, 6 August 2012, http://www.theguardian.com/education/2012/aug/06/michael-gove-own-goal-school-sports; accessed 15 January 2015.

competitiveness, getting rid of the idea of all-must-have prizes and you cannot have competitive sports days. We need a big cultural change in favour of competitive sports.[44]

Two days later, doubtless feeling defensive, given the apparent con-tradiction between the promise to inspire a generation and what his government was now doing, Cameron promised National Lottery fund-ing for elite sport, but, as for the two hours of school sport no longer required, he claimed: 'The two hours that is laid down is often met through sort of Indian dancing classes. Now, I've got nothing against Indian dancing classes, but that's not really sport'.[45] The notion that either British sports teachers or the Labour Party were against compe-tition or that they were counselling 'prizes for all' was a parliamentary shibboleth – something (like being 'soft on crime') of which one party might routinely accuse the other in the House of Commons. But the Prime Minister was able to avail himself of a parallel hare, set running the previous week by chair of the British Olympic Association and for-mer Conservative sport minister Lord Moynihan, who had announced that 40% of British Olympic competitors at the 2008 Games in Beijing, and 50% of British medallists, had been educated in private schools; calling this 'wholly unacceptable', Moynihan stated: 'There is so much talent out there in the 93% [of the population not attending private schools] that should be identified and developed. That has got to be a priority for future sports policy'.[46]

The popular and most convincing response to Moynihan's finding was that this was to be expected, given the privileges of Britain's private schools, and many will have agreed with the chair of the educational charity the Sutton Trust Sir Peter Lampl, who told the *London Evening Standard*:

While we congratulate all our Olympic winners, this research shows that independent school students are more than five times

---

[44] Patrick Wintour, 'David Cameron defends move to scrap compulsory targets for school sport', *The Guardian*, 8 August 2012, http://www.theguardian.com/education/2012/aug/08/cameron-scraps-targets-school-sport; accessed 15 Jan-uary 2015.

[45] Patrick Wintour, 'David Cameron promises extra lottery funding for elite sport', *The Guardian*, 10 August 2012, http://www.theguardian.com/uk/2012/aug/10/david-cameron-lottery-funding-sport; accessed 15 January 2015.

[46] Olympics 'dominated by privately educated', *BBC News*, 3 August 2012, http://www.bbc.co.uk/news/education-19109724; accessed 15 January 2015.

over-represented amongst our medal winners relative to their proportion in the population – which is also the case at leading universities
and in the professions more generally.

This comes as no surprise as children in independent schools benefit
from ample time set aside for sport, excellent sporting facilities and
highly qualified coaches, while in many state schools sport is not a
priority, and sadly playing fields have been sold off.[47]

(At the time of writing, the basic fees per term at Millfield School in
Somerset, the British private school whose curriculum features sport
most strongly and where two British gold medallists at London 2012
were educated, are £11,150.[48])

But, as indicated, the preferred government view was that the fault lay
within the state schools and their neglect of competitive sport. An editorial in the *Daily Telegraph* probably spoke for the Prime Minister in
asserting:

Since the strikes of the Eighties, many teachers have been reluctant
to supervise after-school sport without financial reward. To turn this
round, schools need not just resources – such as pools or playing
fields – but a whole-hearted embrace of sport and its benefits. The
motto of these Games is 'Inspire a Generation'. We must ensure that
it ends up as a mission statement, rather than a slogan.[49]

Similarly, Anthony Seldon, Master of (the private) Wellington College,
called on the government to

[47] 'London 2012 Olympics: private school pupils "five times over represented"
in Team GB medal table', *London Evening Standard*, 14 August 2012, http://
www.standard.co.uk/olympics/olympic-news/london-2012-olympics-private-
school-pupils-five-times-over-represented-in-team-gb-medal-table-8045841.
html; accessed 15 January 2015.
[48] See http://millfieldschool.com/sites/default/files/downloads/Admissions/Fees/
Senior_Fees_2014–15.pdf; accessed 16 January 2015. The fees may, of course,
have been altered since I checked. They are unlikely to have gone down; see
also Rosa Silverman, 'London 2012 Olympics: the private school that produced
eight of the Olympians', *Daily Telegraph*, 7 August 2012, http://www.telegraph.
co.uk/sport/olympics/9459003/London-2012-Olympics-The-private-school-that-
produced-eight-of-the-Olympians.html; accessed 16 January 2015.
[49] 'Raise state schools to Olympic standard', *Daily Telegraph*, 2 August 2012,
http://www.telegraph.co.uk/comment/telegraph-view/9446852/Raise-state-
schools-to-Olympic-standard.html; accessed 15 January 2015.

tell schools that extra-curricular activities should be offered widely to all, and that academic standards will not be jeopardised, but enhanced by doing so. The vision and inspiration that heads could offer their staff and pupils at the start of the coming academic year, inspired by the Olympics, could blow away and delight their teachers and students. May our whole school system be re-forged in steel by these Games.[50]

And Conservative writer David Thomas, while accepting that the 'vast gulf between state and private provision has just been forcibly illustrated by the fact that the Olympic rowing was held at Eton College's private rowing lake', nevertheless insisted that state schools were

actively opposed to competitive sport at primary level and even the best comprehensives seem half-hearted in their commitment. Politicians can say what they like about the need for change, but this isn't a matter of the odd speech here and policy document there. It means an investment of time, money and, above all, the will to create an educational culture that sees sport as central to education.[51]

(These assertions, it has to be said, married well with an established narrative in British politics in the late twentieth and early twenty first centuries wherein, contrary to the conventional political wisdom of the 1960s and 70s, state schools were being depicted not only as inferior to private ones, but as failing the working class child. Educationist Sally Tomlinson, for example, has suggested that a consensus between Labour and the Conservatives formed around 'one of the cruellest and most pointless policies developed in the wake of the Education Act of 1993' – passed by the Conservative administration of John Major – 'that of attacking so-called "failing schools" '.[52] This, of course, became a pretext for privatising these schools – at the Conservative Party Conference one month after the London Games, David Cameron called for: 'state schools given all the freedoms, and carrying all the high expectations,

[50] Anthony Seldon, 'Let the Games inspire a new vision for schools', *The Independent*, 2 August 2012, http://www.independent.co.uk/voices/commentators/anthony-seldon-let-the-games-inspire-a-new-vision-for-schools-7999203.html; accessed 16 January 2015.
[51] David Thomas, 'Come and share my Eton playing fields', *The Independent*, 21 August 2012, p. 17.
[52] Sally Tomlinson, *Education in a Post-Welfare Society* (Maidenhead: Open University Press, 2005), p. 79.

of private schools. Yes – that's my plan – millions of children sent to independent schools ... independent schools, in the state sector'.[53])

Malcolm Trobe, deputy general secretary of the Association of School and College Leaders, protested: 'The prime minister's criticisms of school sport are ill-informed, unfair and fail to recognise the huge contribution that many teachers make to sports in schools. Many teachers, not just PE staff, willingly give of their time to motivate and coach young people in a wide range of sports'.[54] But, political rhetoric aside, the message to those organising and administering sport for the variously 'inspired' young people of Britain was, as they well knew, that they would have to make bricks without straw – that much now relied on their voluntary effort. As Rumi Begum reflected to her interviewer:

> It was a massive change when losing funding. The organization I work with – we started off being the school's sports partnership. We were – you know, we were majorly government funded and we've lost all our funding now, so we've had to cut back on so many things and it's been, obviously, really hard, but if it's something that you're passionate about and something you want to keep going, then you know, you'd find a means to it, I guess.[55]

The British-Cypriot ex-Olympic athlete Fatima Whitbread (born in north London in 1961 and winner of a silver medal for the javelin at the Seoul Games of 1988) was more forthright. Whitbread, who had spent nearly 30 years working on development programmes linking schools and sports clubs in the south east of England argued:

> It is sheer hypocrisy of the government to indulge in the success of the London Olympics, which has seen such outstanding British athletic achievement, to spout the 'Inspire a Generation' strap line and then to cut back on provision for school sports. By scrapping the compulsory two-hour weekly minimum of PE for pupils and abolishing regulation on the minimum size of school playing fields, we are

---

[53] 'David Cameron's Conservative Party Conference speech: in full', http://www.telegraph.co.uk/news/politics/conservative/9598534/David-Camerons-Conservative-Party-Conference-speech-in-full.html, posted 10 October 2012; accessed 18 January 2015.
[54] Patrick Wintour, 'David Cameron defends move to scrap compulsory targets for school sport'.
[55] 'Can East London keep the Olympic spirit burning?'.

doing a disservice to this next generation of potential champions. It is already absurd that some schools within miles of the Olympic Park have to use car parks to play games on. Instead of cutting back, now is the time to invest in the grassroots and capitalise on the youthful interest [in] a broad range of Olympic sports.[56]

A link to Whitbread's article was put on Twitter by Edinburgh Napier University lecturer David Jarman. Responding to the slogan 'Inspire a generation', fellow academic David McGillivray, of the University of the West of Scotland, speaking for many outside of the mainstream media, replied 'If I hear that phrase again . . . '[57] In January 2013 the press returned to Amber Charles, now 22, to ask her reaction to the news that, after the British basketball team's failure to 'medal' in the London Games, its funding had been cut. Charles, who had hoped to represent Britain at basketball in the Rio Olympics of 2016, told the *Daily Mail*:

I am utterly dismayed and shocked by the decision by UK Sport to cut funding to the GB Basketball programme to zero. London 2012 was about inspiring the youth of the world through sport. People like me, keeping my dream alive. I just do not understand how all the great work of the 2012 Games – with so much focus on legacy – can then mean my sport being cast aside so soon after London 2012'.[58]

As proponent of, and subsequent 'ambassador' for, the legacy of London, Lord Coe seemed anxious to distance himself from the details of this. When in March 2013 Olympic enthusiast Alan Hubbard reported that in

Merton, South London, the sale of a public sports hall to a private school by the council has left Olympic medallist Ray Stevens without

[56] Fatima Whitbread, 'Olympic promises to "inspire a generation" look like hot air to me', *The Guardian*, 16 August 2012, http://www.theguardian.com/commentisfree/2012/aug/16/olympics-inspire-generation-fatima-whitbread; accessed 16 January 2015.
[57] https://twitter.com/dsrjarman/status/236141026442616832; accessed 16 January 2015.
[58] David Kent, 'Olympic hopeful "dismayed and shocked" by government cuts to basketball funding', *MailOnline*, http://www.dailymail.co.uk/sport/othersports/article-2270048/Olympic-basketball-hopeful-Amber-Charles-reacts-government-cuts-funding.html, posted 29 January 2013; accessed 16 January 2015.

a home for the judo club he set up six years ago and which regularly attracts classes of 400 over five nights a week, many of whom are disabled or disadvantaged kids.

He noted that Lord Coe was a former pupil of Stevens and asked Coe about the matter. Coe's response was that 'legacy will come good as part of what he calls his "ten year mission" '.[59] Four months later Coe said, enigmatically, that he regretted that the issue of 'school sport became tribal' and was pitching legacy even further into the future: 'My challenge to politicians of all political persuasions is that this is a 20-year mission and a 10-year journey. We're only 45 weeks into it.'[60]

Late in 2013 came convincing evidence that the purported sporting legacy – the next generation of the nation's children engaging in large numbers in sport and physical activity – had not been achieved. Following publication of the Health Survey for England, Alexandra Topping reported that:

> Most children are not getting the daily exercise recommended by the NHS and the promised Olympic legacy of a healthier, happier and more active nation has failed to materialise, according to figures [ . . . ] The 2012 survey of 8,000 adults and 2,000 children found that only 16% of girls aged five to 15 get the recommended hour of exercise a day, despite a nationwide push to get more playing sports. Only 21% of boys get the required exercise compared with 28% in 2008, falling to 14% for 13- to 15-year-olds. Only 9% of boys and 10% of girls aged between two and four meet the requirement of three hours activity a day.[61]

Furthermore, recalling Gordon Brown's improbable undertaking in Beijing in 2008: 'Fourteen percent of boys and girls aged two–15 are classed as obese, and 28% as either overweight or obese. Nineteen per cent of boys and 17% of girls in the lowest income bracket were

[59] Alan Hubbard, 'No doubts over Coe's legacy pledge', http://www.insidethegames.biz/blogs/1013511-alan-hubbard-no-doubts-over-coe-s-legacy-pledge, posted 27 March 2013; accessed 16 January 2015.
[60] Ibid.
[61] Alexandra Topping, 'Olympics fail to create healthier and more active population, says survey', *The Guardian*, 18 December 2013, http://www.theguardian.com/uk-news/2013/dec/18/olympics-fail-create-healthier-active-health-survey-of-england; accessed 16 January 2015.

deemed to be obese compared with 8% and 7% respectively from the richest households'.[62]

It is, to be sure, doubtful that the 'communications' team which concocted and publicised the slogan 'Inspire a generation' ever gave much thought to whether, and if so, how, London 2012 would do so. The ethos of the impression management industry gives priority to 'getting your message across'; it is concerned with the efficacy of the message (its effectiveness in 'winning hearts and minds') and not with the validity or ultimate consummation of that message. Moreover, as demonstrated by a number of the thoughtful responses that were made to Topping's article when it was put on *The Guardian*'s website, the assumptions built into this strapline were questionable. For example, echoing a key point raised in David Conn's radio programme of 2007 by Matt Jackson of the Institute of Public Policy Research, 'OffWhite' wrote: 'the real question that was never properly addressed is how exactly perfect physical specimens winning medals in mainly individual pursuits is supposed to inspire people to take up sport. If you're an inactive individual, what is it about Mo Farah that would make you want to take up running?'[63] Similarly, it was plainly a mistake to equate exercise with sport – as 'AminoAcid' argued: 'When will these busybodies get it into their heads that exercise does not = sport [ ... ]. Many people are put off exercise by all the nonsense surrounding competitive sport at any level'.[64] And '1BeerOnSchoolNights' was one of a number to cite the sedentary lifestyles that Olympic partners help to promote as reasons for lack of fitness: 'Cars make people fat. People, especially kids, are becoming more obese because they are in car-dependent families. Sport is good for fitness if you are committed to doing it properly, but active travel over your lifetime will probably do more for your general well-being'.[65]

One thing which seemed certain, however, is that the provision of post-Olympic sport and physical activity would be subject to the neoliberal logic which British politics had followed since the late 1970s. This logic had dictated a steady marketisation of previously state functions and a correspondingly greater emphasis on political impression management – a growing number of government advisors during this period were specialists in media presentation, and not in substantive areas of administration, such as transport or education; the sociologist

---

[62] Ibid.
[63] Ibid.
[64] Ibid.
[65] Ibid.

Peter Golding wrote in 1994 of the 'public relations state'.[66] The British government had endorsed the 'Inspire a generation' slogan and warm official rhetoric had attended the mission to bring the Games to London, the success of the Olympics as a spectacle and the medals attained by British athletes. But, amid the continued diminution of the state's responsibilities (not to mention the 'austerity measures' instituted by the British government in 2010), it was always likely that those inspired by London 2012 to take up sport, and those helping them to do so, would have substantially to make their own arrangements. Tony Blair, arch-exponent both of the neoliberal political project and of seductive political language, and now an advisor on legacy, made this clear on his website in 2013. 'On the first anniversary of the Games, people', he said,

> are asking: How are we supposed to keep a generation of kids inter-ested in sport when budgets are tighter than ever, especially in this part of the country? And when parents are struggling to make ends meet – let alone paying for expensive sports kit? These are valid ques-tions and there's no easy answer. Times are tough. People are having to make difficult and unpleasant decisions about how to spend money – in Government, in town halls, in schools and at home.

But help was at hand, from volunteers – 'ordinary but extraordinary people – mums and dads, students, accountants, supermarket workers and many more – give up their free time to train and then pass on sports skills to children in their community'.[67] This, of course, was David Cameron's 'Big Society' under a different guise.

## 'A festival of private Britain': regeneration and legacy after London 2012

When in 2012 the American radio station NPR had begun their con-versation about the London Olympics with young East End sportspeo-ple Amber Charles and Rumi Begum, they asked them to comment on a statement by Lord Coe, which read thus: 'Standing with the IOC on a pretty desolate, contaminated, poisoned, underdeveloped, economically challenged 600 acres of East London and trying to explain

---

[66] Peter Golding, 'Telling stories: sociology, journalism and the informed citizen', *European Journal of Communication*, Vol. 9 (1994), pp. 461–484, p. 476.
[67] Tony Blair, 'TBSF [Tony Blair Sports Foundation] volunteers putting Olympic legacy into practice', http://www.tonyblairoffice.org/news/entry/tbsf-volunteers-putting-olympic-legacy-into-practice/; accessed 16 January 2015.

that, actually, within seven years, we would have 3,000 homes, a school, a hospital, world class venues was probably stretching the imagination to about its break point'.[68] The promise to promote a socially beneficial regeneration of this purported wasteland in the East End of London was probably the single biggest factor in securing the 2012 Olympics for London, having been crucial, as we saw in Chapter 1, to gaining the support of then London Mayor Ken Livingstone for the London bid. This final section discusses the outcome of this promise.

As we have seen, during the period before London 2012 there was a good deal of opposition to the Games, both from local residents angry at the perceived threats to their homes, locality and/or way of life, and from commentators, similarly doubtful of the promises of a legacy of regeneration. Such critics, drawn from across the political spectrum, had, generally speaking, been dismissed as 'doom-mongers' and suchlike by pro-Olympic spokespeople and the mainstream media. Even before the Games were over, however, doubts over the legacy to East Enders were beginning to grow. These doubts cannot have been diminished by the refusal of the Olympic Delivery Authority, constituted in 2006, to be bound by the 'ethical pledge', signed by Coe and Livingstone in 2004, that the Games would bring a range of benefits to local communities (see Chapter 2).

If the widely expressed reservations about legacy were to be coalesced into a single foreboding, it would be that public money would continue to be used to regenerate this part of the East End of London not for the benefit of local people on modest incomes, but for corporations and wealthy individuals – as with the nearby docklands of Canary Wharf, developed in the 1990s. There is little ground for doubting the validity of these reservations.

With the Olympics about to begin, Rushanara Ali, the Bengali-born Labour MP for the East End constituency of Bethnal Green and Bow, published an article entitled 'Broken Olympic promises do not bode well for London's East End'.[69] Labour, of course, had supported the Olympic bid; Ali certainly subscribed to the Games' mantra ('I know these Games will be an inspiration to a generation, and especially to so many young people with so many dreams'[70]) and her complaints were comparatively

---

[68] 'Can East London Keep The Olympic Spirit Burning?'.
[69] Rushanara Ali, 'Broken Olympic promises do not bode well for London's East End', http://www.theguardian.com/commentisfree/2012/jul/23/london-olympic-promises-east-end; accessed 18 January 2015.
[70] Ibid.

mild. She regretted the rescinding of a decision to route the Olympic marathon through Tower Hamlets and suggested that, thus far, the aim of bringing 20,000 new jobs to the East End via the Olympics had not been fulfilled. She did claim, however, that 1,700 local people were working on the Olympic site and that 8,500 new jobs had been created in the five Olympic boroughs. She also stated that the new shopping centre – Westfield Stratford City, opened in 2012 – had brought 10,000 jobs. She called for 'much more robust and responsible leadership on the legacy at all levels – from local representatives to national government, from the mayor to the London Legacy Development Corporation'.[71]

This intervention plainly placed great faith in the 'trickle-down' effect of Olympic legacy. However, it begged vital questions – both about Westfield and the nature of leadership in the matter of legacy.

The case of Westfield Stratford City (WSC) strongly implied that the chief benefits of the project would accrue other than in the East End. Westfield was owned by an Australian company which ran nearly forty malls around the world. Following the financial crash of 2008, the British government had bailed out the Olympic development projects and co-opted some of the developers. As investigative journalist Anna Minton told a pre-Olympic conference in October 2011:

> There's a few layers and a few key property companies, but to keep it simple, Westfield will be a huge beneficiary, and also a company called Lend Lease. Lend Lease was the developer that was supposed to be raising the money for the Olympic Village, but then the financial crash happened and they couldn't. So basically the Government said, 'OK, you don't have money, we'll pay for it and we'll appoint you to be the project manager.' And what's particularly interesting about Lend Lease (that also built the Bluewater Shopping Centre) is that its former CEO, David Higgins, went to be the CEO of the ODA [Olympic Delivery Authority]. So all these people are mutually inter-twined. They all know each other and go back a long way. It's the same people and the same companies.[72]

---

[71] Ibid.

[72] Isaac Marrero-Guillamón, 'Military urbanism, surveillance and the privatisation of public space', http://theartofdissent.net/wordpress/wp-content/uploads/2012/06/marrero-guillamon-military-urbanism.pdf; accessed 19 January 2015. Lend Lease had been part of the consortium awarded the contract to build the Olympic Village in the Newington area of Sydney for the Olympics of 2000. The housing fulfilled the IOC's 'sustainability' requirement because it was fully

Cleaners in Westfield centres were low paid. In their Australian malls cleaners received 17.50 dollars (around £9.50) an hour and their union, United Voice, later commissioned a report on the company's tax affairs. The report, compiled by Roman Lanis, a senior lecturer in accounting and tax at the University of Technology in Sydney, found that Westfield, by having a 'highly complex corporate structure', which included 'more than 50 entities registered in tax havens such as Jersey, Luxembourg and Singapore', had paid a corporate tax rate of just 8 cents in the dollar. This was 'far below the official 30 per cent rate levied on business in Australia. On average, the top 200 share market-listed companies in Australia pay 22 cents in the dollar'.[73] The figure of 10,000 jobs brought to the area by Westfield seemed improbably high and seems to have come from the company's press release;[74] Gavin Poynter estimated 8,500 (including 2,000 for local people, 200 of whom were long-term jobless) but these jobs were likely to 'reproduce existing patterns of work inequality, reinforcing the polarised nature of the city's labour market'.[75] WSC was the biggest urban shopping centre but, in an area where, as she herself pointed out, 51% of the population were living in poverty,[76] it was not likely to attract many of Rushanara Ali's constituents. As Jonathan Glancey had observed at its opening in 2011: 'Beyond the walls of Westfield and its offshoot, the 2012 Olympics, lies a very different London. Old streets, old terraces, old businesses. People without the wherewithal to indulge in the mall's 300 and more VIP shops. This was once the hub not of intense luxury shopping, but of manufacturing'.[77]

---

equipped with solar panels, but it was sold after the Games and its units became high-end residential properties, http://www.propertyobserver.com.au/finding/residential-investment/17667-newington-olympic-story.html; accessed 1 February 2015.

[73] Heath Aston, 'Westfield short $2.6b on tax: report', *Sydney Morning Herald*, 29 May 2014, http://www.smh.com.au/federal-politics/political-news/westfield-short-26b-on-tax-report-20140528-394rm.html; accessed 18 January 2015.

[74] Rowan Moore, 'Westfield Stratford City: review', *The Observer*, 11 September 2011, http://www.theguardian.com/artanddesign/2011/sep/11/westfield-stratford-city-shopping-review; accessed 18 January 2015.

[75] Gavin Poynter, 'An Olympic-sized bubble in east London', http://www.spiked-online.com/newsite/article/12739#.VLw4TyoteT1; accessed 18 January 2015.

[76] Rushanara Ali, 'Broken Olympic promises do not bode well for London's East End'.

[77] Jonathan Glancey, 'Uplifting or a vision of hell? Olympic site's giant shopping centre opens', *The Guardian*, 13 September 2011, http://www.theguardian.com/uk/2011/sep/13/uplifting-olympic-shopping-centre-opens; accessed 18 January 2015.

On the other hand, it was soon clear that local businesses were losing out on a lot of passing trade. In January 2012 the *London Evening Standard* reported that

> three months on, local retailers say they are struggling to stay afloat as consumers head straight for the new centre and ignore the old shops and cafes. Some report a decline in trade of as much as 90 per cent since Westfield opened, with others saying the devastating impact it has had on their businesses means they have no future.[78]

Writer Tim Burrows argued that the Westfield centre was in Stratford, but not of it: 'Indicatively, though there are signs directing you to places further afield – central London, Leytonstone, Leyton, Stansted airport – there are none pointing you towards the older end of Stratford, towards the old town hall or the 1970s-built Stratford Centre'. Meanwhile Westfield's predecessor, the Stratford Centre shopping precinct, had become a haven for skate boarders, public space in the area now being at a premium: 'Through the evening and into the night, the Stratford Centre houses a community of skaters, dancers and body-poppers who move liberated from stereo to stereo. It's like being in an 80s version of the future'.[79]

As to the issue of political leadership in the matter of the East End's Olympic legacy, it was subject to little democratic control. Both the major political parties – 'New' Labour and the Conservatives – had been fully committed first to the Olympics and, second, to the Private Finance Initiative, whereby state assets and funds were transferred into private (i.e. corporate) hands. They had been content to see a massive outlay of public money to fund the Olympic project. At local level Newham Council had been equally happy to grant planning permission for the Westfield Stratford City complex on the basis of the company's assurances of benefits to the district. When asked about the damaging effect on local traders, they claimed simply that the WSC would 'transform the lives of our residents by providing them with training and employment

---

[78] 'New Olympic Westfield leaves local traders fighting for survival', *London Evening Standard*, 3 January 2012, http://www.standard.co.uk/business/new-olympic-westfield-leaves-local-traders-fighting-for-survival-7303609.html; accessed 18 January 2015.

[79] Tim Burrows, 'The shopping centre opposite Westfield has become a weird 24-hour haven for London's skate subculture', http://www.vice.com/en_uk/read/the-stratford-centre-is-thriving-in-westfields-giant-shadow-098, posted 26 November 2014; accessed 18 January 2015.

and jobs they can turn into fulfilling and rewarding careers'.[80] Once Olympic and post-Olympic development projects were under way, their disposition was largely outside democratic governance. There were two important and related manifestations of this. First, as writers such as Anna Minton pointed out, formal responsibility for various aspects of the administration of the Olympic districts was vested in a confusion of quasi-governmental agencies and, second, the leaders of these agencies were political appointees, and not elected. For example, Labour peer Baroness Ford was appointed chair of the London 2012 Legacy Delivery Company by the Brown government in 2009 in consultation with the Conservative Boris Johnson, elected London mayor the previous year. Ford was solidly within the neoliberal, pro-business consensus now prevailing in the Labour Party, being a director of both a private healthcare company (Barchester Healthcare) and Serco, a leading outsourcing company receiving numerous government contracts. Johnson had several times made clear his aim to make London a hub for international business and was well aware of the attraction to international firms of various sites in London's East End: in March 2014 he declared his intention to turn the city into the 'tech capital of the world', the centrepiece of which would be a 'digital hub' at the Queen Elizabeth Olympic Park, developed under the supervision of Baroness Ford.[81] According to Minton, far from a beneficial legacy for East Enders, the prospect of this behind-closed-doors conjoining of business and government was 'that a very substantial part of East London will be characterized by new private fiefdoms accountable only to the blurred mass of quangos which are replacing democratically elected local government'.[82] This was part of a pattern of what Minton (among others) had elsewhere referred to as 'the privatisation of public space';[83] the Olympics, she said, were a 'festival

---

[80] 'New Olympic Westfield leaves local traders fighting for survival'.

[81] See Alain Tolhurst, 'Boris Johnson to make London "tech capital of the world"', http://www.london24.com/news/business/boris_johnson_to_make_london_tech_capital_of_the_world_1_3428534; accessed 19 January 2015; Sara Nelson, 'Queen Elizabeth Olympic Park to become world class digital hub', 26 February 2014, http://www.london24.com/news/business/queen_elizabeth_olympic_park_to_become_world_class_digital_hub_1_3367611; accessed 19 January 2015.

[82] Anna Minton, *Ground Control: Fear and Happiness in the Twenty-First-Century City* (London: Penguin 2012), p. xxvii.

[83] Anna Minton, 'The privatisation of public space', http://www.annaminton.com/privatepublicspace.pdf; accessed 19 January 2015.

of private Britain'.[84] The following year she published a report documenting what she called 'the abuses which characterise the operation of local democracy in many parts of the UK with intimidation, bullying or conflicts of interest common practice among lobbying companies, developers and local authorities promoting contentious development'.[85]

Aside from the private space and 'digital hub' that was to be Queen Elizabeth Olympic Park, the Olympic stadium threatened to be a 'white elephant' of the kind much seen with the Olympic venues built for the Athens Games of 2004,[86] but in January 2014 it was announced that

> Balfour Beatty has been awarded the £154m contract to transform the venue into one suitable for football and athletics. The appointment of a contractor to oversee the transformation of the temporary 80,000 seat structure into one with a cantilevered roof, permanent corporate facilities and retractable seats with a capacity of 54,000 was hailed as a 'major step forward' in the project.

Costs on the stadium had thus risen to over half £1 billion.[87] (Every Olympics since 1960 has gone over budget.[88]) As with the Commonwealth Games, the new tenants of the main stadium were to be a Premiership football club (West Ham United) – another decision of doubtful community benefit.

---

[84] Anna Minton, 'The London Olympics: a festival of private Britain', *The Guardian*, 24 January 2012, http://www.theguardian.com/commentisfree/2012/jan/24/london-olympics-festival-private-legacy; accessed 19 January 2015.

[85] Anna Minton, 'The local lobby and the failure of democracy', http://annaminton.com/Scaring%20The%20Living%20Daylights%20March%2027th%2013.pdf, posted March 2013; accessed 19 January 2015.

[86] See Helena Smith, 'Athens 2004 Olympics: what happened after the athletes went home?', *The Guardian*, 9 May 2012, http://www.theguardian.com/sport/2012/may/09/athens-2004-olympics-athletes-home; accessed 19 January 2015; Steven Bloor, 'Abandoned Athens Olympic 2004 venues, 10 years on – in pictures', *The Guardian*, 13 August 2014, http://www.theguardian.com/sport/gallery/2014/aug/13/abandoned-athens-olympic-2004-venues-10-years-on-in-pictures; accessed 19 January 2015.

[87] Owen Gibson, 'Cost of Olympic stadium hits £580m after green light for final phase', *The Guardian*, 6 January 2014, http://www.theguardian.com/sport/2014/jan/06/olympic-stadium-costs-balfour-beatty; accessed 19 January 2015.

[88] See Bent Flyvbjerg and Allison Stewart, 'Olympic proportions: cost and cost overrun at the Olympics 1960–2012', *Saïd Business School Working Papers* (Oxford: University of Oxford, 1 June 2012), http://papers.ssrn.com/sol3/papers.cfm?abstract_id=2238053; accessed 19 January 2015.

The Athletes Village, once again funded by the British government, had already been sold in the summer of 2011 to a consortium consisting of Delanceys, a British developer, and the investment arm of the Qatari royal family. Culture Secretary Jeremy Hunt commented: 'The village will be the centrepiece of a new vibrant east London community'.[89] The likely nature of the vibrancy was spelled out by Gavin Poynter, one of the Olympic project's most temperate critics:

> While this deal enabled the government to recoup some of the costs of the Olympic Village development, the agreement has resulted in a considerable loss to the public purse, and it is not clear how it will fit with plans for creating an 'inclusive' neighbourhood. The pressure to create a desirable environment attractive to those willing to pay substantial rents is likely to shape the tenancy of the 'affordable' housing. Already, there are local-authority interventions to ensure that more 'desirable' groups, such as 'key workers', have access to the housing over those unemployed and dependent upon benefits. Developments on the borders of the Olympic Park are following a similar trajectory. Stratford High Street and plans for parts of the Lower Lea Valley, involving, among others, companies such as Ikea, are committed to the construction of islands of gentrification, designed largely for 'buy-to-let' purposes aimed at young professionals and overseas investors, rather than local, typically poorer communities.[90]

In January 2013 Rushanara Ali reported that: 'The jobless rate in my constituency, Bethnal Green and Bow, remains among the highest in the country...'; many of them, she said, felt betrayed.[91]

## Conclusion

Looking back, with over two years of hindsight and the opportunity therefore to weigh carefully what has transpired, London 2012 seems to

---

[89] 'Olympic Village sold to Qatari developers for £557m in deal that costs taxpayer £225m', http://www.dailymail.co.uk/news/article-2025367/Olympic-Village-sold-Qatari-developers-557m-deal-costs-taxpayer-225m.html, posted 12 August 2011; accessed 19 January 2015.
[90] Gavin Poynter, 'An Olympic-sized bubble in east London'.
[91] Rushanara Ali, 'The Olympic legacy has failed to bring jobs to London's East End', *The Guardian*, 27 January 2013, http://www.theguardian.com/commentisfree/2013/jan/27/olympic-legacy-failed-jobs-london; accessed 19 January 2015.

have been a consummation of the trend inaugurated in Los Angeles in 1984, welcomed as a shot in the arm by the International Olympic Committee and decried as a raid both on the public purse and on civil liberties by the growing cadre of Olympic critics. Like many contemporary elections, the race for the 2012 Olympics was a victory for one candidate and attendant PR team over their rivals, but the result would very likely have been much the same: a heavily policed commercial showcase; a popular and globally mediated sporting fortnight; a curtailment of civil liberties; and a subsequent and contentious disposition of land. The relentlessly deployed promotional slogan 'Inspire a generation' never stood up to much scrutiny and many of the young people wanting to take up sport or other physical activity after the Games were, as was known in advance, unlikely to be accommodated, at least by the state.

Just as importantly, the nature of the political conversation promoted by the London 2012 Olympics was such as to exclude the notions of sport as **unorganised activity** or as **something to be pursued for its own sake – for pleasure, rather than competitively**. This flies in the face of public practice. Helen Lenskyj has drawn attention to research in Australia following the Sydney Games, which, like London and other recent Games, had been awarded partly on the basis of a promise to promote sport participation: a survey in 2008 by the Australian Sports Commission and the Department of Health and Ageing found that 'non-organised sport and physical recreation were the most common forms of physical activity among Australians, and that in the post-Olympic period 2001–2008 the biggest growth areas were aerobics and fitness activities'.[92] Indeed, the Australian Bureau of Statistics survey in 2011 revealed that

> Of all sports or physical recreation activities, walking for exercise had the highest level of participation (23%). Aerobics, fitness or gym was also a popular activity group (14%). Swimming (7.4%), cycling (6.5%) and jogging or running (6.5%) were the only other activities that were participated in by more than one in twenty Australians.[93]

---

[92] Helen Jefferson Lenskyj, 'The case against the Olympic Games: the buck stops with the IOC', in Helen Jefferson Lenskyj and Stephen Wagg (eds.), *The Palgrave Handbook of Olympic Studies* (Basingstoke: Palgrave Macmillan, 2012), pp. 570–579, p. 575.
[93] Australian Bureau of Statistics, 'Australian social trends June 2011: sport and physical recreation', p. 4, http://www.ausstats.abs.gov.au/ausstats/subscriber.nsf/LookupAttach/4102.0Publication29.06.114/$File/41020_Sport_Jun2011.pdf; accessed 5 February 2015.

This runs somewhat counter both to the widely promoted stereotype of the ultra-competitive Aussie sportsperson and to the determination of politicians and commentators in a number of countries to foster will-to-win attitudes through school sport. (When the Crawford Report of 2009[94] questioned the amount of money apportioned to Olympic sport, John Coates, the Head of the Australian Olympic Committee, pronounced himself 'pissed off' and suggested that the report was 'an insult to everyone who has worked to get Australia to where it is on the Olympic stage'.[95])

Similarly, in England, nearly two years after London 2012, the BBC reported the findings of a survey which revealed an apparently widespread antipathy to competitiveness in sport:

> The majority of children would be happy to see the competitive element removed from school sport, a survey suggests. Almost two thirds (64%) of eight to 16-year-olds polled said they would be 'relieved, not bothered or happier' if winning or losing were not a factor. However, 22% of parents said they would have less interest in watching school sport if it was not competitive. The poll, by Marylebone Cricket Club and charity *Chance to Shine*, surveyed 1,000 children and 1,000 parents. Although 84% of children believed experiencing winning and losing was important, the survey revealed that many would rather play sport for fun, or would be relieved if less was at stake.[96]

As to what the future might hold for the politics of Olympic sporting legacy – judgement of which Tony Blair and Sebastian Coe had postponed for a minimum ten year period – a glimpse was provided at a conference in Canada in 2014. A team representing Sheffield Hallam University and the National Centre for Sport and Exercise Medicine

---

[94] http://apo.org.au/files/Resource/crawford_report.pdf; accessed 5 February 2015.

[95] 'Coates "pissed off" by Crawford Report', http://www.abc.net.au/news/2009-11-17/coates-pissed-off-by-crawford-report/1146166, posted 17 November 2009; accessed 5 February 2015. The official response of the Australian Olympic Committee to the Crawford Report can be read at: http://corporate.olympics.com.au/files/dmFile/AOC_CrawfordReport_Response_181209r.pdf; accessed 5 February 2015.

[96] BBC News UK, 'Competitive sport puts off schoolchildren – survey', http://www.bbc.co.uk/news/uk-27113085, posted 22 April 2014; accessed 5 February 2015.

(NCSEM) in Sheffield reported on a project to promote physical activity as a legacy of London 2012.[97] The project had a name – the 'Move More' programme – and it was 'well established within the health and well-being fabric of Sheffield, and leads a physical activity strategy for the City'. The project had a manager 'in place' who was 'funded solely by the NCSEM partners' and 'a full-time project officer' paid for by the local authority.[98] A diagram describes 'The Olympic Legacy Model in Sheffield'[99] and another depicts 'Move More Plan Outcomes, Underpinning Principles and the Brand'.[100] As to progress:

> A significant programme of asset-based community development is now underway, which aims to increase participation from the ground up. The project has successfully supported colleagues from across the city to attain funding for mass participation events, environmental programmes for enhancing active travel, as well as agreeing to a business case to transfer NHS clinics to the NCSEM hub and spoke capital facilities. Furthermore, a partnership has been established between Yorkshire and Humber Academic Health Science Network and Sheffield Hallam University, through which NCSEM-Sheffield has developed and delivered a workforce well-being programme in the NHS. Nationally, learning from NCSEM-Sheffield has informed a number of policy documents, including the Public Health England Moving More Living More framework and the All Party Parliamentary Group on Primary Care and Public Health. NCSEM-Sheffield has also provided a rapid review of workplace physical activity interventions, which will be used to inform the National Framework for Physical Activity, which is due for release in October 2014.[101]

There was little direct mention of actual physical activity but, to a degree, references to 'the health and well-being fabric of Sheffield', 'physical activity strategy', 'asset-based community development', 'hub

---

[97] R.J. Copeland, C.E. King, S.W. Flint and D. Whitney, 'The Olympic Games and sponsors have left town – what about the legacy?', in Janice Forsyth, Christine O'Bonsawin and Michael Heine (eds.), *Intersections and Intersectionalities in Olympic and Paralympic Studies Twelfth International Symposium for Olympic Research* (30–31 October 2014) (Canada, London, Ontario: International Centre for Olympic Studies: Western University, 2014), pp. 47–54.
[98] Ibid., p. 52.
[99] Ibid., p. 50.
[100] Ibid., p. 51.
[101] Ibid.

and spoke capital facilities', partnerships, national frameworks and the rest were telling in themselves. Accounts of enhanced sporting and other physical activity as a result of an Olympics now receding in public memory will, generally speaking, be reports on the spending of public money designated for that purpose. These accounts will therefore be rendered in the language now prescribed by government. This is essentially the language of business plans and performance indication and it leaves scant room for the documenting of flesh-and-blood human engagement. It is also an evasive, corporate lexicon of the kind so skilfully parodied in the BBC's *Twenty Twelve*; it is a language built to seem, rather than to say. Just as Anna Minton found that responsibility for the Olympic site had become lost in a thicket of quasi-governmental bodies, the sporting legacy of London 2012 will likely become buried in a similar morass of official-sounding terminology.

The organisation of the Olympics and their legacy were fully consonant with the established politics of 'Private Finance Initiative' whereby the British state transferred a great deal of money to global corporations, with, as Olympic protocol demanded, no guarantee of a return. Indeed, when pressed to justify the zealous safeguarding of Olympic partners' commercial interests, Lord Coe replied: 'It is very important to remember that by actually protecting these brands, by protecting the companies that have actually put money into the Games, we're also protecting the taxpayer. Because if we don't reach these targets, then actually the taxpayer is the guarantor of last resort'.[102] Richard Giulianotti and colleagues called this 'a broader set of "New Right two step" policies in poor urban areas, involving initial Keynesian investment, followed by a deeper and far-reaching array of neo-liberal measures'.[103] Adapting the work of Canadian writer Naomi Klein, Jules Boykoff has preferred to call mega-events such as London 2012 'celebration capitalism'.[104] In her book *The Shock Doctrine* Klein wrote of 'disaster capitalism' to describe 'orchestrated raids on the public sphere in the

---

[102] On the BBC's *The Andrew Marr Show*, 13 May 2012; quoted in Jules Boykoff, *Celebration Capitalism and the Olympic Games* (London: Routledge, 2014), p. 98.

[103] Richard Giulianotti, Gary Armstrong, Gavin Hales and Dick Hobbs 'Sport mega-events and public opposition: A sociological study of the London 2012 Olympics', *Journal of Sport and Social Issues*, p. 1, http://jss.sagepub.com/content/early/2014/04/14/0193723514530565, published online 14 April 2014; accessed 16 September 2014.

[104] Boykoff, *Celebration Capitalism and the Olympic Games*.

wake of catastrophic events [such as the havoc wrought on New Orleans by Hurricane Katrina in 2005], combined with the treatment of these disasters as exciting market opportunities'.[105] The Olympics, argued Boykoff, offer a similar market opportunity, wherein the bulldozers are commanded by an Olympic Committee expecting new, state-of-the-art facilities; an army of publicists and politicians supplies a rhetoric of sustainability and regeneration; there are heavily protected commercial promotions; and, for the duration, the designated area becomes a militarised zone.[106] (The militarisation, incidentally, is only in part temporary. Dave Zirin recently observed in relation to 'Fortress London 2012': 'Not to shock anyone, but there are no signs that any of the security apparatus has been dismantled since the Olympics were staged. [...] London has been left with a high-tech police force...and a camera around every corner'.[107] Besides, the government's security advisors, as we saw in Chapter 5, intended and recommended that much of the security apparatus brought in for London 2012 should be a permanent investment.)

In the judgement of its critics, the most ironic and disquieting outcome of London 2012 was that its principal intended beneficiaries received not legacy, but social exclusion. The Westfield Stratford City, with its myriad chain stores, was a non-place where a place had been. There were dozens like it in the world; it could have been anywhere. In a classically postmodern gesture, the Olympic site had even been given a new post code, borrowed from the BBC fictional soap opera *EastEnders*.[108] Moreover, local people, in the main, could not expect – and, as we've seen, many of them in any case did not expect – to be able to rent or buy homes in the area after it had been regenerated. They would now be expected to depart, making way for more affluent residents, supermarkets, shopping malls, offices and 'digital hubs'. In a powerful essay Ashok Kumar noted that this was part of an identifiable political pattern in which the Olympics had caused 2 million

---

[105] Naomi Klein, *The Shock Doctrine: The Rise of Disaster Capitalism* (London: Allen Lane, 2007), p. 6.

[106] See Boykoff, *Celebration Capitalism and the Olympic Games*, pp. 108–111.

[107] Dave Zirin, *Brazil's Dance with the Devil: The World Cup, the Olympics and the Fight for Democracy* (Chicago: Haymarket Books, 2014), p. 165.

[108] See Anna Minton, 'Olympic village or private new town?', https://www.opendemocracy.net/ourkingdom/anna-minton/olympic-village-or-private-new-town, posted 23 May 2012; accessed 19 January 2015.

people to lose their homes over a 20-year period. He argued in the spring of 2012:

> The Olympics have always been utilised as a means to pursue what [the radical geographer] David Harvey calls 'accumulation by dispossession,' from visible policies of forced evictions to veiled ones such as gentrification. This violent process is intimately connected to reconfiguring the landscape for capital accumulation and, indeed, is a prime motivation for the very purpose of the Olympics itself. The Games are not simply hosted to 'clean up' the city, but to fundamentally reconfigure it, to 'cleanse' it of its poor and undesirable; to not only make way for a city by and for the rich, but to expand the terrain of profitable activity.[109]

Harvey is one of a number of writers who have campaigned for 'the right to the city', a phrase originated by the French sociologist Henri Lefebvre.[110] In his essay of that title in 2008, Harvey wrote:

> the metropolis is now the point of massive collision – dare we call it class struggle? – over the accumulation by dispossession visited upon the least well-off and the developmental drive that seeks to colonize space for the affluent. One step towards unifying these struggles is to adopt the right to the city as both working slogan and political ideal, precisely because it focuses on the question of who commands the necessary connection between urbanization and surplus production and use. The democratization of that right, and the construction of a broad social movement to enforce its will, is imperative if the dispossessed are to take back the control which they have for so long been denied, and if they are to institute new modes of urbanization.[111]

There was strong urban opposition to London 2012, although it was contained and found little expression in the mainstream media. Rio de

---

[109] Ashok Kumar, 'Want to cleanse your city of its poor? Host the Olympics', https://ceasefiremagazine.co.uk/olympics-opportunity-cleanse-city/, posted 12 April 2012; accessed 19 January 2015.

[110] Henri Lefebvre, *Le Droit à la ville* (Paris: Anthopos, 1968).

[111] David Harvey, 'The right to the city', *New Left Review*, September–October 2008, http://newleftreview.org/II/53/david-harvey-the-right-to-the-city; accessed 19 January 2015.

Janeiro, Olympic host in 2016, is already a different story. Since 2013 often violent protests have been raging across Brazil at the cost (financial and human, given the deaths of construction workers) of the World Cup of 2014 and of the coming Olympics, and seem set to continue.[112] The right to the city was written into law in Brazil in 2001.[113]

---

[112] See, for example, 'Violent protests in Brazil over cost of World Cup and Olympics', http://www.telegraph.co.uk/news/worldnews/southamerica/brazil/10126626/Violent-protests-in-Brazil-over-cost-of-World-Cup-and-Olympics.html, posted 18 June 2013; accessed 19 January 2015. For a full account see Dave Zirin, *Brazil's Dance with the Devil*.
[113] 'Implementing the right to the city in Brazil?', http://sustainablecities collective.com/polis-blog/30417/implementing-right-city-brazil, posted 14 October 2011; accessed 19 January 2015.

# Select Bibliography

Anderson, Benedict (2006) *Imagined Communities: Reflections on the Origin and Spread of Nationalism* (London: Verso).

Andrews, David L. and Oliver J.C. Rick (2013) 'Celebrity and the London 2012 Spectacle', in Vassil Girginov (ed.), *Handbook of the London Olympic and Paralympic Games*, Vol. 1: *Making the Games* (Abingdon: Routledge), pp. 195–211.

Australian Bureau of Statistics (2011) 'Australian Social Trends June 2011: Sport and Physical Recreation', http://www.ausstats.abs.gov.au/ausstats/subscriber.nsf/LookupAttach/4102.0Publication29.06.114/$File/41020_Sport_Jun2011.pdf.

Baker, Catherine (2014) 'Beyond the Island Story?: The Opening Ceremony of the London 2012 Olympic Games as Public History', *Rethinking History*, http://www.academia.edu/6839567/Beyond_the_island_story_The_opening_ceremony_of_the_London_2012_Olympic_Games_as_public_history.

Barney, Robert K. and Anthony Th. Bijkerk (2005) 'The Genesis of Sacred Fire in Olympic Ceremony: A New Interpretation', *Journal of Olympic History*, Vol. 12, No. 2, pp. 6–27, http://library.la84.org/SportsLibrary/JOH/JOHv13n2/JOHv13n2f.pdf.

Blair, Tony (2010) *A Journey* (London: Hutchinson).

Boykoff, Jules (2014) *Celebration Capitalism and the Olympic Games* (Abingdon: Routledge).

Boykoff, Jules and Alan Tomlinson (2012) 'Olympic Arrogance', *New York Times*, 4 July, http://www.nytimes.com/2012/07/05/opinion/no-medal-for-the-international-olympic-committee.html?_r=0.

Boyle, Philip (2012) 'Securing the Olympic Games: Exemplifications of Global Governance', in Helen Jefferson Lenskyj and Stephen Wagg (eds.), *The Palgrave Handbook of Olympic Studies* (Basingstoke: Palgrave Macmillan), pp. 394–409.

Boyle, Philip and Kevin Haggerty (2009) 'Spectacular Security: Mega-Events and the Security Complex', *International Political Sociology*, No. 3, pp. 257–274, http://geeksandglobaljustice.com/wp-content/Boyle-Haggarty.pdf.

Brohm, Jean-Marie (1978) *Sport: A Prison of Measured Time* (London: Ink Links).

Bromund, Theodore R., Steven P. Bucci, Luke Coffey, Jessica Zuckerman and Robin Simcox (2012) 'U.S. Should Assist Britain in Meeting Security Threats to the 2012 London Olympic Games', *Heritage Foundation*, 16 July, http://www.heritage.org/research/reports/2012/07/us-should-assist-britain-in-meeting-security-threats-to-the-2012-london-olympic-games#_ftn3.

Brookings Institution Centre on Urban and Metropolitan Policy, The (2000) *Moving Beyond Sprawl: The Challenge for Metropolitan Atlanta* (Washington, DC: The Brookings Institution), http://www.brookings.edu/~/media/research/files/reports/2000/3/atlanta/atlanta.pdf.

Bruce, Toni and Emma Wensing (2012) 'The Olympics and Indigenous Peoples: Australia', in Lenskyj and Wagg (eds.), *The Palgrave Handbook of Olympic Studies*, pp. 487–504.

Brunet, Ferran (2009) 'The Economy of the Barcelona Olympic Games', in Gavin Poynter and Iain MacRury (eds.), *Olympic Cities: 2012 and the Remaking of London* (Farnham: Ashgate), pp. 97–119.

Burke, James Lee (2005) *In the Moon of Red Ponies* (London: Phoenix).

Cabinet Office (2002) 'Game Plan: A Strategy for Delivering Government's Sport and Physical Activity Objectives', December, http://www.gamesmonitor.org.uk/files/game_plan_report.pdf.

Cahill, Janet (1998) 'The Olympic Flame and Torch: Running towards Sydney 2000', in R. Barney, K. Wamsley, S. Martyn and G. MacDonald (eds.), *Global and Cultural Critique: Problematizing the Olympic Games, Proceedings of Fourth International Symposium for Olympic Research* (London, Ontario: International Centre for Olympic Studies), http://library.la84.org/SportsLibrary/ISOR/ISOR1998u.pdf, pp. 181–190.

Cartledge, Paul (2000) 'Olympic Self Sacrifice', *History Today*, Vol. 50, No. 10, http://www.historytoday.com/paul-cartledge/olympic-self-sacrifice.

Chan, Sophy (2014) 'Unveiling the "Olympic Kidnapping Act" Homelessness and Public Policy in the 2010 Vancouver Olympic Games', in Janice Forsyth, Christine O'Bonsawin and Michael Heine (eds.), *Intersections and Intersectionalities in Olympic and Paralympic Studies Twelfth International Symposium for Olympic Research* (30–31 October, 2014) (Canada, London, Ontario: International Centre for Olympic Studies: Western University), pp. 43–47.

Cohen, Phil (2013) *On the Wrong Side of the Track? East London and the Post Olympics* (London: Lawrence and Wishart).

Copeland, R.J., C.E. King, S.W. Flint and D. Whitney (2014) 'The Olympic Games and Sponsors Have Left Town – What About the Legacy?', in Janice Forsyth, Christine O'Bonsawin and Michael Heine (eds.), *Intersections and Intersectionalities in Olympic and Paralympic Studies Twelfth International Symposium for Olympic Research* (30–31 October, 2014) (Canada, London, Ontario: International Centre for Olympic Studies: Western University), pp. 47–54.

Dave, Chetan (2005) *The 2012 Bid: Five Cities Chasing the Summer Games* (Bloomington, Indiana: Author House).

Emerson, Ralph Waldo (1908) *Conduct of Life* (London: The Waverley Company Ltd).

Evans, Richard J. (2011) 'The Wonderfulness of Us (the Tory Interpretation of History)', *London Review of Books*, Vol. 33, No. 6, 17 March, pp. 9–12, http://www.lrb.co.uk/v33/n06/richard-j-evans/the-wonderfulness-of-us.

Foucault, Michel (1979) *Discipline and Punish: The Birth of the Prison* (London: Penguin).

Gatehouse, Mike and Miguel Angel Reyes (1987) *Soft Drink, Hard Labour: Guatemalan Workers Take on Coca-Cola* (London: Latin America Bureau).

Giulianotti, Richard, Gary Armstrong, Gavin Hales and Dick Hobbs (2014) 'Sport Mega-Events and Public Opposition: A Sociological Study of the London 2012 Olympics', *Journal of Sport and Social Issues*, p. 3, http://jss.sagepub.com/content/early/2014/04/14/0193723514530565.

Golden, Mark (2012) 'The Ancient Olympics and the Modern: Mirror and Mirage', in Lenskyj and Wagg (eds.), *The Palgrave Handbook of Olympic Studies*, pp. 15–25.

Golding, Peter (1994) 'Telling Stories: Sociology, Journalism and the Informed Citizen', *European Journal of Communication*, Vol. 9, pp. 461–484.

Graham, Stephen (2012) 'Olympics 2012 Security: Welcome to Lockdown London', http://www.theguardian.com/sport/2012/mar/12/london-olympics-security-lockdown-london, posted 12 March.

Gruneau, Rick (1984) 'The Chocolate Olympics', *New Socialist*, May/June, pp. 56–59.

Gruneau, Rick (1984) 'Commercialism and the Modern Olympics', in Alan Tomlinson and Garry Whannel (eds.), *Five Ring Circus: Money, Power and Politics at the Olympic Games* (London: Pluto Press), pp. 1–15.

Gruneau, Rick and Robert Neubauer (2012) 'A Gold Medal for the Market: The 1984 Los Angeles Olympics, the Reagan Era and the Politics of Neoliberalism', in Lenskyj and Wagg (eds.), *The Palgrave Handbook of Olympic*, pp. 134–162.

Hargreaves, John (2000) *Freedom for Catalonia? Catalan Nationalism, Spanish Identity and the Barcelona Olympic Games* (Cambridge: Cambridge University Press).

Hatcher, Craig (2012) 'Legacies of Dislocation on the Clays Lane Estate', in Hilary Powell and Isaac Marrero-Guillamon (eds.), *The Art of Dissent: Adventures in London's Olympic State* (London: Marshgate Press), pp. 197–206.

Hoberman, John (1992) *Mortal Engines: The Science of Performance and the Dehumanization of Sport* (New York: The Free Press).

Hogan, Jackie (2003) 'Staging The Nation: Gendered and Ethnicized Discourses of National Identity in Olympic Opening Ceremonies', *Journal of Sport and Social Issues*, Vol. 27, No. 2, pp. 100–123.

Iles, Anthony (2012) 'The Lower Lea Valley: From Fun Palace to Creative Prison', in Hilary Powell and Isaac Marrero-Guillamon (eds.), *The Art of Dissent: Adventures in London's Olympic State* (London: Marshgate Press), pp. 150–159.

James, Mark and Guy Osborn (2011) 'London 2012 and the Impact of the UK's Olympic and Paralympic Legislation: Protecting Commerce or Preserving Culture?', *Modern Law Review*, Vol. 74, No. 3, pp. 410–429.

Jennings, Andrew (1996) *The New Lords of the Rings: Olympic Corruption and How to Buy Gold Medals* (London: Pocket Books).

Jennings, Andrew and Clare Sambrook (2000) *The Great Olympic Swindle: When the World Wanted Its Games Back* (London: Simon and Schuster).

Klein, Naomi (2007) *The Shock Doctrine: The Rise of Disaster Capitalism* (London: Allen Lane).

Labour Behind the Label/Play Fair 2012 (2012) *Toying with Workers' Rights: A Report on Producing Merchandise for the London 2012 Olympic Games* (London: Trades Union Congress).

Large, David Clay (2012) 'The Nazi Olympics: Berlin 1936', in Lenskyj and Wagg (eds.), *The Palgrave Handbook of Olympic Studies*, pp. 60–72.

Lee, Mike, with Adrian Warner and David Bond (2006) *The Race for the 2012 Olympics* (London: Virgin Books).

Lenskyj, Helen Jefferson (2000) *Inside the Olympic Industry: Power, Politics and Activism* (Albany: State University of New York Press).

Lenskyj, Helen Jefferson (2002) *The Best Olympics Ever? Social Impacts of Sydney 2000* (Albany: State University of New York Press).

Lenskyj, Helen Jefferson (2008) *Olympic Industry Resistance: Challenging Olympic Power and Propaganda* (Albany: State University of New York Press).

Lenskyj, Helen Jefferson (2012) 'The Case Against the Olympic Games: The Buck Stops with the IOC', in Lenskyj and Wagg (eds.), *The Palgrave Handbook of Olympic Studies*, pp. 570–579.

Lenskyj, Helen Jefferson (2013) *Gender Politics and the Olympic Industry* (Basingstoke: Palgrave).

Lenskyj, Helen Jefferson and Stephen Wagg (eds.) (2012) *The Palgrave Handbook of Olympic Studies* (Basingstoke: Palgrave Macmillan).

Levitas, Ruth (1999) 'Defining and Measuring Social Exclusion: A Critical Overview of Current Proposals', http://www.radstats.org.uk/no071/article2. htm.

Levitas, Ruth (2003) 'The Idea of Social Exclusion', http://socialpolicyframework. alberta.ca/files/documents/2003_social_inclusion_research_conference.pdf.

Levitas, Ruth (2006) 'The Concept and Measurement of Social Exclusion', in C. Pantazis et al. (eds.), *Poverty and Social Exclusion in Britain* (Bristol: Policy Press), pp. 123–160, http://www.open.ac.uk/poverty/pdf/poverty-and-social-exclusion_chap5.pdf.

Lister, Ruth (1998) 'From Equality to Social Inclusion: New Labour and the Welfare State', *Critical Social Policy,* Vol. 18, No. 55, May, pp. 15–225.

MacRury, Iain (2009) 'Branding the Games: Commercialism and the Olympic City', in Poynter and MacRury (eds.), *Olympic Cities*, pp. 43–71.

McTeer, William (2003) 'Review of Lenskyj (2002)', *Olympika: The International Journal of Olympic Studies*, Vol. 12, pp. 63–64.

Mallon, Bill (1993) 'Qualification for Olympic Games in the 21st Century', *Citius, Altius, Fortius,* Vol. 1, No. 2, Spring, pp. 10–17.

Marcuse, Herbert (1972) *One Dimensional Man* (London: Abacus).

Marqusee, Mike (2000) *Redemption Song: Muhammad Ali and the Spirit of the Sixties* (London: Verso).

Marrero-Guillamón, Isaac (2012) 'Military Urbanism, Surveillance and the Privatisation of Public Space', http://theartofdissent.net/wordpress/wp-content/uploads/2012/06/marrero-guillamon-military-urbanism.pdf.

Minton, Anna (2012) *Ground Control: Fear and Happiness in the Twenty-First Century City* (London: Penguin).

Minton, Anna (2012) 'The London Olympics: A Festival of Private Britain', *The Guardian*, 24 January, http://www.theguardian.com/commentisfree/2012/jan/24/london-olympics-festival-private-legacy.

Oettler, Anika (2014) 'The London 2012 Olympics Opening Ceremony and Its Polyphonous Aftermath', *Journal of Sport and Social Issues*, Published online 1 July.

O'Rourke, P.J. (1991), *Parliament of Whores* (New York: The Atlantic Monthly Press).

Panagiotopoulou, Roy (2009) 'The 28th Olympic Games in Athens 2004', in Poynter and MacRury (eds.), *Olympic Cities*, pp. 145–162.

Pollock, Allyson (2005) *NHS plc: The Privatisation of our Health Care* (London: Verso).

Powell, Hilary and Isaac Marrero-Guillamon (eds.) (2012) *The Art of Dissent: Adventures in London's Olympic State* (London: Marshgate Press).

Poynter, Gavin (2009) 'The Evolution of the Olympic and Paralympic Games 1948–2012', in Poynter and MacRury (eds.), *Olympic Cities*, pp. 23–41.

Poynter, Gavin (2009) 'London: Preparing for 2012', in Poynter and MacRury (eds.), *Olympic Cities*, pp. 183–200.

Poynter, Gavin (2012) 'An Olympic-Sized Bubble in East London', http://www.spiked-online.com/newsite/article/12739#.VLw4TyoteT1.

Poynter, Gavin and Iain MacRury (eds.), *Olympic Cities: 2012 and the Remaking of London* (Farnham: Ashgate).

Poynter, Gavin and Emma Roberts (2009) 'Atlanta (1996): The Centennial Games', in Poynter and MacRury (eds.), *Olympic Cities*, pp. 121–131.

Raphael, Amy (2013) *Danny Boyle: Creating Wonder* (London: Faber).

Rawnsley, Andrew (2001) *Servants of the People: The Inside Story of New Labour* (London: Penguin).

Romney, Mitt and Timothy Robinson (2004) *Turnaround: Crisis, Leadership, and the Olympic Games* (Washington, DC: Regnery Publishing).

Rutheiser, Charles (1996) *Imagineering Atlanta: The Politics of Places in the City of Dreams* (London: Verso).

Ryan, Peter (2002) *Olympic Security: The Relevance to Homeland Security* (Salt Lake City: The Oquirrh Institute).

Ryan-Collins, Josh and Paul Sander-Jackson (2008) *Fools Gold: How the 2012 Olympics Is Selling East London Short, and a 10 Point Plan for a More Positive Local Legacy* (London: New Economics Foundation), http://www.bl.uk/sportandsociety/exploresocsci/businesseconomics/economics/articles/fools_gold08.pdf.

Seabrook, Jeremy (2013) 'Pauper Management by G4S, Serco and Atos Is Inspired by a Punitive Past', *The Guardian*, 25 November, http://www.theguardian.com/commentisfree/2013/nov/25/pauper-management-g4s-serco-atos-poor-laws.

Sengupta, Mitu (2010) 'A Million Dollar Exit from the Anarchic Slum-World: Slumdog Millionaire's Hollow Idioms of Social Justice', *Third World Quarterly*, Vol. 31, No. 4, pp. 599–614.

Shaw, Christopher A. (2012) 'The Economics and Marketing of the Olympic Games from Bid Phase to Aftermath', in Lenskyj and Wagg (eds.), *The Palgrave Handbook of Olympic Studies*, pp. 248–260.

Simson, Vyv and Andrew Jennings (1992) *The Lords of the Rings: Power, Money & Drugs in the Modern Olympics* (New York: Simon and Schuster).

Sinclair, Iain (2008) 'The Olympics Scam', *London Review of Books*, Vol. 30, No. 12, 19 June, pp. 17–23.

Sinclair, Iain (2012) *Ghost Milk: Calling Time on the Grand Project* (London: Penguin).

Slavin, Martin (2012) 'Scenes from Public Consultations', in Powell and Marrero-Guillamon (eds.), *The Art of Dissent*, pp. 214–219.

Sugden, John and Alan Tomlinson (1998) *FIFA and the Contest for World Football* (Cambridge: Polity Press).

Sugden, John and Alan Tomlinson (1999) *Great Balls of Fire* (Edinburgh: Mainstream).

Teixeira, Terrence (2012) 'The XXI Olympiad: Canada's Claim of Montreal's Gain? Political and Social Tensions Surrounding the 1976 Montreal Olympics', in Lenskyj and Wagg (eds.), *The Palgrave Handbook of Olympic Studies*, pp. 120–133.

Timms, Jill (2012) 'The Olympics as a Platform for Protest: A Case Study of the London 2012 "Ethical" Games and the Play Fair Campaign for Workers' Rights', *Leisure Studies*, Vol. 31, No. 3, pp. 355–372, http://dx.doi.org/10.1080/02614367.2012.667821.

Tomlinson, Alan (2012) 'The Making – and Unmaking? – of the Olympic Corporate Class', in Lenskyj and Wagg (eds.), *The Palgrave Handbook of Olympic Studies*, pp. 233–247.

Tomlinson, Alan (2014) 'Olympic Legacies: Recurrent Rhetoric and Harsh Reali-
ties', *Contemporary Social Science: Journal of the Academy of Social Sciences*, Vol. 9,
No. 2, pp. 137–158.
Tomlinson, Alan and Garry Whannel (1984) *Five Ring Circus: Money, Power and
Politics at the Olympic Games* (London: Pluto Press).
Tomlinson, Sally (2005) *Education in a Post-Welfare Society* (Maidenhead: Open
University Press).
Verhulst, Joris (2010) 'February 15, 2003: The World Says No to War', in Stefaan
Walgrave and Dieter Rucht (eds.), *The World Says No to War: Demonstrations
against the War on Iraq* (Minneapolis: University of Minnesota Press), pp. 1–19.
Wagg, Stephen (1992) 'You've Never Had It So Silly. The Politics of British Satirical
Comedy from Beyond the Fringe to Spitting Image', in Dominic Strinati and
Stephen Wagg (eds.), *Come on Down? Popular Media Culture in Post-War Britain*
(London: Routledge), pp. 254–284.
Wagg, Stephen (1996) 'Everything Else Is Propaganda: The Politics of Alternative
Comedy', in George E.C. Paton, Chris Powell and Stephen Wagg (eds.), *The
Social Faces of Humour* (Aldershot: Arena).
Wagg, Stephen (2002) 'Comedy, Politics and Permissiveness: The "Satire
Boom" and Its Inheritance', *Contemporary Politics*, Vol. 8, No. 4, December,
pp. 319–334.
Wagg, Stephen (2004) 'Fat City? British Football and the Politics of Social Exclu-
sion at the Turn of the Twenty-First Century', in Stephen Wagg (ed.), *British
Football and Social Exclusion* (Abingdon: Routledge), pp. 1–25.
Wagg, Stephen (2007) 'If You Want the Girl Next Door...: Olympic Sport and
the Popular Press in Early Cold War Britain', in Stephen Wagg and David
L. Andrews (eds.), *East Plays West: Sport and the Cold War* (London: Routledge),
pp. 100–122.
Wagg, Stephen (2011) ' "They Can't Stop Us Laughing": Politics, Leisure and the
Comedy Business', in Peter Bramham and Stephen Wagg (eds.), *The New Politics
of Leisure and Pleasure* (Basingstoke: Palgrave Macmillan), pp. 169–194.
Wagg, Stephen (2012) 'Tilting at Windmills? Olympic Politics and the Spectre
of Amateurism', in Lenskyj and Wagg (eds.), *The Palgrave Handbook of Olympic
Studies*, pp. 321–336.
Wagg, Stephen and Jane Pilcher (eds.) (2014) *Thatcher's Grandchildren? Politics and
Childhood in Twenty-First Century* (London: Palgrave Macmillan).
Whannel, Garry (2012) 'The Rings and the Box: Television Spectacle and the
Olympics', in Lenskyj and Wagg (eds.), *The Palgrave Handbook of Olympic
Studies*, pp. 261–273.
Whitson, David (2012) 'Vancouver 2012: The Saga of Eagleridge Bluffs' in Graeme
Hayes and John Karamichas (eds.), *Olympic Games, Mega-Events and Civil Soci-
eties: Globalization, Environment, Resistance* (Basingstoke: Palgrave Macmillan),
pp. 219–235.
Yoon, Hyunsun (2009) 'The Legacy of the 1988 Seoul Olympic Games', in Poynter
and MacRury (eds.), *Olympic Cities*, pp. 87–95.
Zervas, Konstantinos (2012) 'Anti-Olympic Campaigns', in Lenskyj and Wagg
(eds.), *The Palgrave Handbook of Olympic Studies*, pp. 533–554.

# Index

'Abide With Me' (hymn), 71
*Absolutely Fabulous* (TV sitcom), 53
Academy of Medical Royal Colleges, 126
Adams, Bryan, 86
Adams, Nicola, 164
Adidas (sportswear), 132, 148
Adlington, Rebecca, 141, 144, 145
   parents of, 145
Agent Orange (defoliant), 123
Aldama, Yamile, 15
Alexander, Meredith, 124
Alibhai-Brown, Yasmin, 121
Ali, Muhammad, 87
Ali, Rushanara, 182, 188
All England Club, Wimbledon, 53
Almanza, Ashley, 114
Alun-Jones, Alun, 58
AMP (Australian financial services company), 47
Anderson, Benedict, 71
Andrews, David L., 148
Aragall, Giacomo, 86
ArcelorMittal (corporation), 59
Arctic Monkeys (band), 70
Armitstead, Lizzie, 141, 145
Armitt, John, 94, 96
ARUP (consultants), 19
*Assistance to Shelter Act* (Canada), 11
Atos (IT company)/Atos Healthcare, 108, 123
Australian Department of Health and Ageing, 189
Australian Olympic Committee, 190
Australian Sports Commission, 189
Australian Tourist Commission, 46
Aviva (insurance company), 116, 148, 149

Bailey, McDonald, 158
Baker, Catherine, 81
Baldry, Simon, 52

Balfour Beatty (construction firm), 94–6, 187
Barchester Healthcare, 186
Barker, Sue, 135
Barnes, Simon, 72
Barnett, Anthony, 74
Barrie, J.M., 69
BBC *Panorama* report alleging Olympic bribery (2004), 24–5, 31, 135, 138
Beadnell, Mary, 100
The Beatles, 68, 70, 71, 75, 78, 86
Beckett, Andy, 39
Beckham, David, 27, 71, 72, 149
Bedford, David, 143
Begum, Rumi, 170, 177, 181
Beijing National Stadium ('Birds Nest'), 92
Berganza, Teresa, 86
Berlusconi, Silvio, 18
Berners-Lee, Sir Tim, 67, 70, 75, 85
*The Best Olympics Ever?* (by Helen Lenskyj), 6
Bhopal disaster, 123–4
*Big Brother* (reality TV programme), 151
Big Society (Conservative concept), 165, 181
*Billy Elliott* (film), 67
Bini, Carlo, 55
Birrell, Ian, 84, 165
Blacker, Gareth, 37
Black Eyed Peas (band), 53
Blair, Tony, 14, 16–19, 21–2, 25, 34, 78, 127, 169, 181, 190
Blake, William, 68, 79
Blankers-Koen, Fanny, 143, 147
Bloxham, Clifford, 154
Bluewater Shopping Centre, 183
BMW (car manufacturer), 118
Bolt, Usain, 144, 147, 151, 155, 163, 164
Bowie, David, 86

Printed and bound by CPI Group (UK) Ltd, Croydon, CR0 4YY